John G. Hughes

If you've read his stuff before you'll know what to expect but WON'T SEE what's coming.

Brim-full of deep wisdom and THOUGHT-PROVOKING insight.

He doesn't write books HE WRITES FEELINGS!

Always has a way of INVOKING DEEPLY PERSONAL EXPERIENCES to give new ways of viewing things.

UNIQUE AND SPOT ON and really makes you think about the bigger picture.

Hitting at the RAW EMOTIONS of love life & death J.G. Hughes is a MASTER OF THE WRITTEN WORD.

BEYOND GOOD ... genuinely BRILLIANT. He hits you in the soft spot with a sentimental blow before taking you to the edge of your seat.

Such WELL-CRAFTED phrasing means delving into his literary pleasures makes it difficult to surface again.

John Glyn Hughes was born in 1968. A former Police National Firearms Instructor and Tactical Advisor, he worked for the UK Government alongside several UK Police Forces and Specialist Military Units as a Subject Matter Expert in the use of firearms, close quarter combat, conflict management & blunt and ballistic trauma.

An RYA RHIB coxswain and powerboat skipper he served overseas alongside the UK's Maritime Warfare Centre and US Military as a national lead on armed maritime policing operations. A published author John is also a certified therapist and adult teacher. He resides on the West-Coast of Scotland.

A semi-professional musician and artist he particularly enjoys keeping fit and the outdoors, graphic design, furniture-making, DIY, and baking his celebrated Pizza's and Bread's.

BATHE MY HEART IN MCAULAY'S BURN

THE MEMOIRS OF A NOBODY

Words & Pictures by

John Glyn Hughes

CHIRON BOOKS
Glasgow

First edition published 2022

Chiron Books
Helensburgh | Glasgow | Scotland
Proud Independent Publishing

johnglynhughes@mail.com

ISBN: 9798365592827

Copyright © 2022
All rights reserved

Cover designed by John Glyn Hughes

Edited by Judy Astbury (New Zealand)

~ The chapter: Meaning of Life is published with the generous permission of
Michelle & Dillon MacDonald ~

Printed and bound by KDP

Typeset in Georgia

Table of Contents:

Index of Pictures:

'The Stickleback in the jar is worth so much more than some Trout in the stream.'

~ J.G. Hughes

Overture

MY NAME MIGHT BE JOHN, but I am

really a nobody. Following the release of my fictional novel 'Sailing Towards the End of the World' in 2021 I resolved to quit writing. The process had taken the best part of two years and entailed incalculable hours of dedication energy perseverance and thought. Essentially the project came at a considerable cost because creation always requires sacrifice.

Life itself consists of time which is the most precious and non-renewable resource of all, and writing requires an awful lot of it. Therefore, to make this book happen I had to similarly put other commitments and undertakings on the back burner. While we are at it being an author also offers little by way of recompense or reward: Given I'm a small independent publisher I know full well this book will only reach a limited audience. Therefore, penning a bestseller is about as likely as catching lightning in a bottle! Still when all's said and done writing is not so easy to relinquish because I enjoy it too much. For this reason, here I go yet again apologising to my long-suffering family.

This book forms my personal memoirs, that is a best effort to develop my craft into the transmission of what I have experienced. Why adopt this biographical approach? Firstly, because I'm told I have done niche things that regularly pique some level of interest.

Secondly thinking is what occurs when the soul talks to itself and having given the matter considerable deliberation mine realised it didn't fully know why I am the way I am. For this reason, my life was incomplete and so this book epitomises an attempt to fill in some of the blanks. To be fair I got more than I bargained for.

Thirdly I consider this to be a legacy document thus have designed it to outlast me. I guess instead of carving 'John was here' in some tree trunk I just went ahead and sculpted loads of words from blank pages instead.

I want you to know everything inside is true aside from some clearly signposted fictional interludes. I also add a light sprinkling of poetic license but only here and there. However real events real places and real people feature throughout, and this means there is potential for causing real harm. I adopted the Hippocratic oath 'first do no harm' to assuage this whereupon I tiptoed through the minefield of potentially offending anyone implicated. I also endeavoured to delimit my mighty pen in evening old scores through making arrows out of pointed words. That said it remains an exercise in point of view and a personal echo of the way I see things. You are entitled to make of it what you will.

Anyway, I shall now end this beginning by verifying an avid reader always picks up a new book full of hopeful anticipation. In this sense I hope this one lives up to being worthy. I figure you are reading it for a reason thus now hope you enjoy discovering why. As for me? I am finally going to focus on the precious people and essential things that I have neglected throughout devising the animated words and stationary pictures you'll discover inside.

Chapter One

'A Force Without Form'

TO LOVE SOMEBODY IS TO see
them as God intended them to be. Then again love does not arrive
when we decide it should nor does it arrive when we think we are
ready for it. Such is the unpredictable quality of love it sometimes
doesn't even resemble love at all. A drive of nature it is an
irrepressible force without form that can't be controlled. A divine
type of madness we are unable to choose who or when to love, and it
has the power to render reason futile whilst reducing the mightiest
of men to their knees.

Indeed this is what it means to be madly in love. Ethereal love
often proves oh so elusive. That said when soulmates meet they
always recognise each other and in that moment two hearts, two
minds, and two spirits intuitively get that their quest is over.

My parents met during the early 1960's. As a handsome young
Welsh police constable stationed in the English Midlands my Dad
was posted quite by chance to Kintyre on the West-Coast of Scotland
for a long-term detached duty. He ended up lodging in what were to
become my Grandparent's house for three-months. It was there he
met the small nineteen-year-old girl with pale skin, jet-black hair,
and striking blue eyes. Beholding my Mother for the first time he

recalled,

"When I saw her I was lightning struck. That was that I had to be with her no matter what."

Adoration tends to shine in many forms and when first introduced solar-flares had kindled from two disparate magnetic-poles. For them this proved to be the headiest sensation in the world. An irresistible natural process falling into love from that very moment had been an entirely unexpected yet mutually exhilarating sensation. As it happened she was engaged to another - a young Irishman - but immediately ended that affair when she met my Father. For obvious reasons I'm glad she did.

Irrefutable complete contraries had unwittingly attracted. He was masculine hardy frivolous and carefree. He epitomised drive determination foolish pride; dynamism and impulsive temper. Yet regardless those traits, from that moment when he thought of her his heart would skip a beat. He often couldn't sleep, but when he did he dreamt of her - his counterpart Venus.

Likewise, the diminutive feminine she imbued grace and gentle charm. She was soft tender musical and quiet; subtle tolerant and creative. Yet regardless those traits when she thought of him her heart missed a beat. She often couldn't sleep, but when she did she dreamt of him - her counterpart Mars.

In union they completed one another in privation each adopting many of the attributes of the other. She was an actress in his role and vice versa. Oh, the insanity and the paradox; yet when joined so completely sane. In the beginning nothing else mattered. In this regardless all else Mars and Venus had merged to epitomise the perfectly flawed union of opposites.

I've noticed that people mostly use words without any deep

thought as to what they imply. Consider the expression 'falling in love'. It's astute because it's entirely appropriate. It's wholly immersive as to let go and fall necessitates an enormous risk. It requires a person to expose themselves as vulnerable thus it's a considerable gamble. Therefore, the act of lowering one's guard seems counterintuitive and even quite mad. Yet physically emotionally spiritually and intellectually love requires you surrender and entwine your soul and ultimate fate unto another, true-self laid bare for your foil to see. Ironically falling into love is the ultimate high.

In their case following a brief courtship his secondment soon ended and he had returned to England. Nonetheless that was just the end of the beginning because afterwards he would routinely make the 360-mile journey to see her on his 500cc BSA motor bike on one weekend every month.

Rain hail shine and gales - over ten hours in the saddle each way: seven-hundred miles and twenty-hours in total on each trip. Fair to say given he'd made those treks on a small motorbike in cheap waterproofs through some of Britain's most rugged scenery before the advent of Gore-Tex or even motorways it is obvious love provided that little motorcycles fuel.

During their courtship they shared countless carefree days touring on that little bike often stopping at various spots on the stunning Kintyre coast to picnic by the sea - and subsequently married the following year before the grass could grow under their feet.

When Mars and Venus collide they tend to explode in giving breathe to new life. Just as their parent's love had provided the spark of their lives so their love would provide the spark of mine. Through it all they parented a family and became accustomed to maintaining what transformed into an unhealthy relationship. They proceeded to grow apart over the many years they were together, even so despite everything they stuck it all out for our sake.

That said on the rarest occasions they somehow pooled a curious and often hard to fathom dedication when they displayed an undeniable tenderness. When it occurred it was utterly disarming and touching to witness.

My Mother suffered many hardships and health problems throughout her life. Following a flawed operation in 1978 she died in hospital for a few minutes. Surviving she would later confide in me by describing in great detail her near death experience as she watched the doctors and nurses fighting to resuscitate her from a disassociated vantage point on the ceiling. Next discerning a blissful white light she'd then irresistibly gravitated towards it however, nearing its blissful eternal promise then heard an indescribably compassionate voice exclaim,

"Mary it's not your time the children are too young. You have to go back."

Accordingly she returned to us. I was aged nine at that time and to be honest needed her more than I could have ever known. Even so our relationship could reasonably be described as particularly strained. Perhaps we were too alike? She was an exceptionally sensitive person but had an unfortunate tendency to fixate upon her painful past in becoming depressed. At these times she would then focus on her fearful future to the extent she was overcome by heady waves of anxiety.

On these occasions self-isolated within the barren pits of her own despair she would habitually retreat beside the framed picture she treasured most of her beloved and deceased Father in her bedroom.

"Daddy what am I to do? If only you were here," I'd hear her tearfully question time and again as I eavesdropped with regret.

You see all I ever wanted was for her to just be happy. This was a wish which would never be granted. Even so when she talked to that picture my Grandads silent image emanated some superficial solace. On one such occasion she'd moved toward her bedroom to sit there when to her astonishment perched right alongside it was a small bird. You might imagine it might have been perturbed at her arrival then likely sought to escape? Oh contraire for it instead tilted its head to inquisitively stare at her for quite some time. This served as what I'd call a 'pattern interrupt' - a surprise which stops a person dead in their tracks. Silently observing one another for an age the little bird eventually just suddenly upped and flew straight out of the open window from whence it had come. Naturally by this time her woes were by now forgotten.

For some reason when we weren't butting heads she inclined to confide in me like no other. Mindful to adjust to her moods I vividly recall her recounting this tale during one of her more lucid moments.

"Son do you think it's possible our deceased loved ones use birds as messengers?" she'd tentatively asked.

I was dubious, nonetheless thought on it for a while. Acutely aware of her need for endorsement I sought to comfort her so after a period of introspection diplomatically offered,

"Mum I think such events appear mundane but represent heavenly things," which appeared to have the intended effect of buoying her no end.

Eventually during their time of greatest need when the young Welsh police constable had become an elderly disabled man I supported them steadfastly. I was determined to do all I could in line with my personal code. After all this was not just my way of helping them but of also of teaching my own children an important life lesson. Family should look after their own in times of need. Stuck in an increasingly difficult house to maintain they were isolated in the country. Hence to my Mother's delight I eventually arranged its sale and the subsequent purchase of a little flat in town close by.

As it happens just two-days before the move she'd yearned so long for she died in her sleep of a massive cardiac arrest right beside the very same picture of her beloved Father and was gone. I was abroad at the time and due to return home that very day to assume responsibility for the move.

Accustomed to leaning on me for support in my absence the stress of the transition had seemingly gotten too much for her. Evidently she'd taken one final trip to the kitchen in the middle of the night for a glass of cold milk, an attempt to ease the chronic heartburn she had assumed she'd been suffering. At her funeral my elderly Dad shook his head and somberly turned to me.

"Damn it we were married for fifty-three years," he sorrowfully uttered in his Welsh drawl. "I wish it could have been fifty-four then again we can't always have what we want."

There was a truism if ever there was one. Alone he now learnt one of life's cruellest lessons. Falling in love measures the assurance of eventual tragedy because one must die first. Therefore, letting go and falling into love is a voluntary act of surrender which always evolves into a barren wilderness. Initially entwining the tender parts of oneself unto your counterparts is spring then becomes summer wholeness, and bliss. The continual familiarity of always being together eventually induces autumn as adulation drops off like the leaves of an old oak tree wailing in the wind. Then in the end befalls the desolate midwinter of concluding grief as the survivor is assured damnation as they are condemned to occupying the now spoiled pleasure-dome that was paradise converted into the lonely wasteland of silent sorrow.

Even so my parents had no choice than to let go, fall into love and interlace to one another. Quite by chance they'd happened upon the matchless union of Mars and Venus. How could anyone pass that up?

A few days after the funeral I was alone clearing out her bedroom when to my astonishment I heard an odd banging against the windowpane. Investigating further I encountered a small bird trying to force its way into the room by belligerently flying at the window. Initially stock-still I eventually came to my senses.

"This might appear mundane but represents something heavenly," I quietly muttered to myself in a stupor.

Experts decree birds fly at windows because they see their own reflection and interpret it a rival infringing upon their territory to be chased off. On the other hand superstitions allege it foretells some bad omen. Well I don't know much about any of that but what I do know is now I'm the one who wonders if birds are the messengers of our deceased loved ones.

☆

I HAVEN'T SHED A TEAR SINCE my Mother passed

away. I've tried time and again but can't. It's almost as though my capacity to cry has become paralysed. Frustrated, at those times I've caught myself thinking,

'What the hell's wrong with me?'

Perhaps having stepped outside my grief during the aftermath I became too disassociated from it. If so it seems my reluctance to experience the lonely wasteland of silent sorrow has restrained my own capacity for expressing her loss.

My goodness then there's the anger. Following her death I felt a tremendous fury towards her. I felt she'd opted out of her obligation to my disabled dad and left it all to me in picking up the pieces. At the time I was already starting to come apart under the sustained strain of my own responsibilities. It seemed unjust and wasn't meant to happen that way. I imitated atlas by taking the weight of the world on my shoulders and for a while felt bitter towards her for adding to my load in simply giving up and dying.

To this end I've reconciled I'm capable of experiencing a depth of emotion that's beyond adequate description here. There's no doubt it is a part of me that can be nourishing however, it's often self-destructive in equal measure. To cope following Mum's death I thought I was being clever in using a nifty therapeutic ruse of mine. Conjecturing the world as no more than a projection of my own mind, instead of being consumed by grief this was my crafty way of averting the hurt by stepping outside it to dispassionately observe it instead. After all no matter how powerful they might feel we are not our emotions. Anyhow in hindsight this was a big mistake because it was a convoluted form of denial.

Psychologists assert there are no wrong feelings. Maybe so nevertheless I've construed there are certainly wrong thoughts. Therefore, it wasn't necessarily how I felt that had proved my undoing – rather how I'd thought about how I felt. Thus in retrospect it is now clear that my coping strategy had backfired in sabotaging me.

Distinguishing this was a start but even so it never lessened the guilt that I felt for being unable to cry. After all I knew everyone else had. Consequentially a heady cocktail of anger guilt and denial were starting to weigh me down.

I discovered a while ago that the universe abhors it when we attempt to force anything through pushing against the grain. Accordingly, in desperately attempting to compel tears I'd inadvertently stifled them even more. You see repressed grief is particularly hazardous as it rages inside your soul before suffocating it. Thankfully quite by accident whilst meditating I eventually grasped that whatever I need to attain acceptance will simply fall into place when the time's right. Therefore, in the meantime I'll patiently wait for it to arrive in its own good time.

By now you've probably noticed I'm a deep thinker. Okay I'll place my cards on the table and just admit much too deep for my own damn good. After all overthinking tends to create problems that aren't there at all. For example I've spent an awful lot of time conjecturing whether or not reality is no more than an elaborate dream. Notwithstanding I've since deduced that even if I am imagining everything I'm going through I must play along by acting as though it's real. Such things are far beyond the influence of mere mortals so who the hell am I to buck that trend?

I've instead decided to focus on influencing what I can in a positive way whilst letting the rest well alone. I've wasted so much life-force being hard on myself and preoccupying with what everyone else was thinking of me. As it happens it was all wasted given barely anybody had been thinking much about me all along. People are just too preoccupied with themselves and their own issues and quite rightly so. I guess now is the right time for me to do likewise. Anyway it's none of my damn business what others think or say about me. As I write this my neuroticism seems palpable but other than hurting myself it has proven a relatively harmless pursuit.

Damn, I wish I knew then what I know now. I never really appreciated what I had until it was gone. In particular I lament rolling my eyes whenever my Mother phoned. It sounds terrible, but at times she could be so emotionally demanding. Yet ironically the thing I now miss about her most is being able to pick up the phone to hear her voice again.

Nevertheless it's at those times I remember myself because I know I can do so any time through the power of my imagination. Resultantly when I want to contact her I sit beside her picture in my bedroom and give her a call up in heaven on my pretend magical phone. In doing so I'm careful to leave the window ajar just in case a bird might want to come in and join me. Thus far I've had no such luck however, patience proves my willingness to live life at the pace it happens.

I firmly believe there are certain things we should all experience before we die. One of the most important is to suffer from a broken heart. It might sound counterintuitive yet there's deep meaningful insight to be taken from such suffering. I also guess if I had to offer anyone advice on how to cope with the loss of a loved one I'd say don't be like me because it is far better to lean into the hurt than to avoid it. The sooner you start the grieving process the earlier it might conclude with some form of acceptance.

Make no mistake grief is the cost of love. Still it's a price we should all be willing to meet. As for me? I'm currently in the process of settling the bill so I am going to have to hang onto life's coattails in the forlorn hope it'll pull me through this soon.

Chapter Two

'The Magical Phone'

AS A THERAPIST I OFTEN utilise my own experiences when assisting the treatment of clients struggling with their issues. Once they enter a relaxed state of hypnotic trance I often tell them metaphorical stories. My reasoning? If something helps me with my own problems – regardless how unconventional the methodology - then it can also help others too. I think I'm onto something seeing as up until now this has mostly proved effective.

Naturally I always tune into the individual sitting across from me and the stories are tailored with them and their unique circumstance in mind. In Greek mythology Procrustes was a merciless killer who tortured stragglers by stretching them or cutting off their legs as he forced them to fit into his iron bed. Hence the term 'Procrustean' is used to describe situations where an arbitrary standard or process is utilised to achieve some end (regardless of what those involved need). Well, instead of forcing them to fit into some rigid formulaic approach the effectual counsellor ought to disregard this and meet the client in their own model of the world. Each interaction should be bespoke and alive in the moment not some two-dimensional clunky scripted routine. I suppose what I'm saying is my own style is that of improvisation.

Being familiar with Gestalt Therapy (the brainchild of the eminent psychiatrist Fritz Perls), I devised the conceptual 'Magical Phone' method for easing my own personal grief by chatting with my deceased Mother following her sudden death. I successively put this to further use through utilising it as a hypnotic tale for a dog owner who had come to see me after losing their dearly beloved pet. I could commiserate given I knew what they were going through.

 After all love is love and grief is grief. A sound frame of reference I reasoned that a direct-line to heaven is just as viable a method of mind-to-mind communication when contacting deceased pets as it is when contacting deceased people. Incidentally the therapeutic story in question shall feature in the second segment of this chapter.

Having owned and adored a few throughout my life I tend to agree with the sentiment 'dog is man's best friend.' Of course, given their lifespans are much shorter than ours I've lost each and every one. My goodness it never gets any easier because a dog is the only thing on earth that loves you more than he loves himself. I'll tell you about one of them right now if you're up for it? This was our mongrel named Prince.

First encountering him at the local rescue centre in Milton as the others ran up barking excitedly he'd caught our eye because he hung back. Interest piqued we then determined he was scheduled to be put-down the following day, so our minds were made up. I guess Prince was a lucky boy we had turned up when we did.

His previous owner hadn't valued him in the least and it was obvious to us he'd been maltreated. In particular he really didn't like men at all. Despite all of my best efforts to remedy this what compounded it more was the fact he remained terribly behaved on the lead. In short this would drive me absolutely nuts whenever I took him out for a walk. It's fair to say we never bonded for the longest time.

Kind strangers do exist and often magically appear exactly when you need them. In particular I recollect one fine summers day when as per usual Prince and I were having our customary tussle. I sighted a curious elderly grey-bearded gentlemen approaching from the other direction and as he espied our scrimmage with a mischievous glint in his eye he tempted me to stop for a brief one-to-one.

"Hello there young man," he'd brightly proclaimed. "If you don't mind me saying you could easily win that naughty lad over by keeping a sliced sausage in your pocket. I'd be willing to wager he'd never want to leave your side if you did!" he declared with a wink.

Graciously thanking him I was next practically dragged home by my eager mutt and for some reason or other the interface stuck in my mind as being particularly significant. Deliberating over what had been said his advice made perfect sense hence I tried it out on our next outing. Lo and behold it worked a treat and from then on

Prince stayed by my side.

Anyway after a few years Mandy had been throwing a ball for him on wet grass. Chasing it he'd slipped then proceeded to suffer a freak spinal injury. His back end was shot and agonising over what to do we decided to clean out our bank account by sending him to the veterinary hospital in Bearsden in the despondent hope of finding a cure. He was there for over a month but was sadly never the same again. From that point on I had to use a rolled-up towel to support his rear legs whenever I took him out which must have been the ultimate ignominy for a proud animal. Ironic, in a tragic role reversal I was no longer tugged around by him given he needed to be heaved about by me instead.

Finally near the end we bonded as I slept beside my terminally ill dog on the living-room floor. I'll never forget his last night when our big brown eyes met and his conveyed a plea for blessed relief. He'd suffered in agony for months and I now realised the only humane option left was to offer him the final act of human kindness: Because we loved him so much we had him put to sleep the following day.

Not long after we subsequently witnessed my beloved Father-in-Law's prolonged illness before he eventually passed away in hospital. It absolutely broke my heart and in some sense I died right there alongside him. Once resurrected the lamentable truth was I found I could never get over it. Simply put he was my hero and the greatest man I've ever known. Unlike Prince at that point I inconsolably wondered why ending his own suffering had been considered taboo. After all if such a blessed release is deemed good enough for cherished pets then why is the same act of mercy not extended to people? For me the offer of dignity in assisted dying at the end of life just seems so right. I only pray when my time comes the law will have changed to allow me this prospect.

Even so by the end Mandy's Dad had become so serene. Almost transcendent the experience eventually served as the catalyst for my own spiritual awakening. I wouldn't be at all surprised if he's currently being tugged around heaven by Prince as they walk once more perfect together in everlasting light.

George Eliot once quoted: *"The dead are never dead to us unless we forget them."* Well as far as I'm concerned John McTernan was a truly special man and as long as I have breathe in my contaminated body he will remain immortal.

★

(A Therapeutic Story about Bereavement)

THIS STORY BEGINS WITH A DOG named 'Lucky'.

Never far from the child's side he was faithful, non-judgemental, and loyal. Sitting by his owner he'd listen endlessly to his chat and could always be confided in. After all he was just a dog. As such he'd earned young Alex's complete trust.

Lucky somehow always knew once he was heading home from school and when the time was right would settle by the door in anticipation. Dogs have a special way of conveying their love for those they care about, thus arriving home Alex would always be met by his eager hound excitedly jumping all over him whilst frantically wagging his tail.

It had been almost two-years since his Mother's death. By the time they'd found the stomach cancer it had spread to her pancreas, and she'd died just before his fifth birthday. Afterward the fun filled energetic boy had completely withdrawn and his widowed Father worried endlessly about him. Of course, there had been counselling and extended family and friends had rallied around however, nothing seemed to help. That is until one day over dinner Alex had taken his Father quite by surprise.

Purposefully placing his cutlery down he'd looked directly at him then cleared his throat.

"Dad please may I have a dog?" he extended.

His Father habitually played with his wedding ring and thought of what Kate would have done in this situation. She'd always been better than him in handling these matters. On balance he'd quickly recognised the positive implications therefore agreed. Not long after they'd travelled to one of those places that re-homed abandoned animals.

Upon entering the compound several dogs bound towards them jumping up and barking excitedly. After a while they'd scarpered off, but one remained. Intriguingly the lingering dog, a mature Jack Russel terrier had simply sat by Alex's side.

"He's the one," he'd jubilantly announced.

The attendant shared a furtive look with his father then tactfully motioned him to one side.

"He's perhaps not the best choice," he whispered. "His name is 'Lucky' but he's quite old. We're actually scheduled to put him to sleep tomorrow."

At this they proceeded to try and coerce the child into choosing an alternative. Then again you know how difficult it is when a child sets their mind on something. Alex remained absolutely adamant so what else could his Dad do?

Afterwards his Father thought of Kate as they made their way home with Lucky onboard. In doing so he again played with his wedding ring. Damn it she was always so much better at this stuff than him. Carefully broaching the subject, he subtly asked,

"Alex you do realise Lucky is quite old? The other dogs were much younger. Why did you pick him?"

At this the little boy looked earnestly at his Dad.

"You don't understand. I never picked Lucky he picked me."

In no time at all they became completely inseparable. Talkative again his Father would often overhear him chatting endlessly to his dumb old pal who would happily just sit at side and listen. Misgivings about Lucky's age aside what really mattered was his son was much more like his old self again. Consequentially so was he. Hence despite the devastating loss of wife and Mother things had settled down ... before the inevitable happened.

Now an old dog Lucky had stopped eating and his health gradually deteriorated. A series of tests indicated he was terminally ill. Finally in the end it was determined the only compassionate thing left to do was to end his suffering.

Once again Alex withdrew and wouldn't engage or open up. Everyone rallied around but it didn't make much difference. Distraught he became remote, and his dad once more found himself fretful.

He'd initially suggested they pick a new puppy only to be informed Lucky was special and no other dog could replace him. For sure this played on his mind until one night whilst musing on how Kate might handle things he was abruptly taken by a flash of inspiration.

The next morning an envelope addressed to Alex arrived by post. On being handed it he was quite taken aback given nobody had ever sent him a letter before. Sat by the kitchen table he inquisitively placed his spoon down before eagerly proceeding to tear it open. Inside was a letter:

Dear Alex,

I miss you and want to let you know that I now live in the 'Cosmic Kennel'. I'm perfect again. I feel great and am so happy to be reunited with my doggy family and friends. I chase sticks in the beautiful, fields, swim in the perfect streams, chew bones, and sprawl by the log fireside. The weather is always great, and the food is just the best.

I notice you are so sad - but want you to know you should enjoy your life ... just as I enjoyed mine. Don't worry we'll be together again. I'm waiting. In the meantime, I'd love to hear from you, so feel free to write.

P.S. sorry about the messy writing - but it's difficult to write with paws.

Lucky (c/o the Cosmic Kennel)

Initially speechless Alex then became suspicious. Sure, he was elated Lucky had gone out of his way to write from doggy heaven, yet something was clearly wrong.

"Dad this isn't right," he blurted offering the letter over for inspection.

"What do you mean?" his Father stuttered concerned his ruse had been rumbled and pretending to sight it for the very first time.

"Look there's no stamp," Alex confusedly replied pointing at the now torn envelope.

Relieved, his father proceeded to feign indifference for a few seconds before extending,

"Oh, that's quite normal. You don't need stamps when posting letters from the Cosmic Kennel. In any case you should write back." he encouraged. "I could help then give it to the postman on your behalf if you'd like?"

Satisfied with this explanation that's precisely what they did:

Dear Lucky,

Hey pal,

I'm so glad to hear that you are okay, have settled in, and are having a great time. That makes me feel better.

I miss you and cry at night when I think about you - but I suppose there's no need now I know you're all better again and having fun with your doggy chums.

Anyway, I miss talking to you. You were great company. I wish I could chat with you again.

Hey, don't worry about the handwriting. Mine isn't much better - I need to work on that at school!

I miss and love you.

Alex (Your best friend)

The letter was successively placed into an envelope addressed to lucky then handed over to the postman who confirmed stamps weren't necessary when sending letters to the 'Cosmic Kennel'. Of course, he was predictably in on the whole thing.

A couple of days dragged past as Alex patiently waited until a large package finally arrived addressed to him in the same scruffy paw handwriting as before.

He immediately knew it had been sent by Lucky so tore it open. Inside was a brown cardboard box with a letter attached to the outside with tape marked, 'Read me first.'

Hey Alex,

It's me Lucky. It was great to receive your letter! I have been having a blast chasing my tail and I even barked and chased the postman after he delivered your letter. Don't worry though, he knew I was only playing and we laughed about it afterwards.

I've been thinking about how you miss chatting to me and it gave me an idea. Instead of me keeping writing with my scruffy paw writing you can call me instead and talk all you like with the 'Magical Phone' enclosed. It works on imagination. Just pick it up. You won't hear a dial tone because it's a magic imagination phone ... but you'll hear me answer in your head.

If you want to hear me reply just use imagination-listening, and you'll hear me talk back inside your mind!

Call me. Love, Lucky (c/o the cosmic kennel)

Eagerly tearing at the box, sure enough inside he found the Magical Phone - an antiquated dial-phone featuring loose wires. Initially speculating how such a primitive thing could be utilised to contact doggy heaven he finally shrugged his shoulders then went to his room.

Determined to give it a try he excitedly dialled random numbers then sure enough in the privacy of his head he heard it ringing. To his delight Lucky soon answered. They talked for what seemed an age as Alex filled his deceased pet in on everything that had happened recently. As before Lucky was a great listener however, this time it was even better because he could talk back by virtue of the fact he was in doggy heaven. Thus, Lucky had chipped in with a couple of quips, a funny joke or two, and the odd piece of advice. Once finished Alex thanked him for sending the magical phone then hung up on the promise to call back the following day.

Meanwhile his father had silently eavesdropped outside. He'd thought of Kate whilst toying with his wedding ring with tears in his eyes.

'It would have been just like her to come up with such a ploy,' he ruminated smiling and shaking his head.

It had been gratifying to hear his son engage once more - even if it was only with an imaginary friend - and over the next few weeks Alex called the Cosmic Kennel each day to chat with his heavenly pet. Lucky would listen intently before sharing the wonderful things he'd been up to in doggy heaven. The overall change in him was incredible to behold. No longer withdrawn his schoolwork improved and he'd even returned to playing with friends again.

The weeks turned into months and things continued much as before with Alex chatting with Lucky. That said with exception the calls were becoming noticeably shorter. This culminated one day when suddenly over breakfast he'd cleared his throat.

"Dad I was talking to Lucky last night on the magical phone," he proclaimed watching him carefully. "He said I should let him retire and get a new puppy instead."

"Well how do you feel about that?" asked his Father following a short pause. In truth he was bowled over by this unforeseen development.

"Actually, it would mean I wouldn't call him anymore," he replied wistfully. "However, he's promised to always keep an eye out for me."

"Well in that case I think it's a great idea," he'd countered before impulsively reaching out to hug his son across the tabletop.

Simultaneously the mail had noisily dropped through the letterbox. Initially ignoring it he had washed the dishes as Alex had finished to go outside and play in the garden. Having concluded clearing up his Father then absentmindedly relocated to the front door and stooped to pick it up.

"Huh more bills," he deliberated aloud as he returned to sit back down by the kitchen table.

Flicking through them there nestled amongst the usual array of brown envelopes was a letter addressed to him. Furthermore, he noticed there was no stamp affixed.

'Hm, that's odd. Where on earth has this come from?' he absentmindedly thought.

He hesitantly used a knife from the table to cautiously open it and removed the letter within. With quivering hands, he then almost involuntarily let it go. Shocked to the core it was clearly penned in the unmistakable handwriting of his deceased Wife.

Dearest Peter,

Thank you for being such a great father, I am so proud of you. I want you to know that I am perfect again. It's wonderful over here on the other side - unadulterated love and light. I have seen unimaginable things and am reunited with my family members. I want you to know I watch you every day and am always close.

Every time you think of me and play with your wedding ring I'm at your side offering strength and encouragement.

I stroke your hair when you are sleeping and kiss Alex's head each night before he goes to sleep. You are the best things that ever happened to me. I love you with all of my heart.

Please live your life. No matter what happens, be assured I'll be waiting. It's all part of 'God's great mystery'.

Oh ... and if you ever want to talk to me just go ahead and use the Magical Phone. It operates on imagination! Such a good idea ... I wonder where you got the inspiration for that? Lol x

Kate (C/O Heaven)

Impossible. It defied all logic. Now wide eyed he attempted to process what had just happened before using his now trembling hands to recover the letter and read it over again and again. He had to eventually remove his glasses to wipe the tears cascading down his face.

After a couple of minutes, he took a few deep breaths then composed himself. Closing his eyes, he held the letter to his heart and arrived at a decision. Standing up he then softly proceeded upstairs to his son's room to open the door. There it was sitting on the bedside cabinet ... the Magical Phone.

Apprehensive at first he pushed misgivings aside to sit beside it. Tentatively lifting the receiver to his ear, he began to dial random numbers and prepared to contact heaven. When Kate answered he was utterly overwhelmed. God how he'd yearned to hear her voice again.

Chapter Three

I'VE MADE SO MANY MISTAKES,

but life doesn't come with a set of instructions. Anyway, be honest even if it had would we really follow them? Therefore, what else can we do than our best as we find our own way. On reflection I guess mistakes are vital after all. If you think about it every mistake serves us a lesson so in theory should make us better. Isn't it strange that through making mistakes we progressively provide ourselves our own instructions for life? Otherwise, all the worlds a stage and as the players we are unrehearsed.

There's considerable value in being able to adopt alternative views regarding the things we're going or have gone through. After all I think you're most unlikely to solve any problem by seeing it the same way as when you created it. I love art and design but wouldn't be so bold as to describe myself as an artist. Even so I do acknowledge artists know when something is viewed from a different angle or seen in a different light it looks completely different. Life is often like that too.

How is any of this relevant? By continually circling an indifferent sun we are involved in the often-difficult art of living. Seeing as the problems never seem to end being able to learn to look at a seemingly unsurmountable difficulty from a new perspective can actually cause it to dissipate. It simply has to because what you were previously regarding has consequently altered.

Alright here's a practical example. I once had a therapeutic client who sought my help with her fear of death. She was young, exceptionally bright, attractive, and very healthy. Indeed, she had the world at her feet and yet it was causing her great concern. I carefully observed as she wrought her hands together and couldn't help but notice her badly bitten fingernails and chipped nail varnish as she nervously revealed her forebodings. Obviously anxious her fear of the future was palpable, so I treaded softly by digging a little deeper.

"Tell me what exactly it is about death that frightens you?"

"Well I don't know," came her initial reply.

"Okay then if you *did* know what would you say?" I furthered.

"I suppose it's fear of the unknown!" she'd eventually replied.

"Well what did it feel like when you were dead before?" I replied without missing a beat. As far as I was concerned it was now game on and this odd rhetoric seemed to stop her in her tracks (which was my plan all along).

"Pardon what do you mean?" she finally uttered after her pupils had slightly dilated during a period of muddled introspection.

"Well it's quite simple," I stated. "Before you were born you were dead so how did it feel then?"

A startling new perspective suffice to say following this simple interchange she went on to become less anxious and frightened of death. I was instead delighted that she just got over it then got on with living out the miracle that is life.

Here's the thing, how would we know we were alive unless we had been dead? Cast your mind back and you'll remember being dead was actually very easy. In fact, so much easier than being alive. Death is commonly underrated in my estimation given it is the ultimate state of comfort. So, what's the problem?

Okay for arguments sake let's just say dying is generally perceived the ultimate calamity. Therefore, it has incessantly troubled mortal minds forever in the silent quietude of inner awareness. Nonetheless when you remove the fear of death there should no fear of life whatsoever. In this way death can actually become life's ultimate safety net. After all grief is a burden exclusive to the living as the dead are instantly over it!

Anyway, contrary to what she had thought I'd known all along my client was essentially scared of life. And with good reason because it's hard.

I find it bizarre when people ruminate over the possibility of an afterlife. They conveniently ignore the fact they know exactly what it's like: it's equivalent to the beforelife we have all experienced. When we were born we woke up and in that instant forgot we'd been asleep. So, surely when life comes to an end we'll fall asleep again then perhaps realise we'd been dead all along? Maybe then we'll dream of being alive once more. I'm just putting it out there. You see when I think back to being dead I'm certain there's something there, but I can't quite put my finger on it …

Okay, I get it. All of this is a bit heavy but please stay with me just a little longer. Who knows what I'm about to share might literally change your life.

A persons reality is born of the subjective responses they have to their own senses. They then become so convinced by these personal experiences that they tend to abide by them. They subsequently accept these perceptions as the fixed reality or the ultimate truth: They then become so convinced by these experiences that they consistently accept their apparent rules. Therefore all of our subjective perceptual distortions become accepted as objective realities. However, consider this - nobody even knows what up is.

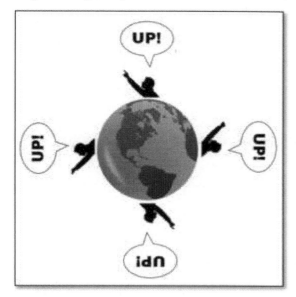

What I mean by that is our planet is a globe yet if you asked four people - one located at the north pole, the other at the south; the other two at opposite median points - to point towards up they will both simply point towards the sky. So then who is right and who is wrong? Are they not all simulataneously correct and also mistaken?

Hence our subjective perceptual distortions are no more than beliefs which are just generalisations. Nothing is ever quite as it seems given our individual generalisations are shaped by our prejudices. They are no more than personal illusions which we hold to be real. Of course, this is not to say that they aren't useful - but by virtue of this life is not so much about how the world is but rather about how we are.

I'll give you another example. I had a different client who was terrified of water. Naturally, he'd never been able to learn how to swim. As a former shipyard welder he was very much a 'man's man' thus hated admitting his shortcomings. Guys generally tend to be avoidant attachment this way (*Note: Avoidant Attachment - when one presents as strong and independent to the extent they won't open up or depend on others in times of need*).

Consequentially, following a somewhat tiresome tete-a-tete he finally explained how he couldn't enter the sea or even a swimming bath to a depth greater than his knees.

"So when was the last time you were fully submerged?" I asked him casually.

The question was rhetorical but essential given it would tee up my next approach.

"Never, I couldn't do that!" he immediately responded. In doing so I noticed him visibly shudder at the proposition.

"Then how did you cope when you used to live underwater?" I probed at which point he became totally bewildered.

"What do you mean? I've never lived underwater!" he eventually stammered confusedly shaking his head. "Hey, are you fooling around with me or something?"

"Not at all," I answered. "There are only two ways to be fooled: One is to believe what isn't true and the other is to not believe what is."

This was a practical application of mind-bending quantum linguistics, a psycho-therapeutic technique which utilises confusion as a method of bypassing the clients critical mind in opening up their subconscious to suggestion. His eye accessing cues indicated he was now bamboozled so I struck by playing the ace I held up my sleeve.

"Here's the thing I think you've forgotten you used to live underwater for nine-months." I concluded deliberately.

He just stared blankly at me for ages before the penny eventually dropped. Suddenly it all clicked that he had once been an amniotic water baby residing in his Mother's womb.

Anyway from that point he began to straighten himself out and overcome his fear. He made great progress by going on to enjoy learning to swim at the Dumbarton leisure centre.

People are immeasurably complex, yet their issues tend to fall into repeating patterns. Hence therapy isn't rocket science especially regarding phobias. Fear flourishes in avoidance thus the remedy is to find enough courage to persistently confront the phobia. Exposure then leads to desensitisation and that's it, job done. It's really just a state of mind. The severest impediment of all is choosing to be blind when you can clearly see. In both examples my clients wore chosen blinkers. I guess it's a bit like voluntarily adopting invisible chains of slavery.

Our perspectives and beliefs are limited to our levels of knowledge and understanding therefore it stands to reason should we increase these our outlook will expand. We all have personal thoughts, prejudices, attitudes, and beliefs however, if we change any of these we change our reality. For this reason, I applaud both individuals. It takes guts to choose enlightenment having discerned you've been living in a self-induced state of deception. A great many people just won't do it.

Some American Indian tribes took part in a ritual known as a Drum Circle whereupon they would sit in a circle and place a drum in the centre. Each individual would gaze upon the drum to notice the light and shade as it fell and pay close attention to the nuance of their unique position. After a while they'd swap places with the next person and follow the same procedure from a fresh place. It would continue this way until they'd viewed the drum from multiple angles. Hunter gatherers closely aligned with the patterns of nature, it was an important process for them. They saw intrinsic value in gaining a deeper understanding by altering their own perceptual positions then making the effort to consider what others might be experiencing. I thoroughly recommend you give it a try it sometime.

☆

GROWING UP IN THE COUNTRYSIDE, I had a

bit of a Tom Sawyer youth in Garelochhead rafting, building treehouses and fishing. At primary school the only thing I excelled at was daydreaming. Trapped I would longingly gaze from the window to pass the day by releasing my imagination to roam free. Upon first attending school I immediately hated it then decided to opt out. Don't get me wrong I was extremely well behaved but didn't try in the least. I subsequently frustrated my teachers, many of whom just assumed I was thick.

In primary seven my teacher was an attractive young woman in the formative years of her career named Mrs. Mathie. She was quite naturally the object of all the developing young boys' desires. A common phenomenon, at the time of writing I've already had this awkward discussion with my youngest daughter Bethan who is herself studying a degree to become a Primary School Teacher. Forewarned is forearmed and all that.

In any case Mrs. Mathie was usually a tolerant sort but had once uncharacteristically completely lost her cool with me.

"Oh for GOODNESS' SAKE John, at this rate you're going to end up being a NOBODY!" she had meanly barked raising her voice.

Despite being shy and awkward I was (and remain) particularly determined and willful. On this occasion I had answered her back.

"Well you have your opinion, but I have mine!" I'd declared with conviction. After all my mean pride had been suitably roused.

Throughout this exchange the unusual wiring in my head had

also confusedly processed, *'Wait, how can someone be a nobody? Surely even nobody is somebody?'* You see on balance I intuitively felt the potential to live life the way I wanted to no matter what it took. My choice at the time was to meet the low academic expectations my parents set which in fairness I never failed at. Nowadays I'd probably be diagnosed with some learning impediment or other. I might even feature somewhere on the spectrum. Notwithstanding, despite innate inattentiveness I never allowed formal schooling to get in the way of my real learning at all.

I lived for school holidays. On one such occasion I spent endless long hot summer day's fishing alone by the stream on the periphery of the village named McAulay's Burn. My family were dirt poor, but I didn't know it at the time so felt rich. Thus I sat contentedly with my little fishing rod with worms on the hook. I could feel the warm ground underneath me as I sat infinitely small on the carpet of grass and would gaze endlessly into the slow, steady flow. The sunlight would twinkle its translucence as tiny flies perpetually teased the surface. This all played out to a gentle soundtrack of flowing water, birdsong, and grass being softly teased by a playful breeze. The occasional white clouds that accompanied me formed shapes only constrained by my imagination.

Looking back besides the sunshine which overwhelmed my heart when cradling my newborn children I acknowledge those halcyon riverside times entail the happiest memories of my life. Just like my books and the endless time I spent at friends' houses they were an escape from the continual troubles of my family home and the difficulties of having to attend school.

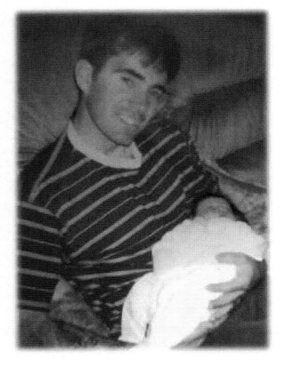

Even now I recall the fascination, deep-joy, and satisfaction of catching little Sticklebacks by the dozen then placing them into an empty jam jar. Of course I never hurt them and always returned them once finished because the thrill was in the chase. Unlike some of the other boys in the village I just couldn't stomach cruelty.

One day a friend an unassuming little lad named Hugh Leech had become intrigued by what I was up to so decided to join me. He was a droll kid, and his comical 'cow's lick' (an everlasting tuft of protruding hair) marked him out as unmistakable. Having never fished before I showed him what to do. He didn't want to sit in the sun with me so instead settled down in the shade beneath an overhanging oak tree a few feet away.

Stunningly within seconds of his first few casts he got a bite and pulled a beautiful rainbow trout from the water. I vividly remember his complete shock unbridled excitement, and joy with the catch. On the other hand I also vividly recall my utter astonishment at seeing such a large, beautiful fish - then my unbridled jealousy and resentment at his stunning beginner's success.

This was a pivotal moment in my life. The memory really stands out because it was the death of my innocence. Little Sticklebacks were now long forgotten as I proceeded to sit alone in the shade underneath that overhanging oak tree for the remnants of summer in an attempt to catch a big rainbow trout and I never even came close. Those tranquil times expired the moment Hugh hooked the big fish and proceeded to take it home in a bucket with his rubber wellington boots squelching as he went. Sticklebacks were never enough for me again and I couldn't be childlike anymore because I wanted more. Man, it's so much better to be grateful for what you have. To always desire what you don't is an acute form of torture as it only ever ensures you never have what you want.

Oscar Wilde once famously stated: *"The two worst tragedies in life are not having what you want and having what you want."* I think that is wisdom of the highest order.

Anyhow you can't turn the clock back. Time might be the cruellest thief of all yet if you're patient enough it can also the greatest healer. This instance aside I'm fortunately neither prone to jealousy nor avarice so I have mostly remained affluent throughout my fluctuating fiscal and material circumstances. That said even I'm not flush enough to buy back my past. Instead, I've stopped looking back and being so sore on my younger self. I think people do this because familiarity breeds contempt and contempt breeds condemnation. We're never more familiar than with the person we can never separate from - ourselves. Intimate with our foibles in a way no one else ever could be, I think it's better to learn to love who you are because this way you'll never be lonely with the person you are always alone with. Of course, none of this is to say we shouldn't aspire to becoming more as any failure in this regard is more like a stagnant tarn than some free running brook.

Sure I'm not perfect by any means but I have unapologetically learnt to accept myself. Having given this a lot of thought lately I've concluded that just like those Sticklebacks I have never intentionally set out to hurt anyone who didn't deserve it. Then again I have inadvertently done so, in particular to those who matter most of all to me.

As an avid reader I always held a sense of excitement when picking up a new book. Even so this was always accompanied by a tinge of apprehension. Why? Because I was afraid of encountering something that I didn't want to know. Well in the interests of fair notice this book might sometimes be that way too including the next few paragraphs.

I vividly remember the first time a person died in my arms. A probationary Police Officer at the time I received an urgent call specifying a mechanic was having a heart attack in a garage nearby.

Accompanied by a veteran Sergeant named Davey we arrived then pushed our way through the crowd to find the victim struggling on the floor. Before the implementation of defibrillators we desperately attempted to save his life with Cardiopulmonary Resuscitation (CPR). As I provided rescue breaths I had to constantly clear vomit from the victims airways as we persisted, and I recollect my shock that people actually did this during a heart attack.

Eventually it became clear he wouldn't make it so panting for breath and now saturated with sweat within our woolen tunics we ceased. Turns out he'd passed away in my arms on what had been his fiftieth birthday and to this day I still don't even know his name.

Aged twenty-two I was at a loss to explain the familiarity of having a sentient being expire in my arms. This was somebody's Son, Husband, and Father ... someone's world. Literally numb, the vestigial remnants of my naivete perished that day. Afterwards I attempted to offload how I felt to Mandy, but I could see it in her eyes she simply didn't understand. I mean how could she?

I saw some awful things throughout my career. Yet no matter what there was never any counselling. Actually any request was always met by the same response.

"For God's sake man up. You're in the Police!"

It's little wonder we instead learnt to arm ourselves with a black form of gallows humour. It's little wonder Police Officers become disparaging, cynical, and suspicious.

One nightshift later I was alone in a vehicle with Davey once more whereupon he recounted being first on scene following the Lockerbie air disaster. Nighttime he explained he had to turn his torch off because each time he utilised it he was met by grotesque repulsions. Worse he outlined the following night he had been detailed to guard the interior of the hanger designated as a makeshift morgue alongside the same charred and deformed bodies and body parts that had previously tormented him. Listening silently I was surprised to hear a sob before glancing to sight floods of tears streaming down his face. The horror. Unprecedented here was a grizzled veteran confiding in a fallow probationer. He had somehow recognised me as a healer long before I had.

Anyhow I recently revisited McAulay's Burn to take the photograph in this chapter. Unsurprisingly like all streams it still repeatedly weeps to sea and hasn't really changed all that much. I stood in contemplation for a while thinking of the unmet potential I once had. As the tree's sighed nearby a beautiful butterfly then landed right beside me. Measuring it against everything I have since gone through a curious thought then entered my head,

'Greed is more gullible than innocence'.

Tears somehow began to jam my eyes whilst I shook my head ruefully.

"Damn you," I mouthed toward the running brook. "Why don't you just rip out my stained heart and bathe it clean?"

Pointless really as water has no memory. Notwithstanding in some way this mentality has helped me throughout the challenges of my life. Whenever desolate enough to cry a river I've learnt to build a bridge then acquire whatever worth I can from the experience before getting over it. Regarding whatever you might be going through you might also take heart from the fact it'll soon just be water under the bridge. Who knows perhaps through reading this chapter you've just assumed a new position in the Drum Circle of life.

Chapter Four

'The Meaning of Life'

ONE OF THE GREAT existential questions is often posed: "What is the meaning of life?" However, the answer is perfectly simple. The meaning of life is discovered through doing the things that give meaning to your life. There it is in a nutshell ladies and gentlemen! It always just seemed so obvious to me then again I often see things in an unconventional way that I suppose most people don't. I have personally come to entitle these insights 'the unseen but obvious'.

I guess I possess a bit of an abstract mind. Despite always being very popular with others I've inwardly always felt quite different and disconnected from the things that seem to turn everyone else on. As a child I was abnormally observant and uncomfortable in my own skin but ultimately grew to realise that being unique is a good thing. As a species I can't help but wonder how much better things would be for us all if we could only accept our own individual quirks whilst placing those differences we find in others aside.

And so I was painfully shy growing up yet thoroughly amiable: An imaginative and whimsical kid if you like. To be candid even now I still find it hard to concentrate on one particular thing for any length of time before my butterfly mind takes off to flutter away on some other flight of fancy. I guess I'm naturally wired to think in an unorthodox way. Then again when it comes to being me I'm the best there is - in the exact same way as you are the best at being you. Come on let's face it nobody does us as good as us!

I established at a young age that my capacity for discerning metaphorical meaning from seemingly innocuous everyday occurrences was unparalleled. I'm not quite sure how or why I'm like this - and remain even less sure that it even matters - nonetheless it's the way I have been from the youngest age.

A confession. I actually found the fact that no one else around me thought to this degree really painful. Impossible to shut off I started to feel neurotic - even mentally ill - for paying so much attention to everything and everyone around me in such an abstract and analogous way. Moreover this was compounded insofar as I was ostensibly able to sense, feel and know a great many things beyond what should have been the limits of my understanding. In this way I always felt 'much older' than everyone around me.

For example one day in class whilst my schoolteacher was busy banging on about sums I instead sat at my desk pretending to listen whilst inwardly assessing the key difference between pain and suffering. Even then I found life an inevitably painful experience but was also getting that I didn't need to suffer from it if I chose not to. I ask you what kind of eight-year-old child thinks that way? It's little wonder I flunked my tests. Simply put I was always in-absentia throughout.

At the time of writing I have experienced many years of chronic pain. Following a nasty bacterial virus I became exceptionally sensitive to the supposed normal sensations relating to light touch before a pain management consultant diagnosed dysesthesia. He then promoted ongoing neurological and rheumatology treatment for my joint pain and spinal cervical/lumbar spondylosis. Yet here's the thing: I have since discovered that my reaction to the pain alters its definition more than any prescribed medication. What I mean by that is my attitude to the pain matters more than the actual pain itself. So instead of suffering from pain I choose to welcome it. Perhaps strangest of all it seems the more I accept my pain the better able I am to truly appreciate life.

On the occasions I have slipped into the quarry of choosing to suffer from the pain I have detested life so much. At those times had there been a button which when pushed would end the world and all of the suffering in it I would have been selfish enough to hit it just to end my own abject torture.

Then again when one cannot transform their situation one must to transform their attitude to the same. Through adopting the 'correct' way of thinking things suddenly balance out as life once more becomes an overwhelmingly beautiful experience. Paradoxically so much so that it actually hurts in an entirely different way. You see I primarily appreciate and cherish my existence so much that at times my heart literally bursts with joy and aches in response to life's overwhelming beauty. A divine source of pain the analogies 'burst', and 'ache' are fitting in supporting the point I'm making. Hence my personal choice is to cherish living for as long as possible.

I've been lucky enough to have some terrific friends and this has helped enormously. I could write about them all to some extent however, for the sake of discretion and brevity it's probably best I don't. In any case they know who they are. I've shared many of life's lessons with them. These never seem to end and have come in all manner of shapes and sizes.

Admittedly a slow learner it has taken me an awfully long time to understand the importance of staying safe within my own lane and life's shallow waters. So far I've been lucky enough to keep my head above the surface just long enough to learn those lessons well. Let me tell you I have had some very close scrapes and things could have worked out oh so differently. As for the teachings still to come? Suffice to say ever since my school days I've straightened myself out to become an avid student and now pay full heed.

★

HIS NAME WAS JAMES MACDONALD, and I

want to talk to you about loyalty, friendship, gratitude, and a little rowing boat.

I arrived at the West coast of Scotland village primary school during 1974 as the new kid with the English accent. At that time there weren't too many of those around. So, for some I was different in the worst possible kind of way, and I guess it was obvious I'd become the target of bullies.

Isn't it odd how cruel children can sometimes be? In fact it might surprise you to know sociological studies have concluded two-year old's to be the most sadistic members of society. Thus it goes without saying that as we mature we tend to become more civilized in all of our behaviours. In any case I remember meeting James for the first time. A gang of laughing bigger boys had surrounded me then repeatedly punched and kicked me to the ground in front of a baying crowd of prepubescent pupils. Holding me there they then humiliated me further by spraying cheap women's perfume all over my skin and now torn clothes.

Almost less concerned with the beating as this played out I remember wondering where on earth they had gotten the perfume from and why its owner hadn't noticed it was missing? Unreal. Anyway it was at that point James intervened and stopped them. Actually in doing so he took a bloody nose for me and in that instant earned my everlasting loyalty.

Even then I reasoned it important to take positives from negative circumstances wherever possible. Oddly enough for this reason I was soon grateful to that gang of bigger boys. You see they taught me a good lesson about my own durability since I'd discovered I was hard to break which would stand me in good stead. Even so in particular I was grateful to James. He'd taught me another good lesson – that nobody is completely bad nor completely good. In fairness like James most of the kids at my school just happened to be far better than those few bad apples so it all evened out in the end.

He was a tall rangy rebellious, and mischievous kid. Somewhat a rogue regardless there wasn't a single bad bone in him. As it happened at the time he could handle himself and couldn't stand bullying. Just as well for me. My ripped shirt stank of woman's perfume, and I wore a few bruises, but had it not been for him it could have been much worse.

James wherever you are now I want to sincerely thank you, and Mum wherever you are now that's why I came home from school that day reeking of cheap woman's perfume sporting a torn shirt. Afterward James and I became close, and we proceeded to embark on some memorable boyhood scrapes and adventures. In these I was to be Tom Sawyer and he Huckleberry Finn. I'm grateful for them all. I remember how he loved to take things apart to discover how they worked whereas on the other hand I simply didn't care as long as they did.

One Christmas he stripped the electric train set I'd just received apart. Man I'll never forget my parents faces when we were discovered struggling to fit the components back together. Me? I wasn't too bothered because I never liked train sets that much anyway. You see I had actually asked Santa for a Scalextric but typically trying to save a few bob my Dad had noticed the train set was cheaper so I guess that was that.

Sometime later we'd been up the woods messing around on a rope swing when James proceeded to take his penknife to cut his thumb.

"Here," he'd said next handing it over to me. "You cut yours too."

I had done similar then he'd placed his cut to mine, and we'd pressed them tightly together.

"You see," he'd announced satisfied with that unmistakable impish look on his freckled boyish face. "Now we're blood-brothers!"

Now flesh and blood I recollect another incident in particular whereupon we'd impulsively decided to 'borrow' a small rowing boat from the shore of our sea Loch one dark night. To do so we'd broken the chain securing it which we somehow managed. After all he was rebellious mischievous and a bit of a rogue and I was shy and easily led. Then again make no mistake I was no innocent. I've always possessed a streak whereupon I can get carried away to revel in pushing my limits, or let's just say living at a pace that kills. To be honest this irrepressible part of me occasionally finds playing with fire making waves and whipping up the wind an irresistible haste. I suppose in some sense it allows me to evade my inborn inhibitions through allowing me to feel more alive.

Thus we launched the little rowing boat onto the deep dark choppy sea loch without even the consolation of a life jacket or paddle between us. Instead all we had was a length of pole which we intended to use as a punt.

We were soon taken by the strong current and caught adrift we were taken further out of our depth as the leaden sky darkened and a rising squall encouraged the sea state to become as badly behaved as we were. This served a crucial life lesson for me, and I suppose that's why I'm now sharing it with you: If you ever find yourself out of your depth then get back to shallow waters pronto. Concurrently realising our predicament we then proceeded to descend into a blind panic as we furiously tried to get back to the safety of shore. Not for the last time I'd found myself in a dire and dangerous set of existential circumstances.

We'd eventually discarded the useless pole to the icy drink. Then almost tipping the pitching boat we desperately splashed at the waves with every ounce of strength that our boyish arms could muster against the cruel depths until they seared with lactic acid. We were by now increasingly desperate to make it back. Neither of us were strong swimmers and even if we were we wouldn't have lasted more than a few minutes in those forbidding icy waters. Plenty of others had drowned in the Gareloch and that night we came ever so close to paying the ultimate price for taking what was not ours to rightfully take. Thankfully against all odds fate decided to offer us another chance and interceded as somehow we eventually managed to save ourselves ... but only just. Thank God. As I splashed ashore in blessed relief I literally dropped to my knees in kissing the shale.

Causality or karma – call it what you like - we both knew the deep icy waters almost took us that night. Afterward I typically became indebted for the experience. After all such events clearly outline the fragility of life to those lost in their complacent prepubescent illusion of immortal youth.

Safely aground we next proceeded to fluster for an entirely different reason. Terrified of being caught for our erroneous deed we frantically relaunched the boat then filled it with large stones in an attempt to sink it - an ill-informed bid to conceal our crime. Then again boats are not so easily scuppered so in the end we instead just gave up and made a run for it.

Looking back I can only shake my head at my younger self's incredible naivety as to what followed.

The next day I returned to the scene of the crime to discover the vessel washed up on the beach full of rocks. Thereafter with the owner nowhere to be seen I simply emptied it and used it for the rest of the summer as my private dinghy. Over the succeeding couple of weeks I punted around the shallow waters and incredibly got away with it until one day I discovered it gone. Upon further inspection I found it chained back up where we'd originally taken it. Finally taking the hint I now left it well alone.

Nobody ever found out about this because James and I made a pact to stick together and hold our tongues no matter what. To our credit neither Huck Finn nor Tom Sawyer betrayed the other as they evidenced there was some honour between those boyhood scallywags. Instead we had learnt an important lesson about the perils of unlawfully appropriating property which belongs to another. Indeed it was a case of lesson learnt.

Despite always getting along extremely well as we grew older we drifted apart. I became less shy and easily led and he became a more rounded character with a lovely amiable manner. As a teenager my amorous eye happened upon a pretty girl named Michelle with long brown hair who lived in our village. After a whole lot of awkwardness my big sister promised to act as a go between in arranging a date. Full of starry-eyed teenage notions this all abruptly crashed down when it was revealed she wasn't keen after all. Of course this caused me a momentary bout of angst before my roving eye quickly moved on to somebody else. I'm sure you know how this teenage infatuation stuff all plays out.

As it happened James also had an amorous eye on her, and she had preferred him. As the age-old adage goes 'all is fair in love and war'. In retrospect she had made a good choice given they were really good together and he was a far better man for her than me. They were eventually married as I moved on and lost touch with almost everyone from the village for several years.

It was later when visiting my Father-in-Law who was ill in hospital at the time that much to my surprise right there in the bed across the ward was James. I hadn't seen him for the longest time, and it turned out he'd fallen down a stairwell to suffer a serious head injury. He was still a young man in relative terms, but his health had rapidly deteriorated. We chatted for a while then as I left I wished him a speedy recovery. A relatively short time afterward I was shaken to the core to hear my boyhood blood brother Huckleberry Finn had finally succumbed to slip beneath the waves. James had tragically passed away leaving my childhood crush a widow with a young child to bring up all on her own. Somehow she managed to muster enough strength to do so before going on to help a great many other youngsters in becoming an altruistic youth worker.

In any case as you can clearly see I still think of James and remain eternally grateful for the boyhood experiences we shared. I'll never forget that small rowing boat or the way in which we almost came unstuck one dark night as the sea threatened to take us. This near-death experience added considerable meaning to my survival: Let me assure you when your life is in jeopardy the meaning of it comes right down to simply trying to stay alive.

Even now the thing I remember most about James is the way in which he stood against a gang of much bigger boys on my behalf. He had no good reason to do so other than the fact he hated bullies. In many ways I'd like to think his blood still courses through my veins. Joined by kinship I still can't believe he stepped up to take a bloody nose for me the new kid in the village with an English accent. Then again only someone as flawed as him could have saved someone as flawed as me.

Isn't it odd that as we age our memory gradually becomes a flickering light, yet unlike people some memories just seem to last forever?

Chapter Five

'When the Unstoppable Force Met an Immovable Object'

VERY SPORTY AGED SIXTEEN I was competing to gain entry to the school athletics team to participate in the one-hundred-metre sprint at the County championships. The problem was only the four fastest boys could make the cut and my best effort placed me at number seven.

The top two were very gifted with the fastest, a boy named Robert O'Neill particularly so. Number three and four were naturally fast but undisciplined and number five and six don't feature in this story again. On the other hand I was naturally fast but neither disciplined nor methodical. No matter how hard I tried I couldn't seem to get better.

At this point I decided to approach things differently and this is when I learnt the importance of coaching.

"You want my advice?" went mister Parlane my P.E teacher. "Then stop running in those tatty old trainers and get some spikes," he said eying up my well-worn plastic Woolworths kicks. "You need to work on your start, rhythm, co-ordination, and breath control," he added before concluding, "... oh, and for goodness', sake build up some upper-body strength, won't you?"

I weighed this all up and it seemed reasonable, so I did. Each morning I'd spring out of bed then do fifty press-ups followed by fifty sit-ups before doing the same at bedtime. I next somehow acquired a pair of second-hand 'Le Coq Sportif' spikes to endlessly practice by sprinting on an uneven bobbled unmanaged country field near my home. Furthermore to develop my base level fitness I would run four-miles cross country each day up to the 'Yankee Road' (a single-track lane built by US servicemen above Garelochhead during World War two). With no access to loose weights I broadened up by endlessly lifting large rocks to develop a muscular chest and biceps. It all eventually paid off as during the final time trials I easily placed fourth to make the team.

As it happened I did represent my school in the County championships at Glasgow's Scotstoun stadium in front of a large crowd. Finishing second in my first heat I progressed to the next however, following a close race I was just pipped to third by a hair breadth. Given only the top two of six progressed it was game over for me. I remember feeling a complete failure but following some reflection a little later I realised the moral of this experience: In my year at school there were approximately eighty boys and I had made the top four. At the championships there were at least two dozen schools represented which equated a joint pool of almost two-thousand boys. At this point I realised I'd actually done well.

Sure I never won a medal but by placing in the top twenty amongst the entire county I'd effectively lapped all those other boys that never made it. Sometimes the variance between success and failure is no more than the capacity to change your frame of reference, or as some might say context is everything.

Incidentally Robert O'Neill won the final with an unofficial time of 11.4 seconds and considering the world record at that time was just slightly over one second faster at 9.93 seconds this was a remarkable feat. My goodness he was not only tall outgoing, and good-looking but an especially talented athlete.

Anyway I later ran alongside him in the 4 x 100-Metre relay team and against all expectations we actually won. Therefore, I had managed a medal after all. Actually, I'd more or less forgotten about all of this until following my Mother's sudden death. As my Sister went through her stuff she ensued to hand me a package.

"Oh look Mum must have wanted you to have this," she said handing it over.

In a clear cellophane bag was a handwritten note in her

distinctive handwriting in conjunction with a small bundle of baby clothes she had hand knitted for me following my birth. Intimate the innermost comment denoted: *"John, this is for* you." Alongside was a black and white newspaper clipping featuring a picture of our County winning relay team with me kneeling front left in front of Mr. Parlane and Robert nearby at the back with one hand holding the trophy aloft. I was stunned. Any type of achievement was always downplayed in our house hence outward expressions of affection praise or encouragement were virtually nonexistent. For this reason I'd reasoned my Mother hadn't even noticed our victory.

Upon leaving school I never met Robert again but overheard he went on to suffer personal problems and serious health issues. By coincidence my great friend and best man Robert MacIntosh met him by chance four years ago and upon mentioning my name Robert O'Neill had fondly reminisced.

"Hey, I remember John very well!" he brightly declared. "He was the school heartthrob whom all the girls swooned over," he graciously added.

I couldn't believe he had even noticed me furthermore his revelation about me being a heartthrob came as quite a shock. Then again I was always a bit dim that way. Damn, the only two girls I'd ever asked out at school had both knocked me back which led to me becoming spurned and crestfallen: *That's it, it's over. I'm never doing that again!'* I had embarrassedly reasoned at the time.

Anyway as I write this I've just learnt that Robert has passed away aged fifty-three from sepsis and a shadow has crossed my heart. Opposites by nature we weren't particularly close however, it seems we did share a mutual respect after all. As top boy in our year I had tremendous admiration for him yet as it happens life isn't like a sprint at all. Dipping for the line too soon Robert O'Neill proved it's more of a grueling obstacle course. I figure somehow as the glorious past slowly dissolves it increasingly leaves you stranded in a bleak future.

As for me? Well because of the fitness requirements of my profession in armed policing I just kept on training. Even so following a debilitating spinal injury during my late thirties an orthopedic consultant informed me I could no longer run and really should consider finding a new career.

At the time I could barely walk, and his bleak prognosis rocked me to the core. To contemplate this potentially life changing scenario I limped for thirty minutes per day. My goodness it hurt like hell, but I somehow ignored it. Within a few weeks I had resumed jogging by basically stumbling one mile per day to mull over this summary some more. Within six months I was jogging five kilometer's a day again as I wrestled how best to deal with being unable to run anymore. Even now well into my fifties I still run each day as I cogitate this conundrum. Sure my legs are like rusted wire as my lungs habitually catch fire. More so, it's neither fast nor pretty. Even so when I run I always jog nearer to good health and farther away from illness.

I'm at a total loss as to how I'll manage now that I have been told to stop running, so in the meantime I plan to just keep on doing it.

★

EVERYONE HAS AN ACHILLES HEEL. Okay I've

actually got a few in particular my innate lack of competitiveness combined with softheartedness. Mild natured nevertheless when I get the bit between my teeth my sheer bloody-minded stubbornness often makes up for it and I become as obstinate as a fixed mule.

Like most young boys I loved playing football. Our primary school team was very good, and I naturally wanted to play a part in it. On the other hand, there was a problem. Like the vast majority I was right-footed, and the team had an abundance of talent on the right-hand side of the field. Well, me being me instead of taking the chance to compete for one of those starting slots (and potentially deny somebody else) I had noticed there were plenty of opportunities on the left. Accordingly, as we broke for the summer holidays I hatched a radical ploy whereupon I would instigate a drastic plan to convert myself into becoming left-handed.

I'd disappear alone for hours over the course of the long break each day to set up obstacles in a secluded area of the village park. I'd then practice dribbling around them with my left foot over and over again backwards and forwards to develop close control of the ball. Initially slow in almost no time at all I'd become extremely proficient with both feet. I'd then practice shooting left footed hitting the dead ball time and again into imaginary goalposts from a variety of angles. I furthermore began to change everything I did including swapping the way I held a knife and fork to simple actions like brushing my hair carrying things, and even writing.

The school holidays came to an end, and I'd entered my final year of primary. At that time our janitor who was a smallish ageing man named Archie McCuaig managed the football team. Ably assisted by the effervescent Augusto Vitrano (a local Italian restaurateur who'd once been on the books of Juventus) Archie was hard but fair. With two older sons of his own rumour had it he affixed broom handles down the back of their shirts to train them to stand and walk straight. I recall his youngest Gus as an exceptional athlete who went on the represent Scotland as a sprinter.

Anyway, looking back I vividly recall the first team meeting of the season.

"Okay boys we've got a tournament in a few months," he'd barked like a military commandant. "All of the primary schools in the area will be competing and we need to win it," he'd announced as though it was the World Cup itself.

"First on the agenda there's a problem," he continued pausing for added effect. "It appears we need a full-back on the left side of defence. Is anyone here left-handed?" he requested in what I perceived as more hope than expectation.

Silence amongst my peers. I was one of the biggest and fastest boys but remained softly spoken and painfully shy. Nonetheless this was my moment to step up. I'd prepared all summer and wasn't going to let it pass me by, so had haltingly raised my hand.

"Erm I'm left-footed and can play full-back Mister McCuaig," I'd sheepishly announced after clearing my throat then pensively surveying the room.

I remember being embarrassed and blushing profusely as he'd stared perplexed long and hard at me through his thick lensed glasses. No doubt he had vague recollections of my prior right-footedness the preceding year. He eventually screwed up his eyes and exhaled.

"Really? Hm. Okay then Hughes we'll give you a try."

At our first training session we'd all clip-clopped out of the pavilion in our studded boots and gotten down to business. I'll never forget Archie's face as I surged up and down the left like greased lightening with nothing getting past me on the counterattack. Afterwards he had me wait behind then proceeded to regard me with a slow and purposeful inspection.

"Aye alright. I suppose you'll do," he'd declared without cracking a smile. "I'll see you at the next gathering. Off you go."

From that point I proceeded to make the position my own. Time passed and we'd persisted with football practice. On one occasion I found myself up against a much smaller boy in a foot chase for the ball. Easily outpacing him I could hear him to my rear panting and grunting in desperation as he endeavoured to catch me. He was also trying to make the team and in that split second I felt incredibly sorry for him, so slowed down enough to allow him to get the ball. Afterwards a visibly roused Archie pulled me aside.

"I saw what you did," he'd stated with barely suppressed anger. "Why did you let him beat you?"

"I didn't I swear," I'd mumbled unconvincingly averting his stare to look at my cheap muddied plastic boots.

"Yes you did, and I now want you to tell me why?" he'd insisted.

"Well, I suppose I did it because it meant more to him," I'd falteringly confessed.

Becoming wide eyed he'd shifted closer to hiss to my adjacent ear.

"WHAT? You need to toughen up son. If you ever do that again you'll be OUT of my team do you understand?"

He was right. I felt inconsolable. In being too nice I'd let him and my teammates down. Then again little did I know at the time he was trying to teach me a valuable lesson to stop letting myself down. A repeating pattern in my life I had put others first yet again and in the process betrayed my own prior hard work and sacrifice. I promised myself there and then never to repeat that mistake on the football pitch at least. This was a promise I would go on to break many times again in my life.

Eventually the 1979 tournament arrived. As we kitted up and walked out none other than my pal the venerable James 'Huckleberry Finn' MacDonald was in goal. Our first match pitted us against the favourites led by someone we'd all heard whispers about.

Tipped as the star player I picked him out as they limbered up. He was a really cool confident looking kid wearing a multi-coloured love-bead necklace, brand new expensive leather Adidas boots with screw in studs (I mean, wow!) and nonchalantly chewing gum.

"Listen up son you're up against Keving Ross," Archie avowed pointing to the very same boy. "They all say he's the best player around and unstoppable when he gets going. Take my advice and don't hold back. Give him an inch and he'll skin you alive so get stuck right into him ... got it?"

By this time my knees were almost knocking as I somehow

attempted to fire myself out of my normal languid state. Then once the whistle went they immediately controlled the ball. After a period of possession, it was fed out to Kevin. He easily danced a couple of challenges as graceful as a gazelle before dribbling through our midfield to spring down the wing like a livewire straight towards me. This was it. Now baring down with Archie's words still ringing in my ears I grimaced then made my move by going in full force.

Clattering him hard time slowed as I won the tackle and our heads clashed. The beads of his now broken necklace scattered the air in slow motion as he bounced off me backwards to the ground in agony holding his hands to his face. I more or less ended up standing over him seeing stars as the ball meanwhile trickled out of play.

Forehead cracked open like the shell of an infringed hardboiled egg I was shocked to sight blood pouring from my opponents face. Looking confusedly across to Archie at the side of the field for some reason I registered he looked really pleased with me. Albeit shaken I'd only ended up with a minor cut above my eyebrow and as I was given attention and a plaster poor Kevin was being carried off effectively ending his tournament after less than two-minutes.

Archie never uttered a word to me about it but at half-time made sure I received two slices of orange to suck on whilst the rest only got one. We went on to defeat the favourites and win that game three to one and I recovered enough to continue to play throughout it and the remaining fixtures.

As it happens much to Archie's annoyance we never won the tournament. We instead drew our second game then fell apart in the final group match. Ironically because of injuries I'd ended up playing an unfamiliar right centre-half position and we'd shipped seven goals to go out on goal difference.

What's the moral of this story? I'd found out winning meant far more to most than it does to me. More important still I'd discovered what happens when the unstoppable force meets an immovable object. Not for the last time it proved my robust physical toughness far exceeded my fond forgiving heart.

In Secondary School it's no real surprise I excelled in Physical

Education and Art and Design. After all these were the only subjects I was even remotely interested in. For the sheer hell of it I persisted with football and now playing in attack ran rampant. Actually, everyone touted me the best player in the school which was mildly flattering at the time. Even so the truth was I wasn't all that bothered about playing football anymore. By this time, I was discovering about much more important things including pretty girls, playing loud music, and consuming the alcohol I'd regularly pilfer from my unsuspecting (or was he?) Father's drinks cabinet.

In later life I discovered I had been naturally blessed with an exceptionally high speed 'fast twitch' muscle response all along. This inborn anaerobic advantage became evident again during my police handgun shooting whereupon I could draw and accurately engage any 'threat' exceptionally fast. Seems those endless youthful hours of shooting targets up in the woods of Garelochhead with my Diana SP-50 air gun hadn't been wasted after all.

We were pitched on my National Firearms Instructor Course into a shooting competition. Placed in pairs I combined with a Londoner from the Metropolitan Police called Nick. In a head scratching coincidence after a brief chat, it turned out his parents originally hailed from Campbeltown, and his Mother was a distant relation to my own! Anyhow each twosome were to take turns in shooting a two-by-two wooden post in half from a distance of fifteen metre's: A key stipulation was that one firer must use their weak hand. The duo managing to accomplish this with the least number of rounds would be declared as winners. I volunteered to take on the challenge weak handed and guess what? Yup we won. Turns out I was an exceptional left-handed firer. Hey who knew?

Chapter Six

'Turn it Up, or Turn it Off'

MY PARENTS WERE BOTH very
musical therefore it was always a bit of a thing in my childhood
home. Mum played accordion and Dad as a founding member of the
Machynlleth male choir had a tremendous voice.

My Mother had mostly given up playing when she'd married. As
such her accordion resided in a cupboard and hardly saw the light of
day. That said she regularly sang each day as she went about her
strict regime of daily chores. Although not bad by any means she
certainly wasn't a patch on my Father who had sung tenor.

"Huh listen to him," she'd meanly whisper as he belted out
melodic paean whilst shaving in the morning. "I'm much better
aren't I?"

By now adept at adjusting to her erratic mood swings I'd mostly
agree just to keep the peace yet in all honesty inwardly disputed her
claim. Naturally my Father knew about this however, her criticism
never seemed to bother him in the least. Let's just say he wasn't one
for emotional displays.

Reflecting on their relationship given he was always at work it's
now obvious to me my Mother was isolated and desperately
lonesome. When he did make infrequent appearances she'd often

lower herself into deriding him to his face and I can now fathom why. An intensely emotional woman it was her attempt to make him react in some way ... to at least show her something. Even so he usually wouldn't take her bait which only served to exacerbate the situation through frustrating her even more. Of course her moods would then blacken which unsurprisingly had a trickle-down effect upon the overall ambiance and the rest of us.

A record player was situated in our living room, and it would be frequently fired up to fill the house with an eclectic variety of sounds. My Mother preferred traditional Scottish tunes and my Father's choice would be the madrigal hubbub of resplendent Welsh choirs. I liked neither so upon reaching my teens would take over and play my own choice, which in particular drove my Mother nuts.

"Pfft that's not real music," she'd condemn screwing her face up as though she was being mercilessly tortured by my seventies and eighties pop and rock tunes.

Upon visiting the dentist during this time he informed I was grinding my teeth. I couldn't openly admit I'd actually been chomping them in imitating drumbeats to accompany the never-ending melodies which always filled my head.

It might sound peculiar yet for as long as I can remember music has perpetually enacted within my mind. As a child I've no doubt this compounded my inability to concentrate on anything for too long. All things considered I suppose it was almost a forgone conclusion I'd become a musician.

When young I absolutely loved wheeling and dealing swaps with my pals. Aged ten I received my first guitar in exchange for something or other. It was an old acoustic strung only with two strings as the rest had long since snapped. Even so I found it a fascinating object and soon figured out that each fingerboard position – or 'fret' - represented a different note. Always glued to the radio I would soon pluck out the bassline to The Police's hit, *Walking on the Moon*, and from that point I was off and running. I guess I have never really looked back.

It turns out I was endowed with a terrific ear and perfect pitch so had little difficulty picking out basslines from songs. Sometime later together with my great teenage friends Robert MacIntosh and Ian MacAndie we had agreed to form a band. They were eager to take on lead guitar and I'd excitedly volunteered for bass. We would often haunt our familiar hangout by a bridge traversing McAulay's Burn about a couple of hundred metre's downstream from where I used to fish to talk endlessly about how we were going to make it big in the music business and conquer the world.

I later heard a guy at my School nicknamed 'Smiler' was selling an old electric bass, so I went hungry for several months to save my dinner money before finally being able to afford it. Never let it be said I wasn't willing to suffer for my art. By this time my buddies had sourced similarly cheap guitars and we'd frequently jam by playing through our parents record players to Black Sabbath, Iron Maiden, and Deep Purple. In doing so we'd occasionally surreptitiously sip vodka from their drink cabinets then conceal our crime by replacing the liquor with water.

I was utterly obsessed and practiced endlessly in my bedroom; sometimes quaffing cans of cheap lager pinched from my Father's poorly concealed stash. Seems alcohol and music combined pretty damn well. My taste in music gradually progressed to include just about every genre as I challenged myself to master the instrument. Developing a taste for modern electric jazz I was particularly entranced by an interview I caught on late night TV (another new concept) featuring the legendary Miles Davis.

"You played a thirty-minute jazz improvisation at the Isle of Wight festival recently. What was the song called?" went the plainly English upper-class interviewer in a particularly plummy tone.

"Call it anything," Davis replied dismissively.

"Oh. Alright then. Eh, who are your influences?" next queried the now slightly unnerved presenter.

"I don't have influences. I AM the influence," rasped Davis from behind mirror shades without missing a beat.

"I see. Then what advice can you share with any young up and coming musicians who might be watching?" he persisted.

Now looking directly at the camera Davis uttered something that really struck a chord in resonating with me.

"To all you young cats out there, if you're going to do it you gotta turn it up or turn it off."

I was tremendously impressed by this cool exotic man with beautiful deep dark blue skin. Even today it seems to me his advice applies to almost any undertaking in life: If you are going to do something then go all in or don't bother doing it at all. This mindset was tailor made for my discreet teenage all or nothing ethos. I guess it still is as I loiter the fringes of late middle age.

Go figure I was a peculiar creature given painfully shy introverted traits mostly governed my younger self. But man if you showed me an empty stage something deep down inside of me burned insofar as I felt the insatiable urge to get right up there and light it up by showing off. In any case music was to become the perfect vehicle for my self-expression. And why not? After all by now I knew I was especially talented and let me tell you I thought it was about time everybody else found out.

★

I MET MY MUSICAL PARTNER Jack Aitken in 2008

when we were both serving Police Officers. When we first jammed it just clicked right away and together we combined in an almost telepathic way. Given music is at its best when it's a collaborative endeavour it's just great when that happens. We only recently discovered our Dad's share the exact same birthday. What's the odds of that? Seemingly some alliances are preordained. I've got to say we've had some real adventures playing around Scotland. One example being when we were booked to play 'The Argyll' pub in Paisley for the first time.

Driving past it looked a right old dive and we had both become more than a tad concerned.

"Just keep driving dude," I'd urged Jack at the time only half joking.

Notwithstanding we pushed foreboding aside, parked up and then went inside. Upon arrival we found nobody there.

"You know it's okay if you want us to cancel. It's totally cool," Jack said to the manager before we'd begun to unload our gear.

"No, not at all," he'd replied. "You guys have made the effort to be here so if you're happy to play we're happy to pay you."

We did just that and the staff made it truly memorable by proceeding to get up onto the bar and dance the night away. They were even so kind as to buy us chips during our break! Funnily enough we have played there a few times since. Never judge a book

81

by its cover as the staff and clientele always gave us a warm reception and treated us brilliantly. Let me tell you it's not always that way which puts me in mind of my very first gig.

It was 1985 and a real crossroads for me. Robert and Ian had since left for university, and I felt mislaid and lonesome without them. I was condemned to working hard for peanuts during the day as a general dogsbody in the local Helensburgh Advertiser printworks. Even so I must confess that I loved that job. A few weeks after starting the foreman had requested to see me in his office. I nervously went in and sat there unsure as to what I had done wrong. For no reason whatsoever I was expecting some sort of earbashing.

"I've been watching you very carefully," he declared scrutinising me closely through the thick lensed glasses he wore.

"Oh, erm, I'm sorry, is there a problem?" I tentatively answered blushing boyishly and awaiting his telling off like some timid church mouse.

"On the contrary," he continued, narrowing his gaze. "There's something unusual about you that I can't quite put my finger on. Even so I've noticed every time you have a spare moment you pick up a brush then busy yourself sweeping the floors. You have a great work ethic so hang in there a while longer as I'm going to push you forward for a printing apprenticeship."

I was taken aback and delighted. Remember this was the economic wilderness of Thatcher's mid-eighties and jobs never mind apprenticeships were like gold-dust.

In any case this would be abruptly snatched away several months later when the company was unexpectedly bought over, and we were all made redundant. Bloody hell I was back to square one. At least there was the consolation of a generous severance pay out which I used to buy a top notch bass-guitar and amplifier.

And so, I reconciled myself to the situation and continued to practice by myself for a while before out of the blue two guys I'd gone to the village primary school with approached. Seems they'd been writing some songs and wanted us to hook up. Steven Barr played keyboard, guitar, and drums, whilst Graham Kirkness played keys and sang lead vocals. Importantly he also owned a small four-track Tascam home recording system, so we set about laying tracks down. These would later be recorded as a demo in the famous Glasgow 'CAVA' studio in our fruitless bid to secure a record deal with Ian returning to make a guest appearance on guitar and Grahams pals girlfriend Laney Lloyd-Jones adding backing vocals.

Word soon got out before we were offered the opening slot at a gig planned for Helensburgh's Victoria Halls supporting the popular local rock band 'Perfect Strangers'. No further information was forthcoming nonetheless we accepted the invitation before starting rehearsals in the Garelochhead church hall.

Oddly enough James 'Huck Finn' MacDonald and his girlfriend Michelle (my unrequited crush) would occasionally sit in and listen as we played, debated, and sometimes argued.

After three-months the gig finally arrived. First on we set up our gear and did a soundcheck before watching on as the headline act did likewise. I couldn't help but notice as a heavy metal band they benefitted from a sizeable following. We on the other hand were a new romantic pop band from the sticks doing a mix of chart covers alongside our own tunes. For some reason only now did this strike me as a problem and Graham evidently agreed.

"Uh oh this could go badly wrong" he worriedly sited nervously observing from backstage as the hall filled with metalheads.

"Just relax. Go out there and enjoy it. Show them how good you are," I encouraged attempting to settle his nerves through concealing my own.

Meanwhile Steven seemed totally oblivious and was simply happy to be there at all which seemed fair enough.

We jointly wore white jeans, sleeveless t-shirts, and sported elaborate hairstyles carefully styled with lashings of gel. Furthermore, I sported long Adidas boxing boots that stretched halfway to my knees. Hey, come on it was the eighties after all. Fashions come and go!

Always one for crooning from the throat Graham had by now developed a penchant of drinking milk before singing insisting it coated his pharynx to make his voice better. Loitering together in the wings the ambiance of the hall was now discernible, and he'd just begun his pre-show ritual of guzzling a large beaker of milk. All of a sudden the organiser abruptly burst in.

"Guys there's been a change to the schedule. Quick I need you on stage right now," he'd blurted.

Shocked Graham lost his grip and spilled the contents of his beaker all over the groin of his white trousers.

"F**K! he cried out in alarm. "Oh shit, what am I going to do now?" he desperately groaned.

I shrugged my shoulders. Nobody had spares and we were now expected to perform. Instead, I threw him the towel I had planned to wipe sweat from my brow between songs under the bright stage lighting.

"Look just try to mop up the worst of it. Come on we've got to hustle!" I'd urged him.

Moments later we walked onto the large stage as the home crowd watched on in silence. It almost looked as though they wanted to hurt us. Regardless I strapped my black Musicman Stingray bass on as Graham walked up to the microphone.

"Hi there, we're 'Strength to Strength' and are going to play you some songs," he'd cheerfully declared.

Silence then they noticed the wet patch on his groin and a discernible collective snigger went up. Shaking my head, I felt bad for him but at the same time sensed my temperature rising. Albeit a slow burn I've always possessed a bit of a temper and once again my mean pride was kicking in. As far as I was concerned we were a unit, and I did not like being part of the joke. It was at this point Miles Davis's advice echoed around the otherwise empty chamber in my head.

'I AM the influence ... Turn it up or turn it off.'

That Stingray bass had a really hot pickup and wailed when cranked, so I swiftly altered the mix by turning my amp up a notch. Spontaneously deciding to get back at them they had compelled my inner injunction to let them have it, so I ripped into the intro for the Go West song: *'Don't look down'*. Off we went as I slapped the axe hard, and I was gratified to sight a few startled faces near the front.

Concluding the opener Graham now approached the microphone.

"Thank you!" he tactfully proclaimed.

Complete silence. We looked at each other nervously for a few seconds in that sizeable venue before I shrugged, and we immediately launched into the It Bites song: *'All in Red'*.

At the time I recall reasoning the crowd of rockers would at least have enjoyed this number given It Bites were something of a crossover band and quite heavy in their own right in a progressive sort of way. Nope, the audience were not having a bit of it.

In any case this particular tune included a few bars presenting a musical breakdown in the last section at which point a complex three-part vocal harmony played out. We totally nailed it since we had rehearsed so hard which I found gratifying.

As the beat thundered on Steven resplendent in shades and by now grinning like a Cheshire cat impulsively stuck his hands to the air to repeatedly clap them over his head.

"Cone on everybody join in with us," he cried encouraging the audience to participate.

'Steven, nnnnnnooooooo ...' I inwardly groaned having already read the room. Arms crossed they stood passive and glared at him as though they wanted to drag him kicking and screaming from the stage and beat him up. Again, as the song finished an eerie silence ensued. Then all of a sudden it was shattered by a lonesome voice from high up in the circle reverberating across the hushed hall.

"HEY JOHN, NICE BOOTS!!!!"

Flushed the venue reacted anew as they now burst into laughter at my expense. It continued this way right until the end of our set and I have to say it felt like we died a slow painful death up there that night. We had played flawlessly. Nevertheless, it was no real surprise they'd hated us. We simply hadn't known our audience.

Afterwards Perfect Strangers went on to kick up a storm as we skulked backstage before retreating to lick our wounds over some Pizza from Helensburgh's Lido chippy at Kidston carpark. As it happens unbeknownst to us a music journalist from the local rag had been in attendance to write a review of the event. It just so happened he held a flame for my big sister at the time and wanted to win her over: Once published he slated Perfect Strangers whilst instead raving about our talent. My goodness cue an angry response in the letters page from their fans over the next couple of publications.

Look, I personally had mixed emotions about all of this. Sure, I was thrilled at such high-profile public validation then again I found his criticism of the others really embarrassing. They were a great bunch of lads and had been gracious enough to offer us the slot in the first place. Furthermore, my big sister didn't fancy him in the least, so it turned out he had completely wasted his time. This all served as my first introduction to the slings and arrows of the music business and let me assure you it wouldn't be my last

It came as no real surprise that we eventually split to go our separate ways. My bandmates had subsequently fallen in love then given it all up to move onto pastures new. Notwithstanding at least we'd gained some national radio airplay when a DJ heard our demo tape and really liked it.

I moved on to play in the popular folk singer Finnian McGurks band for a while and was later offered an audition for a high-profile

Glasgow group who had a UK top ten hit at the time. Turns out having produced our earlier demo the sound engineer Gordon Rintoul was now working on their second album and the bass player had left to go and work with Midge Ure as an alternative. Having earlier dug my sound he remembered it to then recommend me. I was in the now defunct Helensburgh Garth Inn when tipped the wink the gig was mine if I wanted it. By now typically inhibited the offer really unnerved me and I panicked before turning it down. Even so I have no regrets. By this time, I felt a real need to drop anchor in seeking the security of a steady income as opposed to scratching out a living as a musician. After all there's a good reason why 99% of those in the creative arts are mostly poor. Anyhow I recently bumped into a guy I used to go to school with and catching up we then reminisced about the good old bad old days.

"Wait, didn't you play a gig in the Victoria Halls back in the late eighties?" he unexpectedly asked at one point.

I suddenly became cagey because I wondered where this particular line of inquiry was going.

"Erm, yes that's right. Why do you ask?" I delicately responded.

"Yeah I thought as much," he nodded thoughtfully scratching at his chin. "I recall Graham Kirkness pissed himself in fright before going on stage!" he recollected smiling sentimentally without any trace of satire. "I must say your bass was awfully loud that night too!" he concluded screwing up his face as if the memory had somehow traumatised him.

I really couldn't be bothered clarifying what had actually happened with Graham's trousers or why I was so loud. I reasoned he wouldn't have believed me even if I had.

Chapter Seven

'Once Upon a Us'

LOVE IS JUST A WORD until you meet someone who gives it meaning. Like most guys I was always fascinated by girls. I found them mysterious and complex but intensely compelling creatures. Sure, I didn't understand them in the least however, always found myself helplessly gravitating towards their allure. In any case the truth is that a great many boys are scared of pretty girls, and I was no different. It's a linear equation - the terror a young man feels towards a girl being directly proportional to his attraction for her.

It was the late 1980's and the times were changing. A somewhat hedonistic era was drawing to a close and I recall distinguishing a pendent vibe implying nothing would ever be quite the same again. Having had a few casual relationships, the juice had never been worth the squeeze, and I hadn't enjoyed those failed dates at all. Having had just come out of a long-term romantic affair with a girl named Yvonne to this day I'm still at a loss as to what transpired. Nevertheless, I'm glad it did. One of those tough life lessons she effectively taught me never leave room in your future for those who abandoned you in the past.

We'd gotten on like a house on fire. I'd spent my entire wages treating her extremely well and I thought the world of her. As far as I could tell things were really good. Then without warning she stood me up on a prearranged date. Before the advent of mobile phones, I found a phone box to call her and make sure she was alright. Her sister spoke to me instead.

"John please give it a day or two before calling back. Yvonne promises she'll talk to you then to explain what's going on."

Odd. Anyhow I did so only to get the exact same spiel again. This same process then played out a few times over a couple of weeks. I know I know. As daft as I was I simply couldn't face the fact that I was being played by someone I cared about.

"Listen John I'm so sorry," her sister eventually confessed with discernible authenticity. "For what it's worth I think you did really well to last as long as you did. Yvonne has told me to pass on she won't speak to you or ever see you again. Please don't call back."

I was absolutely gutted. Combining insult to injury the bitterest pill to swallow was that she wouldn't even tell me herself. It was particularly cruel, and I certainly didn't deserve that.

At the time I was strung out working dead end jobs on building sites then as a doorman in Helensburgh's lively Commodore hotel disco at night for extra money. My band had broken up, I had a turbulent homelife, little prospect of a meaningful career, and my friends had all either moved on or settled down. If the truth be known ... I was lost.

In a nutshell opportunity wasn't knocking at my door therefore I had to get a grip of my own coattails to haul myself up. The bottom line was I somehow had to find a way of making something happen.

In between times I took a girl named Fiona out for a date. An attractive blond even so I just felt there was no spark between us.

Nevertheless, we had shared an obligatory kiss on her doorstep after I escorted her home.

"Listen I'll give you a call next week to see if you fancy going out again," I uttered as we exchanged phone numbers before parting. The thing is I actually never bothered and ghosted her instead.

'I'm not chasing after her she can call me if she's interested,' I had immaturely reasoned at the time.

Naturally she didn't and why would she. Alternatively, a couple of weeks later she walked into the same pub we'd gone to hand in hand with another guy.

"Uh oh watch out big man," voiced my pal Chris MacFarlane. "She's trying to make you jealous,".

I wasn't convinced. He was very handsome, and it looked like she was having a far better time with him than she'd had with me. Anyway, I deserved everything I got for being a total prat.

To be frank because of Yvonne I was actually still seething and had gone sour on females in general. Seeing no other option, I was instead inclining towards joining the army. Then again it was during this period whilst working on the door that fate decided to intervene one night as I was waylaid out of the blue.

"Hi there how's it going? Listen, my pal really likes you and wants to know if you'd be interested in taking her out?" a chick said sidling in close to me.

"Nah," I replied arrogantly shaking my head, chewing gum and barely giving her any notice. I next slipped her what had become my dismissive stock reply to such queries,

"The thing is I'm not really looking to go out with anyone right now."

"Oh. Well, that's a shame ..." she tailed off loitering awkwardly unsure as what to do next.

"In any case for what it's worth who is she?" I'd extended. For some strange reason my interest was suddenly piqued, and I was now curiously glancing around the lively venue. Proceeding to point her out I then saw her for the first time.

There on the dance floor was a skinny little girl with long lustrous dark hair, green eyes, and impossibly high cheekbones. Watching her dancing in a plain purple t-shirt, jeans, and high heels somehow in that instant everything changed. I know how crazy this sounds but it's true. Even now I can't explain the premonition I had within me as something voiced,

"You're going to marry her".

Startled I swear it took me like an electric shock. Composing myself I coolly turned back to her pal intimating she move a little closer because of the loud music.

"Hey there, I'll tell you what maybe I was being a little hasty," I'd said cupping a hand to her ear. "Sure, why not. Tell her I'd take her out."

A few days passed then I saw her again and my heart skipped a beat. She slowly walked past a couple of times and made big green eyes at me offering ample opportunity to make a move. Old foes, by now I was crippled by my introverted and indirect traits. God how I hated that inhibited part of my younger self. Shy, I was reluctantly stalling. Eventually she'd evidently become fed up so just walked straight up to me to break the ice.

"Right, you, are you going to ask me out or not?"

"Erm yes, I'd like that," I'd stuttered totally taken aback by her directness.

"Good. I've got nothing on next Thursday, so I'll meet you at the train station at seven o'clock okay?" she'd casually continued now sauntering back to her pals who were stifling laughter and watching closely from the periphery of the bustling dancefloor.

"Erm ... great," I called after her. "Oh, by the way I'm John. What's your name?"

"I know," she called back over her shoulder. "I'm Mandy ... and don't forget, Thursday, seven o'clock. Be there." she continued meandering off.

We met as arranged and I was completely taken by her. Refreshing, unlike my former girlfriends she wasn't temperamental vague, or overly complex. Instead, she was really straightforward quick-witted, and great to be around. I'd never met someone who had it as together as her and we agreed on almost everything.

As it happened the only emotional drama that played out during our courtship was mine. Even so she helped me straighten that out. With her I had discovered a sense of purpose and for the first time in a long time I could envisage a positive future. Discarding the army, I joined the Police Service instead and we were married two-years later when she was just twenty years old with me twenty-three.

Once upon a us Mandy gave me two beautiful talented and intelligent daughters as we sadly lost another. Indeed, like any couple we have had our fair share of trials and tribulations. When working through these I always find a cute way of getting around her though through gifting a bouquet of her favourite white lilies.

"I don't think we can really live without each other do you?" I then playfully ask.

Possessing a staggering intuition her eyes customarily intertwine mine for a brief eternity as brown bleeds to green. Like some ancient queen of inner space, she always knows how to soundlessly delve my infinite soul and up until now she has always uttered,

"No."

We then hold each other tight as I always promise we shall grow old together. Had we not met I would have waited forever to be with her again because she's the best thing that ever happened to me and the essential ingredient of my life.

Look, marriage is incredibly hard. How so? Because life is incredibly hard, and you have to do it together. But I find having two hearts minds and souls to solve it is invariably better than one. A good marriage is when an imperfect couple learn to enjoy each other's differences and a great marriage is when you are able to fall in love with the exact same person over and over again. Unusual for a writer I find it hard to articulate how much she means to me.

My debut fictional novel: *'Sailing Towards the End of the World'* (2021), was the first book I had written which I was proud of. Throughout I partly used it as a vehicle for encapsulating what it is like when restless young romantics entwine in what becomes a tragic love affair as life gets in the way. My best attempt to capture the weight of devotion soulmates share, like the principal characters Jonathon and Elisa most long-term couples will go to hell and back at some point. In that case what really matters most is you both make it back. Statistics today measure that 42% of all UK marriages end in divorce therefore I guess a great many don't.

In any case looking back when I was a young man I would often tell Mandy that I loved her when what I mostly meant was "I need you." Now I frequently her that I need her when what I'm really trying to say is, "I love you."

★

(An extract from 'Sailing Towards the End of the World')

HER LONG BLOND HAIR was blowing in the summer

breeze and her mercurial blue eyes seemed focussed upon another time, another place. Those eyes. My God, those eyes. He could easily drift into them and bathe there for an eternity. She always seemed able to get in touch with some deeper reality, to shift to some far away alternate plane of being. So powerful was her perception that he'd instantly recognised she possessed some sort of psychic-power, just like him.

In the beginning, she'd been engaged to another - but after trailing her track for some time she'd finally come around and capitulated to his tender persuasion. Despite her repeated refusals he wouldn't take no for an answer. She was glad of that. Even as she had been rebutting him, she'd been secretly scared that he would. Shortly after she'd begun to clandestinely court him instead. She just couldn't help herself, for his irresistible allure somehow made it easy for her to lie uncharacteristically.

Her fiancé was a good man: plain, respectable, straightforward, dependable ... predictable. More than that, he'd treated her extremely well and she'd convinced herself that in time she could learn how to love him in some way if that was what it took. Fair to say, he was the sensible option and with him she was demure, a flower forever constrained by polite leaves under his shade.

... and then Jonathon Palmer had entered her life. She hadn't needed to learn how to love him at all. Instead, loving him had instantly happened. Like a bolt from the blue - or a foreign being sent from another celestial place - it was as though he'd been guided by destiny to shake up her comfortable but unexciting existence. He was twenty-years old. She was seventeen – and he sent shockwaves right through her carefully mapped-out future.

Sure, he was undeniably humble, quiet, and kind, but he also possessed a mysterious, dangerous, and electrifying edge. An unfathomable aura surrounded him, and she'd instantly felt they'd been reunited once again, after parting from prior undetected lifetimes together. Suddenly, exposed to the warmth of the sunshine of his radiance, she'd blossomed.

Fair to say, he was intoxicating and tantalising. Unlike many of the gentlemen of the time, he wasn't artless, vain, or pristine – he never even bothered trying to be. Instead, he was effortlessly attractive and everything a man should ever be. She knew all of the other girls felt it too. She'd heard them talk about him as girls always do when alone in each-others company. They all fantasised about being with him. What made him even more fascinating to them was the fact that he never even seemed to notice. After all, he'd made it clear to her from the outset that he only had eyes for one, and one alone ... her.

Somehow, the illicit time they spent together always felt precious and never quite enough, as though there was no tomorrow, nor another moment to waste.

As for him, he knew from the very first instant he'd set eyes on Elisa that she was the one. He knew there and then that she was the girl he'd marry. In some strange way, he'd always known, long before they'd even met. As far as he was concerned, they simply had to be together regardless the cost. Often conjecturing how men could be stirred enough to write poetry inspired by the object of their affection - suddenly he understood completely. She was a work of art.

Moving towards her, she'd presently reoriented to the moment. Absentmindedly biting her lower lip, she'd then smiled to tentatively reach out and take hold of his hand for the very first time. He remembered how curious it had felt as that peculiar tingle of pleasure had spread up his arm, travelling along his veins to cause his heart to quiver a beat. The best he could do was to liken it to being tinged by the divine feminine energy, as though the Goddess Aphrodite herself had stretched out and stroked him. For her, no less. She had felt a flutter in her lower belly and became lightheaded in the same instance as their passion then proceeded to outpace them both.

After a while he'd held her close. Cheek to cheek and utterly lost to the heavenly scent of her gardenia perfume, at that point he'd decided to never let her go, so gently whispered to her ear,

"I would have waited forever to be with you."

She could feel his physical power, but he always used his strength carefully with her, appropriately – softly. Lost in the infinite universe of his mottled hazel-coloured eyes for the longest time, the best she'd eventually been able to muster was to softly murmur,

"I'm glad you didn't have to."

It would be entirely unfitting to say that he'd taken her virginity. Instead, she had willingly gifted it to him just as he had gifted his to her.

They'd only known each other for several weeks, yet soon after, they'd absconded together to avoid the resultant scandal. In doing so, she'd inwardly thought,

'My God, what am I doing?'

They were married four-days later at short-notice in the simplest of ceremonies. Afterward they'd sat together in a meadow near the remote church on that fine summer day. They'd then stayed up all through the night to witness it become the morning light. Settled beneath the stars, they'd held each other tight and confessed their hopes and dreams. At some point or other, he'd tenderly placed his hand upon her stomach and sworn an oath upon the head of their unborn child that he would always look after them, always be true.

Of course, the years had passed, and life got in the way. Oscar was born and growing up fast. Jonathon was barely ever there anymore. When he was, he often drank too much in a bid to try and block out whatever confidential woes were ailing him. Eventually they'd come to fight just as much as they'd used to laugh.

No matter his undeniable and undying adulation of Elisa, she sensed he remained possessed by a restless inner compulsion that just wouldn't let him be. He carried ghosts from past lives, and she found him increasingly emotionally detached. Unable to gather moss, he seemed illogically caged within the four walls of the wonderful home she'd made for them. Thus, despite his repeated assurances to the contrary, he'd always been coerced into chasing some stupid venture or other 'just one more time', and it had placed their relationship under enormous strain. The infamous jaunt which had culminated with his near fatal clash with the tiger had been the thing which captured the public's attention. Thus, it had begotten his ascension to recognition. Sadly, it had also been the beginning of the end for her.

The finale, she simply couldn't take any more and at her insistent behest they'd eventually separated.

Devastated, it was during that time he'd eventually slipped into the arms of another for comfort, to try and fill the empty void of Elisa - a yawning chasm left within his soul. Paradoxically, he was now surrounded by ever more people and had received more attention than before. But he hadn't changed. Everyone else had. As such, he always felt tragically lonesome amongst the burgeoning crowds of socialites and fawning admirers.

Illogical, throughout their time apart Elisa wore one of his favourite shirts he'd left behind to bed each night. She concurrently wished to never see him again, whilst hoping that she would. Naturally, she'd heard rumours he'd seen someone else. Hurt, she'd pretended to pity her, whilst also wondering who the lucky girl was.

She loved him so much that she hated him. Yet still, first thing each morning she'd rise and quickly glance out of the window into the empty courtyard below just in case he was there. Met by an empty space each day, she would quietly mutter, "Good," to herself, whilst her heart simultaneously betrayed her resolve by briefly sinking anew.

So, it continued like this for almost ten-months. Then one morning she had looked out and he was there, standing soaking wet in the torrential rain.

Her heart had skipped a beat as he looked up at her, before she had inwardly summoned every ounce of strength to then mutter,

"Oh no you don't Jonathon Palmer. Not that easy. Not that easy!"

Finally awakening from his stupor he'd gotten a grip of himself and realised his ultimate truth: He had to be with her again, no matter how; no matter the cost. Quite simply, he always had.

Following a week of leaving bunches of her favourite White Lilies on the doorstep each morning, she'd finally given in and agreed to see him.

He'd watched her cradle the latest bouquet by way of his newest apology, but would it be enough to win her back? At that point neither of them knew. He begged her forgiveness – making sincere promises to forgo any further escapades. At that, she'd finally broken down with tears welling in her once-innocent gorgeous blue-eyes to sorrowfully utter,

"I've come to realise there's a part of you deep within that I just can't reach. No one ever will... so, I'm not sure I even want to try anymore."

Even so, whilst simultaneously making that declaration, her resplendent psychic eyes had merged with his, then lingered for the longest time searching for the truth. As always, they conveyed his inner awareness. They transmitted he was truly sorrowful, that he meant every word. Admittedly, she had also been confused to discern something else. An unfathomable disruption. Nonetheless, she pushed it aside for she sensed him to be true.

"Please, if you want me to, I'll get down on my knees and beg," he'd finally pleaded with her.

Damn him. Her hard-head had already decided their relationship was a lost cause, but he always had a knack of talking her soft-heart round like no other ever could. She'd sighed a long sigh, before haltingly replying,

"That won't be necessary."

Contrary to her hurt pride, she'd given him one last chance and also resolved never to mention her knowledge of his fling. Why would she? She reasoned they'd been separated. There was simply no profit in it, so she swallowed her vanity to cast it aside.

Together again, he proved as good as his word. No longer boozing, once again she had her considerate and attentive husband; Oscar his doting father.

After trying unsuccessfully for the longest time, and the sadness of several miscarriages, at the beginning of the year 1640 he'd softly placed his hand upon her stomach and sworn an oath upon the head of their second unborn child. A promise to find them a better life away from the political instability of England which would eventually lead to the civil war.

With her agreement, he'd composed a letter to his best-friend from the army, and former sparring-partner and second Ben Cribb on their behalf. He'd quickly replied. More than that, he'd been utterly delighted to hear from him and was eager to facilitate their request. So, it was then agreed. They would next make the suitable arrangements to travel together to Liverpool forthwith, to catch the sail which would ferry them toward their new life overseas.

Heartbreakingly, the unfathomable disturbance that she'd been unable to foretell was that the voyage was pre-ordained as doomed. Of course, she'd been unable to apprehend this for a good reason. As much as they were fated to be together, destiny had also pre-determined that other unavoidable events would soon abruptly separate them again. Similarly, it was just meant to be.

☆

INHABITING A WRAITHLIKE PLANE, he strolled barefoot awhile across the beach hand in hand with his decedent wife. As the waves faintly rolled forth to goad the shoreline, he felt the dampness of the sand between his toes, and it was utterly indescribable to be reunited with her once again.

Truly sublime. She momentarily drew to a halt, then looked up at him with her resplendent gaze. At that he felt pinwheels go off in his head, as his heart proceeded to ache with the gravity of the love that he felt for her.

Her lengthy soft straw-coloured hair was teasing him whilst floating at the behest of an effortless draft, so he reached out to lightly run his fingers through it. He simply had too. He couldn't resist.

She tilted her head and briefly closed her eyes, smiling in ecstasy at the texture of his touch, and he became momentarily lost to her recognisable scent.

Proceeding to move close, he tenderly placed his hands either side of her head to employ a tender kiss on her forehead, then did likewise to each of her sealed eyelids. She paused in time as the smile framed her exquisite face, then slowly opened them again. Becoming coy, she gazed up at him and now bit her lower lip in that inimitable way of hers. He adored that about her. God, he adored everything about her. He soaked every small detail of it up. He'd missed her so much that his soul was fetching aflame at the mere thought of having to part with her again. He knew they would soon have no other option. After all he was alive, and she was dead. Even so, she was the most alive woman he'd ever known.

She put her arms around his back, and now drawing him close they stood skin-to-skin as they held each other tight in a loving embrace for the first time in several years. He noted how warm and soft she felt; how well she fit him. They'd been made for each other. There could be no other explanation. He was her Perseus, and she was his Andromeda.

Much shorter than him, although slight he could feel her suppleness as he lightly stroked the small of her back. Next embracing her tightly, his arms braced around her waspish waistline. Contrasting the dense solidity of his own physical form, her feminine lack of muscle-mass made her feel yielding, malleable ... almost velvety. Just cuddling her in this ethereal place decreased his physical pain and melted away all of his earthly woes.

Ineffable, he'd almost forgotten how fulfilling it could be to engage in simple touches and bodily contact with the person that you were supposed to be with. Such a truly healing impression. A restorative state, in that moment nothing else mattered. Focussed solely upon his partner, he had become fully in touch with the magnitude of the emotion that he felt for her. The sentiment was totally overwhelming him, and it was further heightened by the fact that he subliminally grasped she felt the same way too. Connected, it was just so right: a timeless fusion of total intimacy.

If he'd been granted the choice, he would have elected to remain like this for the rest of time - two statuesque marble lovers, frozen in an infinite devoted embrace.

They presently kissed, and he tasted her again. She had closed her eyes once more – but this time he elected to keep his open. He wanted to take it all in. He wanted to remember this for all times-sake, so he simply had to watch. Familiar, this was what he had missed all along. It was apparent she was the essential ingredient of his life. She'd made the world turn; the stars come out at night, the seasons change, and the tides rise and fall. As far as he was concerned, without her they'd become cliched, dismal and devoid of any joy.

Breaking, they proceeded in silence again, together hand in hand. Their footfall was light, more analogous a drift than whatever else. Undeniable, something sinister loitered nearby – he could clearly distinguish it – but he was somehow wordlessly bolstered by her presence that it could not incumber him in the privation of this spectral place. No. Never with her.

They drew to a close and she turned to look at him. In doing so, she mildly took his hands and spoke for the first and only time to utter in her unmistakable silken timbre,

"Do you remember, you told me not long after we'd first met that you would have waited forever to be with me? Well, now you must prove it.

"I'm waiting for you, but you must do one thing for me. Persist until the time is right. You must persist."

And at that she had gone, fading away like a ghostly apparition at the behest of first light. With heart-broken anew, he inwardly swallowed his woe and then determined,

'I must remember her words at all costs!'

Then the scene brusquely altered, and he found himself attended by most of the others that had consisted of the landing party. Bolstering them further brooked the unfortunate matelots prior waived on this disastrous quest. In stark contrast to his divine liaison with Elisa, together they now entailed a solemn assembly. Distraught, he realised they collectively tolerated in silent reverence to a swamped hulk. Recognising it as the Mothership, he had become overwhelmingly sad. What on Earth could this peculiar fantasy mean?

★

AWAKENING FOR A SHORT TIME in the early hours of darkness, he found the little vessel taken alike a fallen leaf in a keen autumnal stream. The sea's glib slap playfully tanned the freeboard as yet again his thoughts had inevitably shifted back to Elisa. Naturally, the multitude of white lilies lay passive on the silent sea as he floated on through them. All but out of reach they vaunted their satin leaves toward him. Another hallucination? Well, of course. They simply could not be real.

Regardless, he apprehended their tacit design. Her favourite flowers, he presently understood they'd been sent to remind him she'd been the love of his life, and the best thing that had ever happened to him. Thinking back, he'd never quite understood why, however her delight whence presented with them had always required no further explanation, so he had no proper reason to do otherwise. For this reason, he had persisted in gifting them to her right unto the end of their incomplete time together.

Self-sacrificial in nurturing him whilst he'd chased foolish lost causes, she'd always been there. It was for that reason he'd naively come to take her presence and dedication utterly for granted. This was to be his imperishable shame. True to her wedding vows, she had stuck by him through it all and bestowed him a gift beyond price - a perfect son. Cited a 'hero' by some, it just so happened he was actually no more than a heedless fool who'd failed them both when it had counted most. To think, the only battle he'd ever truly lost also just so happened to be the only one that had ever mattered to him.

In a maudlin state, once more he bitterly gazed over the edge of the transom to outwardly slur toward the now floret-littered ocean, "Damn you. It's not fair!" he spat. "Why consume all that is pure and innocent, yet spare one so foul as me?"

Five-years after the tragedy, the injustice of it all still left him dumbfounded, particularly in this present soused mess. In verity, he'd never really understood what she'd seen in him. As far as he was concerned, she'd been much too good for a cretin like him. Indeed, even when his ego had become intoxicated during that mad time following his ascension to relative fame - and he had come to neglect her most – it was then he'd actually needed her more than ever. Paramours entwined, as it transpired their blend had equated a higher plane. They were two-halves become two-wholes. Retracting with frowzy head now in hands, he knew her to forever be his paradise lost.

Dissimilar those fair-weather friends he'd ignored her for, once turbulent times hit it was her that had kept him from falling apart during his most complicated moments. True, those sometime associates had evaporated, whilst she'd offered him enough affection to enable him to feel better. A shoulder to cry on, she'd sought naught else in return other than seemingly obtaining tangible satisfaction from witnessing him finding the emotional relief he'd so desperately craved. Therefore, as it had transpired, she had not only been his one true love, but his truest friend.

Albeit immeasurably sensitive, imaginative, shy, and softly spoken, in privation she was certainly no pushover and as spirited as a finely-honed blade. Like all good spouses do, she had plenty about her to provide him with more than enough of a challenge to force him to get his act together, sharpen-up and become a better man.

An example was his return from the ill-fated expedition which had culminated with his infamous encounter with the Tiger. Following his protracted homecoming, he'd wholeheartedly expected her to run into his arms with warm tears of relief and joy – to meet him with an ardent embrace. Instead, she'd strode forward to shock him by slapping him hard across the face, before condemning,

"You damned fool. I told you not to go! Don't ever scare me like that again, or I'll be the one doing the mauling, do you understand me?"

He next recalled one summer afternoon several months following the birth of Oscar. Pinpointing it the happiest point of his entire life, they'd held hands before he'd chased her slim-waist and long fair lace skirts through the lengthy grass as the pink silk ribbon adorning her chapeau had trailed behind.

Catching up and gently wrestling her giggling to the ground, as they'd lain together under the canopy of a mature Elm, she'd mischievously wiggled her nose and gritted her teeth to roll him over and momentarily pin him down palm to palm. As he'd laughed then longingly gazed up into her breath-taking blue eyes, he'd impulsively freed one hand enough to push her bonnet aside and run his fingers through her newly unbound flaxen hair. At that, she'd cuffed at him to tease,

"Why, how dare you, Jonathon Palmer! You certainly know how to spoil a girls carefully crafted look in no time at all!"

They'd playfully wrestled then impulsively kissed awhile before he'd roguishly turned her back over. She always had the tendency to catch him off-guard with her quicksilver acuities, and he remembered she'd momentarily broken his tender embrace to stare inquisitively at the cobalt sky for a moment, before catching him out by proclaiming a most unforeseen reflexion.

"You know, it's just occurred to me. I'm a Pisces, and Oscar is a Cancerian! Ha, ha, I'm a fish and he's a crab. We're both children of the sea!"

At the time a throwaway remark, how her astute rumination had stuck in his head and subsequently come back to haunt him in the years following their ill-fated passage across the Irish Sea, as they bid to start life anew on Ben Cribbs estate in County Cork.

Time now equated the unquantifiable precious material of life, and he'd let his past slip by too fast. He ruminated, if only he'd been able to slow down those all too fleeting moments of delight – to savour them further. Unable to turn the clock back, at least he held onto some good memories renewable enough to last forever.

Water on the other hand possessed neither memory nor moral compass. The same indifferent brine that presently convoyed him inexplicably through dozens of her phantasmal favourite white lilies had heedlessly swallowed her whole, whilst conversely expelling him out.

He presently reoriented himself. In the lessening grip of an opiated high, he piteously looked toward the eavesdropping Aquarian Moon, as tears jammed his eyes.

"My love. My life. I'm so, so sorry. Please forgive me," he sentimentally whispered, before becoming overcome by sadness.

With his heart now breaking afresh, the ocean heard him cry for a few seconds. Throughout the slings and arrows of life, he'd found out the hard way who had deserved to be by his side - to share the best of times with. It was her. It had always been her. To this end, she'd been the one who'd served his anchor to reality, the loving source of support which latched his life onto the good things she had revealed that it could hold if you only opened up your heart.

Like no other could, she'd always been able to read between the lines. Thus, had ever been the only one able to somehow coax him into expressing his most anguishing emotional experiences.

As for his sometime lover? She'd just been another unintended casualty of his jarring fate. Collateral damage, beyond any shadow of a doubt he had undeniably loved her for a time too, albeit differently. Thus, the reason he had come to demonise her. In truth, it was the only way he had been able to bring himself to stay away from her and commit fully to winning Elisa back.

As it happened, alone following the maritime tragedy, the everyday sadness of his grim reality had come to paint the canvas of his life in infinite shades of grey and black. His misery was beyond all adequate description and the improper guilt and bitterness he felt had intensified his sadness ever more. It had consumed every waking minute of his tortured continuation.

Like any parent, his love for his child was unconditional and infinite. Bad enough to lose his soulmate - the pain of losing his son and the unborn child they had created together was an unbearable aggravation that would n'er let him be. Commonly perceived the greatest terror of all, death e'er shadows the dark recesses of each mortal mind. Yet, in truth - as only a parent that has lost a child can truly attest - there was far worse than that. Indeed, mourning the loss of his son and unborn child was the most devastating and soul-crushing pain he, or any other grieving parent could ever possibly know.

Jonathon Palmer would never get over it. Instead, it was something that he just had to live with. Unimaginable, to awaken each day and witness the sunrise, while all he had ever loved would n'er have the opportunity to experience the same again. A black hole where his heart should be, it had disbursed his soul. Indeed, the grief was a malignant worm that had burrowed beneath his skin to infect his very being - before becoming a truculent wasp within his head - an inescapable whirlwind inside his mind every time it took to frenzied flight.

Each new day ordained his heart must break afresh. He had no other option than to live on without those he ached for most. His earlier temperance had subsequently waned. Obviously, he'd then been introduced to a new way of numbing himself. Opium had superseded alcohol as his favoured poison of choice, quickly replacing his forsaken wife as his best friend. Next it effortlessly proceeded to become his only friend – before it finally revealed its true form as a Trojan-Horse and his worst enemy. At that point it had assumed control and he had plumbed new depths of what was already a living hell.

Here, hopelessly lost at sea, he chanced another peek overboard only to discover the tiny dinghy now completely surrounded by dozens of buoyant floral reminders of his one true-loves delight. A slight breeze had also picked up and had begun to rustle a simple crimped refrain over and over again in Elisa's unmistakable voice,

"Forget me not... do this for me... persist... persist... persist."

Was this real, or another hallucination? It was so hard to tell. He retracted back into the boat, then listened for a while as the almost imperceptible mantra eventually waned off into the distance, then ceased. As it faded away, he pitifully pled aloud,

"Please, don't go."

Met by silence, sadly it had been to no avail. He next decided to chance another glance overboard. The lilies now littered the sea for as far as the eye could see. Incalculable, odd that each and every one had wilted.

Suddenly afraid, he hurriedly retracted in fright. Then he saw it. A single white lily was placed upon the bow-loader of the dinghy. Gobsmacked, he stared at it for the longest time, before finally making a move to reach out for it. As his fingers finally closed around its stem it proceeded to fade away, leaving him with naught else but a grip of fresh air.

Moaning, the ocean heard him cry again until he eventually waived to the effect of the poppy once more and dropped into the refuge of an entheogenic oblivion. Sadly, he was now well-versed in the truism when all you love is unexpectedly smothered out there can be no such thing as healing. You must instead endure a spun-out life which is befallen an abominable disease of the heart.

Chapter Eight

'The Animal Within

I ABHOR CRUELTY AND violence which might seem ironic given my former expertise as a Police Firearms Instructor. Then again I suppose the entire point is there are those who don't in the least, so there has to be a time and place for it otherwise you run the risk of becoming a victim. It's pretty obvious you need to keep your wits about you in eschewing that.

From the off let's just put this right out there: Life is intrinsically unfair and often brutally difficult. Moreover a significant part of the underlying tragedy is that it is also fraught with those who are inherently malevolent and always on the lookout to spread their own particular sort of misery onto unsuspecting others. I guess that's what bullies teach kids at school - they forewarn if you don't push them back then they'll just keep on pushing you. Simply put if you're not at the table then you're on the menu.

That said it adds up to a significant failure on your own part if you allow any of this to demoralise you, knock you off your path, or make you bitter cynical cowardly, or even a bully yourself. The antithesis can be found in the fact we are remarkable creatures capable of shouldering unthinkable burdens. We have an inherent capacity for seeing through the rough times thus are capable of taking the biggest of hits to somehow rise again in moving forward towards our goals. Indeed unless you've been born into some power assisted and privileged background any success you gain is usually defined by your ability to take the knocks regardless all else. Anyway, with regard conflict you can usually avert trouble through just looking the part. Even so I have also found out to my own cost that this doesn't always work.

Situated on the River Clyde it stood to reason Helensburgh's Commodore disco would be frequented by servicemen from the local military bases including sailors, marines, and soldiers. As expected local lads would seek to take them on at the weekends. It's probably like that anywhere civilians and servicemen mingle socially. Once combined with alcohol it often reaps a volatile brew.

One incident in particular sticks out when I was working the door as a bouncer. Liveried up in black trousers shoes white shirt, and black bowtie there were four of us and we'd often split up to various locations throughout the venue to keep an eye on things. You know how it can be when you have a large congregation of drunken young people who are out for fun. There's always someone who revels in causing hassle and spoiling everyone else's enjoyment.

Anyway, I was near the dancefloor and noticed three sailors annoying a group of young women. They'd obviously had too much to drink and just wouldn't take no for an answer.

"Hey guys come on," I'd intervened. "Enough already give the girls a break or I'll have to ask you to leave."

"F**k off," the nearest snarled dismissively after turning to gauge me. It just so happened he was the brashest and nearest my size.

"Look knock it off nobody wants any hassle," I'd continued tactfully. "Take the hint. They're not interested and you're starting to ruin everyone's night," I'd reasonably continued.

Suddenly turning he'd pushed out with both hands and shoved me in the chest. Rocking backwards I shook my head but kept my feet. Gathering myself I stepped forward to place a hand on his shoulder.

"Listen," I said to his adjacent ear over the thumping music. "Enough is enough ... "

"I've already told you just p**s off," he replied, and attempted to push me again.

This time I'd anticipated it and swiftly moved aside.

"Right touch me again and we'll be fighting do you understand?" I warned trying to sound tough but by now trembling with adrenaline.

At this his they'd sighted one of my colleagues who'd noticed this unfolding heading across, and their demeanor unexpectedly altered to become friendly. They shared a look then abruptly agreed it was perhaps best to leave after all.

"Everything alright?" my coworker inquired eyeing them up.

"It's all good," I'd replied starting to usher them toward the doorway whilst indicating I had it in hand. "These guys have decided to go elsewhere. It's cool."

The loudmouth had now become extremely pleasant and reassuringly placed an arm around my shoulder as he proceeded to apologise – that is, until we got outside. As the door closed behind us I realised too late I was isolated, and it was an ambush. Any predator knows the best way to attack its quarry is from behind and they did so by proceeding to weigh in with a flurry of rabbit punches and kicks. Cheap shots I instinctively hunkered down in an attempt to become a smaller target. I was in trouble and in-between blows impulsively reasoned my best chance was to take them to the ground so grabbed out at the leader and tripped him down. Another intervened and attempting to stifle his assault I hauled at him too. Together the three of us proceeded to brawl on the pavement as the remainder occasionally ran in to aim kicks at me before retracting back to the wall. Absurd throughout he kept squawking,

"Leave them alone, leave them alone!"

Surreal, it was almost as though I was the one doing something wrong. Scuffling it felt as though I was fighting for my life. I'd lost buttons from my shirt and my bowtie was gone. True I was taking a beating but the longer it progressed I at least started to prove a match for my assailants and was somehow holding my own. An eternity I guess it only really lasted a couple of minutes or so.

Eventually straddling atop the leader's waist to suppress him the second was back up along with the other. Momentarily focused on them circling me I was unexpectedly taken by absolute agony. Looking down the guy on the ground had strained his head to sink his teeth into my ribcage like a rabid dog. At the time I absurdly remember thinking,

'Shit this isn't fighting fair!' through the agony.

No matter how hard I tried he wouldn't let go. I must have beaten his head a dozen times in complete desperation in between fending the others off. I hadn't felt pain like it before. He eventually let go by rolling me over and regaining his feet. A stand-off then ensued as I did likewise, and we screamed profanities at each other. Then as quickly as it all started the leader collected the Adidas Samba training shoe he'd lost in the scuffle, and they ran off. Thank God it was over.

When we fight we openly express the primeval feral animal that lurks mostly dormant in the dark recesses of our psyche. Battered black and blue at least it had been a score draw and I'd taken satisfaction from noticing the ring leader's swollen eye. Assessing my torso his bite had broken the skin into an angry purple welt even so I went on to finish the shift in an attempt to impress my workmates.

I'm not ashamed to admit that once I had gone home to become isolated in my bedroom I let it all out by crawling naked into a ball on the carpet and bawling like a child.

I wore his fierce teeth marks for weeks until the nasty wound eventually healed. However, the psychological scars lasted and surprisingly manifest again during the spring of 1990. Upon joining the Police I was undergoing recruit training at the college in Medmenham, Buckinghamshire. We'd often put theory to practice through role play whereupon students would be selected to play Police Officers whilst others wore civilian clothing to play criminals engaged in some nefarious activity or another. This necessitated closely following a surreptitious script. Experiential learning the remnants would accompany the instructor nearby to observe how the trainee cops coped throughout and make notes.

Anyway I'd been selected to play a criminal. Briefed accordingly I was to agitate two officers before being arrested for assault. The precept was I should verbally withstand until they placed hands on me then acquiesce. It all went as planned until they attempted to take me into custody. As they both grabbed hold of my arms something deep down took over as I suffered a jarring flashback to being attacked and bitten. Ensuing to ragdoll both of my shocked colleagues around for a time I then wrestled them both howling and disheveled to the ground before standing over them wild-eyed and panting like a madman.

"STOP, STOP, STOP!" raged the instructor as I was abruptly

brought back to the moment. "HUGHES WHAT THE F**K ARE YOU DOING? HAVE YOU LOST YOUR MIND?" screamed the scouse Sergeant Ray Peel obviously furious. "You f*****g idiot you're meant to lose, remember?" He scolded in a rage.

"I'm very sorry Sergeant," I muttered by now back in the moment and beaming bright red in front of my watchful peers on the sideline who were struggling to suppress their mirth.

"Get out of my sight," he spat, pushing his index finger into my face.

"Change back into uniform and I will see you back in the classroom do you understand me?"

Crestfallen I had trodden back to the dormitory and then changed before making my way back to class. I'd blown it and reasoned I was about to be told to pack my bags.

I nervously reached the door then paused as I resigned myself to fate. Sighing I opened it and walked in. Seated by their desks my pensive classmates consecutively turned to look at me as Peel stood ashen faced by the front of the room. You could hear a pin drop.

"Well, well, well," he eventually muttered in his sardonic scouse drawl. "Look everybody if it isn't 'No-Lose' Hughes!"

Tension broke in an instant as the entire room erupted into a fit of hysterics including him. As it happens I did go on to pass the course and the nickname stuck with Black Class of 2/90. Up until retirement I'd occasionally bump into those that remained in service and without fail they would usually chirp in,

"Alright 'No-Lose' how's it going?"

Labels often stick and I drew on this disclosure and the initial disco assault for the main character Jonathon 'the Tiger' Palmer who featured throughout my debut novel: '*Sailing Towards the End of the World*' (2021).

As for Sergeant Peel? He turned out to be something of a scoundrel himself. An open secret he permitted a bit of an anti-establishment streak and I later heard he'd seemingly enjoyed the farce so much he'd gone on to entertain future courses by regaling that infamous incident. My goodness he was particularly sore on us throughout those fourteen weeks, so much so we certainly received a far rougher ride than our counterparts in Orange Class. With an old-time instructor who wanted to shine success on their part reflected well on him - hence he fed them the answers to their weekly law exams well in advance. Alternatively Ray ensured we worked our socks off for it. Finding the injustice of watching my fellow recruits from Orange Class hit the bar each night insufferable it was only later on reflection that it dawned on me Ray was essentially doing it for our own good.

Eventually kicked out of training he had seemingly lost his cool during a trainers summit to throw a punch at a high-ranking officer. If I'm being honest this made me like him even more. Anyhow I've never disclosed what caused my irregular behaviour during that incident therefore, just like my schoolteachers I guess he must have simply assumed I was too thick to follow simple instructions.

Throughout writing my debut novel I was suffering health issues and heading for retirement. The UK had entered a national lockdown as a means of countenancing the Covid-19 pandemic and to be honest my coping mechanism included not only writing the book itself but taking solace from the bottom of a few too many bottles. The chapter I'm about to share was actually penned whilst I was hungover and feeling particularly blue. It's reasonable to say my turmoil at the time bled onto the page through the main protagonists own struggles. Actually unloading my misery onto him helped me immeasurably. As you are about to find out Jonathon Palmer was an apple that hadn't fallen too far from the tree. In truth I ensured that he took ownership of my own personal angst, so in this sense I owe him an awful lot.

★

(An extract from 'Sailing Towards the End of the World')

TIMELINE: SEPTEMBER, in southeast Asia, the year of the lord 1645. Not that it mattered, but he knew it to be his birthday. The one known as 'the Tiger' also knew if he didn't cease, then the poppy would devour him for all time and that he would be forever rapt. However, it was simply too good. In fact, so much more than that. In the same instant common-sense and logic were downright annulled. Former good allies, they'd certainly been afforded momentary reflexion – before subsequently being discarded in little more than a jiffy.

Immersed as he was in his own travail, living for the moment seemed a much better discretion, for now at least. In any case he could always stop after just one more time. As he stared at the pipe with an almost uncontrollable entheogenic urge, this concept made him feel somewhat better. After all, he was in control ... wasn't he? Of course, he knew deep down that he was hoodwinking himself. It was a futility - a paltry self-deception ultimately designed to afford his morality no more than a sub-optimal delusion of choice. He'd conceived the idea no more than to ease his momentary misgivings about being in an unmanageable state – which, if the truth be told he undoubtedly was.

He briefly caught his diabolical naked replication in the grimy mirror. A gaunt, grey face bereft of life, framed by unkempt beard and dishevelled hacked locks stared back from gormless eyes. He purposely strained a counterfeit smile, only to reveal pallid-tarnished teeth. As it appeared to him, the likeness masqueraded an inferior doppelganger openly manifest to mock him.

Caught by his own inferior copy, such was his shame that he became lost to an aberration - momentarily pondering exactly who was watching who. After a period of solipsism, he was suddenly overwhelmed by sadness for the person that he had once been – vibrant, fetching, proud and full of zest. Ruefully, he briefly wished the despicable, opiate addled wretch in the mirror would just reach out and drag him in, consume him and be done with it. Nonsensical, at that repugnant thought he suddenly became petrified, hence instinctively lashed out. Shattering the glass with a well-placed thrust, of course this achieved no more than littering the parquet floor with menacing shards and further soiling the erstwhile fouled wooden boards with rubicund nurds of gore from his now abraded right-mitt.

Indifferent, it mattered not given the numerous disfigurements adorning his body were testament enough that he regularly cut himself anyway, just to remind him he was still alive.

"Seven-years bad luck?" he slurred to nobody in particular, "Hah! I've had thirty-seven already, another seven matter not ... that is, if I'm doomed hapless enough to behold them!" he pettily appended.

Finally, he self-piteously slumped in a ball to the ground. An utter wretch, he had settled upon suicide several times and had meant it. Yet, odd that when it came to the deed some primal constitution always proved just enough to serve preventative. Conclusively, instead he next decided upon adhering to one of his couched meditations by slurring out aloud,

"I will gladly expire, but not by my own hand, nor from a damned lack of trying to live on."

In any case, after a moment or two he presently pushed all deliberation aside. He was merely wasting time - delaying the inevitable, so to speak. Resolution anew, he roused, assembled the paraphernalia, then quickly lit-up the oil lamp to vaporize the drug. Without further ado he greedily sucked at the pipe and deeply inspired.

In what seemed an instant the misery of his agitated state - the pointlessness of his life, the nausea, craving, aches, and pains - were replaced with a feeling of deep relaxation, as the familiar ecstatic sensation of calm-bliss flounced through his frame like a fast-flowing incoming tide of warmth and illumination. Such was the efficacy of the hit, he presently felt as though he were being affectionately enfolded by God-almighty himself.

After a few seconds of savouring the exquisite high, he contentedly smiled before longingly gazing at the pipe with glazed pupils to declare aloud,

"My prized friend I humbly request you disregard my prior misgivings ... you really are truly sensational!"

Wholly elated he lessened his rancid cranium against a squalid old sylvan partition wall. Cloying humidity, effulgent perspiration, and filthy surroundings (including his own horrid reek) now seemed altogether extraneous. Odious guilt, grief and pain were currently superseded by euphoria; he was now oblivious to it all and quite simply cared not one iota.

If he had been remotely bothered anymore he might have regretted ever conceding to the analgesic prescription that had set him on this erroneous path what seemed a lifetime before. Perhaps even chastised himself for daring to question his indissoluble dependence upon the opiate a few moments hence. But he just wasn't. He simply didn't care anymore. In that instant it could have his eternal soul for all he cared. Just like everything else what had seemed important mere moments before had now become entirely whimsical: Life itself inconsequential, superfluous ... a tawdry, paltry onerous affair.

When sober, he was never able to satisfactory sleep. The burden of mental malady and physical pain that bore down upon him was akin the globe forever propped atop Atlas's figurative shoulder. Enduring trauma relating to the battlefields of Europe had affiliated with his personal tragedy – and together they combined to plague his waking consciousness. Reminiscences of his tragic Elisa and Oscar combined with the abdominal bullet-wound and once shattered wrist and damaged vertebrae to perpetually nag him. Yet, in this transcendent stupor, he now found himself tantalisingly fatigued.

As usual, he would not contest it too long. He craved death and already knew that prior to tripping toward the deep drug-induced slumber his last remorse was going to prove another familiar mantra. To this end he proceeded to openly solicit his maker for eternal repose by uttering,

"Please God, I beg you allow me silent darkness - the abyss of senseless bliss. Take pity on my awful soul and ensure I never wake up".

Alas, as it so happens, existential crises and self-piteous pleas seldom combine more than some hollow, vacuous catcall. Thus, he would inevitably return from the fleeting bliss afforded by the drug induced drowse to find the familiar anguish of his disturbed existence patiently awaiting his return. It always unwearyingly abided nearby, like some everlasting insidious attendant. Consequentially, the ongoing cycle of guilt, grief, pain, trauma – substance abuse – and self-loathing persisted unabated.

He dearly beseeched inner peace: yet, dissimilar the fledgling stems of a sapling e'er stretching toward the sunlight of life, instead his yearning mimicked dank, soiled roots forever forging ever lower to dank loam and lull.

Yet worse would soon succeed. Unbeknownst to him they were about to disembark with the sole purpose of hoarding his life. Following limpid instructions, they'd successfully sought him out. In all honesty, this proved no tangible coup whatever considering tall English opium addicts were never too tricksy to pin-down in Southeast Asia at this point in history.

Furthermore, recent gossip had spread like wildfire and conspired to lead them straight to his cloistered den. Patently, he'd recently fought off four opportunist thieves who'd mistaken him for an easy target then jumped him in a dark alleyway. It was reputed they'd mercilessly set about him with staves - before he'd permanently disabled one by snapping his leg at the knee, ripped another's braided ponytail entirely from his head (including a significant portion of his scalp) ... and proceeded to beat one more to death with his bare hands, as the remaining ruffian had scarpered screaming for his life.

During the attack, the suppressed shadowy part of him that had until now condemned his post-war curtailment for wreaking mayhem had taken over ... and in this state of unleashed wrath he was not a man to be trifled.

Smashed thru a heady cocktail of liquor and poppy, he'd torpidly gotten their tiresome spiel. Barely affording any notion concerning the implications, he'd ambivalently condoned whatever the hell they peddled by signing the contract they'd pushed under his nose - as much to placate them and make them go away as anything else. Abrupt, what had followed was an enforced cessation from his corrupt vice.

Cold turkey had been a devastating, gruesome experience. The intense throbs, stultifying pain and perpetual movement of his thrashing only served for starters. Snot endlessly poured from his nose, and the green sickness, endless diarrhoea and cold sweat seemed eternal. He felt a restive mannequin being cast in twain by some vindictive puppeteer on invisible filaments for aeons on end. These vile symptoms combined with chronic dehydration to ensure his misery was exclusively entire. Suffice to say, if Hell could manifest to represent Earth, then this was surely it, and he was convicted an inmate within its unforgiving fiery walls of damnable distress.

Repetitive piteous implorations for release aimed toward those professing aid - shameless begging of retraction bereft personal dignity - fell upon heedless ears. He had begotten an assassination through what felt like the affliction of a hundred-thousand harrowing papercuts.

Naturally, that apogee would have been altogether expedient if he had been slain. Notwithstanding, he wasn't. Rather his life was being inexorably extended and it was proving an altogether racking physical, psychological, and emotional episode.

Naturally, they held a schema toward someone else's venal end - thus were more than a tad disinclined to trouble whatsoever for his penn'orth. Indeed, just plain proxies of the company the mercenaries expediated good reason for conveying him near restored. Hence, for the time being this once irrepressible force of nature instead likened no more than a scant gnat: upturned, struggling for release upon the torpid grip of a marshland consisting of the direst of dirge. Indeed, if the inopportune cost of his life was to now bear more suffering, then it had become a penalty which he would have no other option than to extend.

His long-forsaken Father had previously amassed reasonable wealth by virtue of his sharp business acumen. Therefore, he'd gifted considerable alms to charity before absconding incognito to patronise these far-flung sordid dens. He hadn't even told anyone he was going – but in fairness, nobody would have really cared anyway. His clandestine intent, he'd determined to over-indulge in opium until it literally killed him. Nevertheless, that disposition was now befitted badly awry. Unbeknownst to him, instead he had unwittingly acceded toward being primed for an unforeseen passage into the unknown. Indeed, a quite frightful voyage awaited him: one which guaranteed much more trouble than the mere glitch of this obligatory process of sobriety.

Chapter Nine

'Agents of Chaos'

DO YOU BELIEVE IN GHOSTS or

haunted houses? In the cold light of day this question is easily laughed off. However, I'd defy you to do so quite as effortlessly at night once isolated in a creepy old property. I know because I've experienced it.

Before our marriage we purchased a property situated in a red sandstone fronted Victorian tenement building constructed during the latter part of the 1800's. It had several benefits including expansive views over the river Clyde and surrounding countryside, an outbuilding, and clear access to Helensburgh's local park. Records showed it once consisted larger flats which formed residences to accommodate servants from adjacent affluent town houses where the well-heeled had resided.

I would live there alone until I'd renovated it and initially everything seemed perfect. During the day I was busy and had plenty of company but at night I developed an unsettling notion I wasn't alone. Once darkness fell the atmosphere would change and because of this I'd double check the door was locked and inspect the empty rooms before going to bed. Uneasy I would often find it difficult to sleep.

Of course, during daylight hours I'd laugh at my own ridiculous nocturnal fears, rationalise them, then renew my resolve to dispel these stupid notions. Yet each night the feeling would return, and I couldn't seem to shake it off.

Our dog Prince had also been behaving strangely. He'd suddenly sit bolt upright then start whining as his gaze would dart around the room as though watching some invisible flying object.

The situation soon escalated. My sleep had become more troubled, and I was experiencing odd phenomena.

On several occasions I was awoken by strange knocking and footsteps within the bedroom. Yet when I turned the light on it would instantly cease and there was nobody there. On another occasion as I lay in bed dozing on and off I was sure I'd witnessed the bedroom door half open of its own accord before softly closing through the gloom. Forcing fear aside I arose then proceeded to check the property was secure, searching it from top to bottom. Of course, it was empty. My imagination was running wild therefore I persevered.

The situation finally culminated one night. Turning out the lights I'd eventually succumbed to sleep. I had a vivid dream whereupon my name was incessantly whispered. Ever so slowly I began to drift back to waking consciousness. Because I was so tired I was initially resistant to leave the refuge of my deep slumber. Suddenly to my abject terror I realised the voice was not exclusive to my dream after all. Finally awake but with eyes held tightly closed I lay in the dark for a few moments, before a voice clearly whispered in my ear,

"John!"

Paralysed, I forced my eyes open to find an old grey-haired man in Victorian attire indignantly looming over me. Staring into my face, he lingered there for a few seconds before gradually fading away. Breaking the inertia, I screamed to fumble for the bedside light only to find an empty room.

Okay take a deep breath. H.P. Lovecraft once guided: *"For that which is mysterious, never explain anything."* Actually, on this occasion I am going to overlook his advice in ruining the suspense.

In fact, the phenomenon I underwent can reasonably be explained as Rapid Eye Movement (REM) sleep/paralysis whereupon rapid shifting of the eyes is accompanied by other physiological changes. This is accompanied by vivid dreams/hallucinations that cross over with the individual as they shift into a full state of wakefulness.

Throughout my early life I displayed a penchant for this together with sleepwalking. Growing up it was a bit of a running joke in my family as fast asleep I would frequently alight bed before proceeding downstairs to hold bizarre conversations with whoever was around. Going back to bed, in the morning I would have absolutely no recollection of this.

Actually, there are no haunted houses – only haunted people. This phenomenon manifested consequential as a symptom to the psychological and emotional trauma I had frequently met as a child which I'll discuss later.

As for the flat? Once married we lived there for three years until moving on. Despite being far more emotionally stable than me Mandy was unsettled there and particularly disliked being alone when I was working night shifts.

The oldest and strongest emotion of all is fear especially that of the unknown. For this reason, we are sometimes compelled to conceive the eerie the macabre and the inexplicable. After all a pinch of intrigue tends to add a bit of spice to the humdrum recipe of daily life don't you think?

As a child Garelochhead seemed an awfully mysterious place. A local legend related to the 'Green Lady', a spectre who roamed the field's and woodland adjacent to our housing estate at night. For no good reason she'd apparently appear as translucent green before haunting anyone unfortunate enough to have straggled into the countryside during dusk.

I recall one particular incident. Darkness had fallen and a group of youngsters had been caught playing there when the Green Lady manifested to chase them. Playing with my friends under the streetlights the terrified kids then burst from the undergrowth and breathlessly proceeded to share their horrifying ordeal with us.

What did we do? Obviously we armed ourselves with battery powered torches and sticks and stones then set off into the darkness to confront her of course! Several of the group were subsequently terrorised by glimpses of her. Certainly, nobody witnessed this thus I decided to join in by describing in detail how it had also happened to me. Eventually absconding home, we would go on to regale each other with inflated accounts of this incidence for weeks to come.

Here's the thing. We'd actually convinced ourselves of the validity of the encounter because if we'd admitted the truth life would have just been a lot duller.

Unsurprisingly as we grow up our imagination becomes more and more constrained. Consequentially as far as I was concerned the village just became plain old boring. It was at that point I wished I really had met the Green Lady after all. Logically none of us had experienced anything at all that night. Even so you should never undermine the basic human requirement to be scared now and again. When all is said and done let's just say imagination is our best weapon in the war we sometimes need to wage against cold reality.

★

NOWADAYS PEOPLE CONSTANTLY demand

respect. Personally I think there's a bit of confusion about this because respect is commanded not demanded. Instead it's best to strive towards treating each other with the utmost courtesy and good manners - which although seemingly similar are entirely different things altogether.

Transactional I would never dream of treating anyone with anything other than politeness and consideration. However, if you want my respect then you have to earn it. I'd expect nothing else from you in return. In this respect (no pun intended) quarter should be neither sought nor given. The bottom line is respect isn't freely conferred upon the insistence of someone else's demand - it has to be earned.

Self-respect is no different. How can one respect oneself unless deep down one feels they've done enough to merit it? In short you still have to prove yourself worthy in both regards. Confidence is comparable. I've had loads of therapeutic clients and students asking,

"*Give me more Confidence,*" as though it's some complimentary commodity waiting to be plucked from thin air.

It isn't. To be precise confidence comes at a high cost and the price you must pay is in developing sufficient aptitude in whatever context is in question. Having done so you then need to consistently apply the fundamentals. Listen it's not easy but definitely worthwhile. Therefore its relatively easy to assist 'capable' clients or students to tap into this in becoming more assured. Alternatively, for those lacking I always explain that to become more confident they must first invest in becoming more competent. To put it bluntly they just need to get better. There are no shortcuts.

Don't get me wrong I know there are plenty of bluffers out there who are full of it. But unwarranted self-respect and confidence is a castle built upon shifting sands. It is a hollow pretense which is fine right up until the point it isn't. Then when it's too late it usually measures a sobering affair. Rather, I think it's better to be realistic and keep one's ambition ranged within one's own capability then adjust both accordingly in line with their respective evolution. Perhaps it might save a lot of hassle if more people recognised this?

For example my daughters learnt Karate from a young age. Developing physical and mental conditioning and advancing through the belts enabled them to acquire greater confidence in their increasing aptitude. Importantly they also learnt the virtues of courtesy, discipline, and restraint. Counterintuitively I wanted them to be able to fight in order to avoid confrontation. After all bullies never seek opponents they only seek victims. Similarly any state which maintains a functional army by way of deterrent always wins each war that it averts. Paradoxical, the most successful armies are those which never have to fight at all.

When I joined the Police discipline dress and bearing were paramount. A strict height limit at the time ensured Police Officers had sufficient physical presence. (*Note: The reasons for this were not as extraneous as those who brought about its cessation would have you believe*).

We wore a flat cap woolen tunic white shirt tie and carried a whistle with a wooden truncheon secreted in our woolen trouser leg pouch. Furthermore hair had to be closely cropped and if you wanted to wear a beard or moustache you had to apply in writing for permission. Footwear had to be polished to the extent you could see your face (i.e. 'bulled'), and the arms of all upper garments and legwear had to be pressed to a razor edge. At the beginning of each shift we would parade. The Inspector accompanied by the Team Sergeant would arrive to announce,

"Prove appointments!"

This meant we stood in file to attention extending our truncheons erect in our right hand (a subliminal sexual undertone of vitality and vigour if ever there was one) whilst presenting our open notebook warrant card and whistle in our left.

At this point the Inspector would progress down the line checking these along with our hair and shaven faces creases, and shoes. Woe betide anyone that didn't meet the yardstick as this would likely result in a month-long punishment of some kind or another. Furthermore to appear outside of a building or vehicle without wearing your hat was considered unthinkable as the individual was deemed 'out of uniform' thereby similarly punishable.

I recall an officer - a keen rugby player from a different section who didn't parade as much as ours – once joined us for overtime. Typically our Inspector arrived then compelled us to do so. At this I heard our visitor mutter *"Oh, shit!"* under his breath.

Walking down the line our boss abruptly stopped then spent ages staring at his clearly dirty boots.

"I've heard you're a really good rugby player?" he eventually questioned in a friendly tone without averting his scrutiny from the filthy hacks.

"Erm, yes Sir that's correct."

"They say you play for Glasgow that's really quite impressive!" he went on now meeting his regard by being seemingly sincere.

"Thanks very much Sir!" he replied proudly dropping his guard.

Abruptly changing our boss now erupted.

"NEXT TIME DON'T WEAR YOUR F*****G WORK BOOTS WHEN YOU'RE PLAYING!"

The rest of us attempted to contain our hilarity as he continued by whispering menacingly,

"Turn up on my shift looking like that again and your ass will be grass and I'll be the lawnmower, have you got it? Get them polished NOW!'"

This may or may not surprise you however, this was no hollow threat. Not in the least. That very same Inspector once had a probationer manhandled into a metal equipment locker whereupon it was locked then carried outside by four officers at his behest. Positioned at the top of a flight of four concrete stairs he proceeded to roll it down with a firm kick to teach him a lesson. On another occasion I witnessed him punch another full force in the solar plexus sending him winded to the ground. Trust me this kind of stuff did happen and in those days prisoners were assaulted too.

So what was the point in all this fuss? Standards. They were exacting and had to be maintained for a good reason. If you are going to hold the public to account you need to uphold the same. Think about it. How can you affect the big issues – those largely outwith your control – unless you first establish maintenance of the small things, or those within it? Doing so was considered a good starting point for us. It meant we were more likely to earn the respect of those we served alongside and more importantly those we actually served.

Generally speaking chaos reigns in the absence of order. Towards the end of my career standards had deteriorated to a near catastrophic 'everything is permitted but nothing is forgiven' mentality regarding dress and appearance. This contaminated almost everything else in-between. The decline had an adverse effect upon the service in general and the public's perception of it.

Here's the thing. You ought to be very careful when forgoing the small foundational structures that underpin a functional society. To do so only leads to creeping subsidence and eventual collapse. To not take care of one's appearance is a blatant outward expression of lack of self-control. It not only undermines the base arrangements of your own self but on a grander scale society itself.

A while back Mandy and I were heading for a holiday in the Canary Islands to celebrate her birthday. During the car journey to the airport I approached a roundabout featuring something of an obstructed view. Checking right to duly give way to oncoming traffic it appeared clear thus I proceeded. Suddenly a car travelling at high speed entered from my offside. Unavoidable I was already committed and despite taking evasive action our cars briefly met in a glancing blow.

Getting out to assess the damage by now the other driver had done similarly.

"YOU F*****G CLOWN LOOK WHAT YOU'VE DONE!" screamed the small bald aging driver angrily. I noticed he was unsuitably dressed much too young for his age like some sort of overgrown toddler in trendy sports apparel.

"Alright take it easy," I replied trying to placate him. "What matters most is there's hardly any damage and we're all alright!"

"That was your fault!" he continued irately still highly charged.

"Actually it's not that simple," I replied evenly. "The speed limit is forty miles per hour for a reason and I think you'll find I couldn't give way because you were traveling far too fast."

I fully accepted my part in the collision, yet he was also at fault. Nevertheless this tete a tete went on for a bit before he calmed down enough for me to phone 'Crazy K' Divisions Police control room in Paisley. I confirmed nobody was injured and the vehicles were still roadworthy at which point they gave me an incident number and advised we exchange insurance details before resuming our respective journeys.

Having done so we were just about to leave when a Police car roared up with its blues and two's blaring as though it was responding to some dire emergency. As it happened another motorist had seen the incident then notified this Police car which had been loitering at a loose end relatively close by.

'Oh, here we go!' I thought, noticing it was a Traffic Unit. Essentially a fierce rivalry existed between different Police Force's and specialisms and Traffic (or the 'Black Rats') were known for booking their own grannies given half the chance. Just before the advent of the amalgamated Police Scotland force two of Strathclyde Police's finest jumped out and chose to pull me aside first. I couldn't help but notice they weren't wearing their hats their boots were scuffed and dirty and their appearance was overall shabby. As far as I was concerned this wasn't a great start.

"Right my friend what happened?" one of them arrogantly queried hands in pockets chewing gum and gauging me like some sort of lowlife.

I politely explained my version of events before they sauntered off towards the other driver. Fuel to the fire out of earshot I watched the hot head reignite to become angry throughout by generally waving his arms around whilst animatedly gesticulating in my direction. After this they both returned to me. As one chatted away the other started to go over my car with a fine toothcomb. Damn. It had obviously become a fishing expedition and I knew I was the catch.

"Listen mate we've heard both versions of events and the collision was your fault," he proclaimed removing his pocketbook and clearly getting ready to write.

As far as I'm concerned quickly apportioning blame in complex situations such as this indicates a lazy person hastening to make sense out of confusion.

"I disagree. That analysis is too simplistic." I courteously rejoined. "He was well in excess of the speed limit and entered the roundabout like a bat out of hell. How was I supposed to evade him since I'd already begun my manoeuvre?"

"Doesn't matter because he had right of way," he replied, scribbling away.

"Come on. Although you're technically right you do realise your assessment also insinuates that speed limits don't matter then?" I stated incredulously. Coming from a Traffic officer I was more than a tad surprised.

"Nah I'm not having it pal," he asserted sighing dismissively. "In any case you'll have your day in court. So what do you do for a living then?" came his next line of inquiry.

"What does it matter?" I invited now breaking my own rule of never conversing with the Police when off duty any more than absolutely necessary.

"I suppose it doesn't. I'm just asking," was his nonchalant come back. "So, are you going to let me in on your little secret or not?"

I knew all too well I was about to brighten up his day.

"I'm a Ministry of Defence Police Officer," I confessed.

"Oh really? General police duties then?" he went on glancing at me differently as much as his eyes were now lighting up in anticipation.

"Firearms," I responded.

"Aha, an ARV officer then?" he queried smiling.

"No I'm a Firearms Instructor," I answered taking his lure hook line and sinker.

For him this was even better, and I knew what was coming. As he reeled me in I couldn't help but befall riveted to the dark stubble dotting his unshaven face.

"Well then you really ought to know better shouldn't you?" he quantified delivering his glib punchline with a grin, and barely concealed glee.

At this his colleague appeared by his side so they went off to have a brief conflab before returning to me.

"Buddy did you know your front near-side tyre is just under the legal limit?" officer two asked chipping in for the first time.

"No I thought my tyres were absolutely fine," I responded, genuinely surprised as my car had only recently passed its MOT.

"Okay we're reporting you for driving without due care and attention and having a bald tyre," he added before his partner stepped back in.

"Right you're not obliged to say anything but anything you do say will be noted and may be used in evidence. Do you understand?"

Silent I looked blankly at him.

"Do you understand?" he repeated once more looking at me expectantly for a few seconds.

Silence.

"Look you know the score," he impeached dropping the formalities. "Do you understand or not?" he attempted again now bringing his pocketbook back up and looking at me questioningly.

"I don't speak to the Police or answer questions under caution," I illuminated. "Stick me down as 'No reply'."

"Seriously?" the other one chipped in screwing up his face as though I was somehow besmirching the new friendship he'd imagined we were forging. "Ach don't be like that!" he continued.

Having by now received all kinds of mixed messages from them nevertheless I had ascertained two important factors. One they were lazy and impolite; two if I didn't get a move on we were going to miss our flight.

"Are we finished here?" I finally asked after they had written me up. "May I continue on my journey or not?" I coolly requested.

"Yeah off you go you'll hear about this in due course. Oh and have a nice holiday!" officer two countered waving me away with a grin as he attempted to wind me up.

So I went back to my car where Mandy was still sitting. Completely mortified she was glaring daggers however, I ignored this by moving to the boot to uncover the spare tyre. By this time the other driver had screeched off by laughing and firing a rude gesture my way in the process. Moments later I was genuinely surprised to discern Tweedle Dee and Tweedle Dum appear at my side once more.

"Hey mate off the record," officer one whispered, " ... do you mind telling us what you are doing?"

"I'm changing the illegal tyre of course. I need to get a move on to the airport to catch my flight. I'm going on holiday remember?" I spikily stated not even looking at them.

"Listen don't be daft," the other returned softly in flip flopping yet again. "Just go," he whispered. "You're only a couple of minutes away it'll be alright."

Abruptly stopping what I was doing a silver lining to this sad episode had suddenly presented itself. Only now I chose to look across at them.

"Really? Alright then if you insist!"

Jumping behind the wheel beside my furious spouse we continued in simmering silence to fortunately make the flight by the skin of our teeth. This put a dampener on the holiday, and I understandably found myself in the doghouse for a day or two. Actually she needn't have bothered as I was kicking myself quite enough for being so damn stupid. Nevertheless once we returned home I was subsequently cited for the offences.

My lawyer advised I accept whatever punishment came my way. In the end I took three points and an £80 fine on the chin. Even so it could have been much worse. You see the tyre offence was dropped once my lawyer informed the prosecution I'd been compelled to continue on the public highway with an illegal tyre by the Police after the officers had reported me for it. Indeed at the time I do recall thinking,

'Dear oh dear, that's a schoolboy error right there chaps. Under caution nothing's off the record!'

I'd had the last laugh and maybe if they'd been able to polish their boots and shave or go so far as to introduce a hot iron to their uniform they might have been able to do the rest of their jobs properly. Even so I wasn't complaining as it had mostly went my way.

It seems to me the world contains plenty of agents of chaos and they come in all shapes and sizes. Thus it's vital to be able to quickly identify and then proactively avoid them at all costs if at all possible. As it happens you get the good the bad and the ugly in any walk of life. How can you tell them apart? Let's just say it's the little things which give them away.

———————————

Chapter Ten

'When the Past Collides with the Future'

ODDLY ENOUGH AS A child playing 'Cowboys and Indians' at school I always wanted to be an Indian. Furthermore I had a small collection of Dinky toy painted metal figures, and my favourites were always the Indian braves resplendent on horseback. I also recall sighting an artist's impression of *'The Battle of the Little Big-Horn'* for the first time and becoming deeply fascinated by it. I guess this is attributable to a shared tendency we have for mostly favouring the underdog.

Many years later we had lost our second child and then my Father-in-law in quick succession. To add to it all Mandy then became seriously ill. I ended up disoriented and cast adrift in a stormy sea of fate I would go through a phase whereupon I became overly enchanted by religion and spiritualism. Looking back I was obviously bereaved on top of being afraid and just needed to fix onto something to get me through. Although not sure what to expect I spontaneously attended a medium named Colette based at Strathaven for a reading in her shop 'The Blessed Bee'. This was also the base of the Scottish school of Tarot which she had founded. Fatefully I would later go on be taught there by her in how to interpret the cards especially during 'clairvoyant' readings for others. Indeed she claimed I was an especially spiritual person with an unusual talent for it. Even so for whatever reason I always remained suspicious. *'I'll bet she says that to everyone'* was the thought which always loitered around at the back of my mind. My pragmatic wisdom reasoned that if she was right - and I was especially gifted - then my gut instinct was becoming a damning indictment on her but then again who knows. I guess I was torn between daring to hope and making haste to escape my grim reality at the time.

Mandy deplored my new fascination which undoubtedly cranked the tension up between us a notch. Christians, she couldn't see how any of this was congruent with our faith in the least and we had argued about it a lot.

In any case as I tentatively walked into the Blessed Bee accompanied by the sound of the chimes that framed the doorway Colette sat behind the counter and had inquisitively glanced up. A large friendly woman she had once been a pharmacist however given it all up to follow let's just say a more holistic career path.

"Oh ... that's a bit unusual," she murmured placing the book she had been reading moments before down and removing her glasses. Seemingly taken aback she looked me up and down for a moment then continued, "Wow! A spirit has walked in by your side,"

'Yeah, right!' I glibly thought chuckling to myself as she proceeded to converse with this invisible person. Meanwhile I just stood there bemused as I tentatively glanced to my left and right.

"Oh, really?" she went on talking to empty space, "Ah yes I see. Uh huh. Well, can I just say that's really nice!"

Next turning her attention back to me she declared,

"Now then it seems you've brought your Grandfather along with

147

you. He explains his name is David and wants you to know he's around you a lot and offering his support!"

Holy crap. I was stunned. I had secretly yearned for a message from Mandy's Dad however, this information was absolutely spot on. Given she knew nothing about me whatsoever I was mystified. Was it some elaborate scam? Even if it was she now had my full attention and afterwards she proceeded to deliver an incredibly pertinent piece of information from 'the other side' regarding my domestic situation (which shall remain private).

In concluding her reading she once more took me off guard through further revealing my 'key spirit guide' had now decided to make a guest appearance with a message to impart. She attested he was a native American Indian named 'White Cloud' who had been killed during 1886 by blue-coat soldiers on the shores of the Red River in what is today the USA. He further claimed I had once been a Cherokee holy-man and warrior in a former life and that we had spent many lifetimes together in different guises helping each other.

Sheesh as goofy as this all sounds funnily enough I had always imagined an unseen guardian angel accompanying me throughout my youth and would secretly talk to him. I think a lot of kids do this.

The winters of the 1970's were always so much colder than today. Contrary to the current global warming planetary crisis alongside nuclear war the mass medias insistence of that time was to scare us by insisting the world was heading for a new ice age. Call me cynical but the more things change the more they stay the same! Then again my upbringing featured a particularly spartan environment insomuch as we never had any luxury's at all. For example unlike many of the other kids in the village my family home never featured a coal fire central heating double glazing or insulation. Therefore I was constantly freezing throughout the winter months. Our solitary source of warmth came from a small two bar electric heater which was situated in the living room. Even so its use was strictly regulated to a single bar by my parents. I would sometimes sneak the second bar on then sit in front of it to soak up the extra heat but had to be extremely careful: On a bad day my Father's temper could be like a short fuse burning all the time and if caught he would have hit the roof. This was all compounded by the frequent power cuts and my Mother's bizarre insistence on opening all of the windows each day regardless the temperature outside. Whenever I protested I would always be met by the same rebuke,

"Stop complaining. If you're cold then go and put another jumper on!"

This was all a bit rich given I already sported about seven of them.

At night I'd crawl beneath a pile of multi-coloured hand me down blankets in bed to watch my icy breath like some sleepy white dragon before burying my head below the heavy shroud for some blessed relief. By then my body temperature would have slowly warmed the crib and next morning I'd alight my bunk to open the mismatched curtains. Met by ice on the inside of the window my daily routine meant I would proceed to carve a happy smiling face on it with my index finger whilst sincerely hoping the milkman had been able to make his deliveries. If not there'd be no alternative than to pour water over my cornflakes for breakfast, which I can assure you was not nice in the least. For sure we were considered amongst the poorest families in the community however, this was compounded by my Father being as tight as two coats of paint with money.

I once recall attending school after it had snowed for several days without end. By now the climate had changed enough to start melting the snow to slush and a sizeable snowball fight had erupted in the playground. Compacted into an icy projectile someone had cried my name before launching one at me. As I turned I caught it directly on the forehead knocking me clean from my feet. Of course the kids proceeded to panic before scarpering. I eventually regained my senses to somehow struggle up to the teacher's restroom for help. Now sporting a goose-egg sized lump they were unable to conceal their shock as I stumbled in before flustering in sending for my Mother. All alone awaiting her arrival in an empty classroom my eyes had welled-up then I had started to openly chastise my invisible friend.

"Hey, you! What happened? You were supposed to be looking after me," I sobbed aloud. "... and now look what's happened!"

I then caught something in my periphery and turned to catch my Teacher and Mother standing quietly on the threshold listening inquisitively.

"John are you okay? Who are you talking to?" inquired my Teacher.

"Nobody Miss, I'm just talking to myself," I'd unconvincingly replied before being taken home to have a bag of frozen peas placed onto my head for some more brain freeze then sent to bed under the familiar pile of blankets for a day of BBC Radio Two.

They obviously thought I was concussed which I probably was given I experienced double vision for a couple of days.

Anyway I guess the point I'm trying to make is you'd be forgiven for scoffing at the notion of mediums spirit-guides and invisible friends as utter stuff and nonsense. After all this is the default convention of societal norms regarding the supernatural and related matters. I actually found this out firsthand through catching considerable heat when openly discussing this stuff before. In short I do remain a bit skeptical but am mostly openminded. After all I consider this a far better utility than being closeminded which is to be completely dismissive or cynical.

One of my greatest psychological inspirations was the legendary Carl Jung. As it happens he himself enforced he held chats with his own spirit-guide on a daily basis. Therefore for right or wrong I reasoned if it was good enough for him then why was it not good enough for me? To this day my rationale maintains the same: It doesn't necessarily matter if what you believe is real or not - what actually matters most is whether or not it's useful.

The Buddha once said: *"Just as a candle cannot burn without fire a man cannot live without a spiritual life"*. In this regard let's just say I've always felt the presence of the divine throughout my life and park it there. I don't need to broadcast my faith because it is mine alone to sense in the quietude of my inner awareness. It seems unfashionable to follow a religion nowadays - especially for Christians - yet I took tremendous inspiration from Jung's own assertion: *"I don't believe in God, I know in God."*

If anything, this simple turn of phrase perfectly exemplified his genius. Henceforth my own deeply personal conviction in God is the same. I don't need to believe because I already know. A formidable scholar and man of science Jung's assertion someway illustrates the act of believing to be a suboptimal form of devotion. Indeed, he underscores knowledge as being even more devout than faith. In this sense true devotion is never a proving thing it's a knowing thing. I agree with this thesis. Why not compel yourself completely to go all in because a great many people drift through life committing barely fifty percent at best to any of their schemes and dreams. I mean it seems to me when all's said and done that if you fully commit to that which really matters to you then it will at least imbue your life with some true meaning and sense of purpose.

Anyhow let's return to Native Indians and tie the loose ends together. Many of the reservations where they were eventually shepherded still exist to this day. Notably the inhabitants remain amongst the most deprived demographic consisting modern society in the United States. Unlike many other minorities they just don't seem to have much of a voice. I reason this is probably because they are an inconvenient reminder of the genocide which was meted upon them – and the truth that they combine as one people under a banner symbolising an original ethnic majority.

I've read many Indians take particular exception to the phrase 'native Americans'. I guess this should come as no real surprise. They inhabited the plains and fertile landscapes of the old-world long before any of the expatriate settlers known today as Americans arrived or the term 'America' was even devised. Parallels can be drawn to other indigenous peoples who suffered a similar fate. Desmond Tutu once cited: *"When the missionaries came to Africa they had the Bible, and we had the land. They said, 'Let us pray' and we closed our eyes. When we opened them we had the Bible, and they had the land"*.

The Native Indian tribes were similarly powerless in halting the inbound wave of advancement and eventual colonisation. Alike tragic king Canute precariously perched upon his shoreside throne they were eventually engulfed by a similar uprising swell of encroachment. How ironic during the colonial era that a similar unstoppable surge of indifference would eventually lave away what were up until then considered brave new technologies of the time. One perfect example being the Steam Engine. Then again in the context of progress everything and everyone has a shelf life.

A segue my Father's lineage belongs to North-Wales. In fact it might surprise you to know English is actually his second language as he exclusively spoke fluent Welsh (one of the world's oldest languages) right up until he began school. English was then rammed into him so hard that his grasp of it became far superior to most English people I know.

As it happens both of my Parents were especially talented regarding grammar. My Mother in particular was a total whizz at crosswords and my Father always loved to play with words. One indulgence I will attest to is that lots of books cluttered my childhood home. These fascinating objects provided me with plenty of food for thought. I reason my parents must have possessed an inbuilt proclivity for linguistics as both were country peasants who never received much formal schooling.

So then what's the link here? Well, my Fathers first job was as a railway signalman and all of his family including his forebears were deeply embedded within the railroads as one of the post-industrial revolutions most important technologies. The same not only furthered the pioneers' schemes relating to conquering the wild frontiers of the American West, but also provided continual employment in the heyday periods throughout most of the developed world during the industrial revolution. It was for this reason I wrote the following fictional story in my second book: *"This Dream, Reality"*, (2017). It was my way of blending all of the aforementioned together and I would like to share it with you now.

⭐

(A Short-Story of Spirituality)

THIS TALE EMBARKS WITH the portrayal of White

Cloud's petition:

"Oh Wakan Tanka whose voice I hear in the wind and whose breath gives life to the world. Please hearken me. I am but one of many of your unassuming children. I am humble small and weak. Please offer your wisdom and loan me your strength. Let my people walk in peace and enjoy each sunset. Allow our hands to respect all that you have made and make me wise so that I might guide your children well.

"Hear me. I do not wish to conquer my enemies. Instead I must overthrow my greatest foe ... myself! When my time comes in the fading sunset of this life allow my spirit to come to you with neither shame nor sorrow. Let me enter the happy hunting ground a place the Paleface cannot steal."

The year was 1886 and the native Lakota Sioux Screaming Bird and White Cloud presently scouted the gigantic metal monster they coined 'the Iron Horse' plough across the sacrosanct plain far beneath them. From their vantage point held high in the rocks it was seen to chug a path along the metal tracks before sounding a cry born of thunder to spew a mighty plume of grey smoke in its wake. Akin the legendary Thunderbird itself the shrill cry of its whistle resounded throughout the valley manifest as impressive and devastating in equal measure. For them it was a truly terrible sight to behold.

Holy-man and warrior White Cloud instinctively knew what this meant. The implications were laid bare to him thus he convened a dismay deep within his gut. Dark brown eyes set deep within a truly tanned face he watched at length with a heady mix of awe burden and resignation.

Inspecting by his side the renowned brave Screaming-Bird witnessed the same spectacle however, lacked his companion's foresight and wisdom. Of course he knew how to abide the warpath. Notwithstanding the intricacies portents and omens of the Buffalo Woman and the mercurial means of the Great-Spirit were quite beyond his capacity. It was for this reason he conclusively turned to his companion.

"Ach it still endures. What might this mean?" he questioned.

Without affecting his scrutiny from the tableau below White Cloud purposefully replied in a steady voice.

"It means there are now two ways for us. One leads to hunger fever and death and the other to where we endure life as emaciated poor relations to even the poorest White Man."

Screaming Bird considered these words before replying.

"But surely we can still prevent it? If we avert the Iron-Horse then the White Man will be chastened from the hunting grounds and things would go back as they were!"

"You're wrong," his companion cut back in respectively. "My vision-quest decreed we cannot alter the events now set in motion. Regardless our actions more will come - more than there are blades of grass stars in the sky snowflakes in the winter air or grains of sand on the summer plain," he outlined mournfully.

They sat a while longer watching the cumbersome beast recede beyond the far side of the valley in silence. A man of action the brave wondered why the holy man was so lacklustre. Surely there was always another way to defeat their enemies. Presently White Cloud continued,

"Brother pay heed. Even if we do manage to break the Iron Horse they will just fix it or bring another. I know the Paleface's heart. Like an illness inside him he is fanatical with greed. Instead we should parlay for our women and children's sake and for our old ways. Failure in this regard means we will forever be wiped from our homeland".

White Cloud felt great love understanding and connection with the land upon which he had been conceived and then born from loving parents. Self-conscious shy sensitive and kind with a gentle humour he was truly in tune with himself and others. He loved his family and his tribe and way of life - but had also seen the prophecy of what would come to pass in the sweat-lodge of his vision-quest. He already knew he was destined to die a violent death upon the sanctified soil of this land. Wise he knew only fools wished unpalatable truths away or covered their ears to deny that which cannot be forfended ... and to his eternal credit he was certainly no fool.

Nonetheless in privation he also questioned his own prediction and had often inwardly queried,

'Great Spirit have I merely dreamt my prophecy, or shall it actually come to pass?'

Naturally he could never voice these doubts aloud because holy men were taught to internalise such matters. For them it simply equated 'the burden of knowing'. After all he was born to walk tall and proud amongst the rest as one truly hallowed. He possessed an obligation to steer them in line with the creed a position rightly handed down from his previous incumbents. He had become familiar with the ways of the interlopers but had to admit he could not fathom them out at all. Their nature was alien to him and their understanding of the natural order was narrow.

For sure he understood why they coveted the land because it was fertile and yielded much – but they never cottoned on the land does not belong to man, man belongs to the land. Having previously met them to broker a deal an agreement had eventually been made whereupon they would all share. Yet despite the White Man always uttering honourable words his deeds spoke otherwise. Having spent time with them they lacked integrity and genuine spiritual depth. In this way he had concluded them to be untrustworthy peddlers of half-truths.

They were obsessed with expansion ownership and self-indulgence. The promises and agreements they had brokered were first broken "Just this once" before soon after becoming always. To this end their renewed pledges always seemed to mirror the ever-shifting sands of the prairie itself. He had been wooed with whisky coffee and the most powerful medicine of all sugar. Witnessing its effect he had been astounded. Nonetheless in spite of their shallow attempts to win him over he knew they furtively considered him an uneducated savage for he was nobody's chump. He had then carefully observed the lurid effect of the White Man's medicines once openly distributed amongst his kinfolk and it had profoundly shocked him.

Most important of all he knew that the interlopers could not only invent and build incredible machines of metal, but also cause ruin and wage war in a staggering way. He had concluded them far more debased and crueler than even the Comanche as the tribes traditional enemies. Indeed if a nomadic tribe lost two or three braves in a battle it would be considered a devastation. Yet the Paleface seemed not to care if they lost two or three hundred at a time. He immediately noted this was contrary to the sacred teachings contained within their own Holy Bible and to him this made them hypocrites. In fact their chaplain had once tried to entice him into the rustic little church they had newly constructed nearby from mesquite wood.

"I will never go inside your church," he had vehemently declined meeting the inquisitive parson square in the eye.

"But why not? It teaches us all about God," came the reply as the parson gently coaxed him by taking his arm.

"No," said White Cloud pulling it back from his grasp. "All it teaches the White Man is how to fight about God," he asserted.

Almost as bad was their wastefulness. The tribes only took what they needed from the land and never wasted anything. Every hair sinew and bone from a fallen Buffalo was appreciated before being put to good effect. The White Man only took its hide then left the rest to rot in the sun. Tragically they consumed huge quantities whilst wasting an equal amount with seemingly little regard for the consequences.

The accord had soon broken, and the tribe had fought him hard in a prolonged campaign. They harried and harassed the laying of the Iron Horses tracks as it passed through the sacred hunting ground of their forefathers. They scored much celebrated coups resulting in significant damage to the metal runners that defaced the hallowed turf, yet to their dismay within days more arrived accompanied by ever-greater numbers of the blue-jacketed Soldiers.

Protected by rifles which spat fire progress had resumed at a truly irrepressible pace.

White Cloud had partaken in several raids against the settlers. However, he intuitively knew that pride fueled primitive arrows stone knives and spears would never be enough. They were no match for the callous guns that defended the Iron Horse. With its shanks of steel fearsome breath and incorrigible wheels it was now unopposed as it trampled around the plains like a monstrous elk.

A tribal gathering had now been called and was attended by all.

"These are our lands. We tend them well and they have been sacred for generations," impeached an animated brave named Eagle Claw whilst pounding his heart with a fist. "The White Man threatens our way of life therefore we must destroy the Iron Horse once and for all. Failure means they will not only steal our land but decimate the prized herds of the plains."

This resulted in a loud whooping from the gathering. As it finally subsided Kicking Bird was next to step forth.

"Bah the wretched pale skins are unworthy," he angrily spat. "A single Brave is worth more than a ten of them" he snorted dismissively which was met by more fervent whooping before he concluded,

"I say we launch an all-out assault and destroy the Iron Horse for all times sake!"

"I agree," declared Silver Ear interjecting. "They lack integrity and lie and cheat at every turn."

Listening intently the renowned squaw Green-Eye Owl allowed the agitation to subside somewhat.

"My people the Great Spirit will surely aid us to chase away the interlopers," she softly opined. "Righteousness is on our side," she concluded as her words relit the now delirious collective.

After the chants and whoops had finally subsided she next turned to her brother White Cloud.

"I see you remain cowed what might the omens say?"

Such was the esteem and reverence which he was held the gathering had become noiseless. In response he silently stared into the crackling fire then after a pause cleared his throat to purposely stand up. His steady voice resonated in response to his familiar deep timbre.

"Brothers and sisters your words are familiar to me. Yet my prophecy reveals we cannot stop the tide regardless what course of action we now decide. The spirits reveal our time presently ebbs and our light will soon begin to fade. This is what I have been shown by Wakan Tanka."

The Subdued group sat sullen in deep contemplation. After a pause he carried on.

"Sadly there are now but two ways left, the way things were, and the way things are going to be which will be the White Man's way. Wherever he stands he always declares 'This is now White Man's land!' so be assured he will surely take our land too because I have seen it."

A hiatus followed as he allowed his words to stew. Despite not being what they wanted to hear his words were not exactly news to them for he had already dispensed similar before. The holy man respectfully cleared his throat then continued.

"He is the new order and will never let us be. Things will never be the same again. No matter what from now on we will forever be staring down the barrel of his gun. We can now either choose to wash with the Paleface's flood and make the best of it or stand tall and proud against him in the likelihood we will be washed aside. No matter what I will respect the consensus. If you choose to fight I will fight for I am not scared to fight him in the least. Then if you choose to barter further I will smoke the pipe of peace and parlay for neither am I scared to talk with him. But the time has now come, and we must decide."

In due course the decision was made to fight.

A fearsome sight they had finally emerged in line-formation on the brow of the savannah. Often overlooked at this time the plains Indians consisted the best light cavalry in the world. Having spied the Iron Horse for a time they'd scoped its defences for potential weaknesses and planned their assault. Mounted upon his white and brown pony with his handprints marked in chalk upon its loins White Cloud proudly perched in full war regalia including face-paint and full Eagle feather headdress. They held true awhile in a bid to intimidate their opponents before eventually charging whooping to battle from their posture of tactical advantage on the high ground,.

Descending like an avalanche they swept into the plain as an avenging falcons talon would seek to purge the soft pelt of a dove. The long grass encouraged them by wafting in the airstream as the sound of one hundred and thirty-seven sets of Lakota Sioux hooves, and just as many of their Cheyenne accomplices screeched their war-cry towards the steam engine rumbling along the tracks beneath them.

In that instant White Cloud felt the familiar rush of excitement sense of belonging fear and hope as adrenalin coursed through his veins. Every nerve was alive as each brave was spurred on by fellow warriors on this suicide mission. It was now all or nothing on what

White Cloud already knew to be an impossible charge. Primitive and idealistic they represented the past and they were about to collide head-on with the future.

Nevertheless they would fight them hard in honour of their ancestors for the Great Spirit and for a cause they felt to be just. On they rode bearing down upon the obstinate coal-fed machine as it forged a path along the tracks like a belligerent bull. Closer now he felt the rumble of its shanks rattle his pony's hooves and became acutely aware of the grey plume of smoke spoiling the clear air in its wake. Alike a recently roused firedrake its whistle suddenly shrieked a shrill plea much as they imagined the legendary thunderbird would screech in fury.

Next the smell of its burning throat infused his dry mouth: impressive and devastating in equal measure he suddenly became aware of the cracks of rifle fire as the defenders opened up in repeating volleys of spiteful ire. By reply he whooped alongside the rest in fear and joy as he let fly with arrow after arrow. Throughout it all he ruminated,

'I am Lakota Sioux. I am a Warrior. I am a Holy Man. This is for my ancestors, for my children, for my people ... for my Mother Earth!'

He brought his pony to a halt and briefly noticed the terror in its panoptic eyes as he turned and poised to hurl his spear. Suddenly a crack emanated from one of the soldiers' rifles and the resultant bullet stopped him as it tore straight through his skull like a hot knife through butter. Falling from the near delirious pony he was almost dead before his body even met the long grass of the same plain on which he had been conceived and was born of loving parents.

Self-conscious shy sensitive and kind with a gentle humour he was in tune with himself and others. He loved his family his tribe the land and their way of life - but White Cloud died right there in that long grass as it now blew at the behest of an indifferent draught.

Just as his spoiled cadaver slowly seeped gore toward the soil he suddenly found himself as an ethereal being gazing down upon his spent body as his spirit soared ever higher. To his joy the blinding eternal light of amity was patiently summoning him home hence he paused to take one last look in wonder at the mortal scene unfolding below him. Satisfied as the spirit of White Cloud finally began to make his final approach towards the happy hunting ground of eternal life he felt neither shame nor sorrow for he knew his final destination to be a place the Paleface could not steal.

Finally enveloped in the all-consuming radiance of God he telepathically inquired,

'Great Spirit ... please tell me is this a dream?

At that a heavenly voice answered him with immeasurable compassion by proclaiming,

"No my child this is reality!'

As White Cloud transitioned unto the universal all-loving consciousness back in the material realm the Iron Horse disregarded the broken bodies now littering the prairie to sound its whistle once more as it insensibly thundered on regardless.

Chapter Eleven

'Tears Are a Magical Potion'

LIFE CAN BE INCREDIBLY hard yet remains a mystery to be lived not a problem to be solved. Here's another new perspective: it's generally accepted the capacity 'second sight' is no more than some fictional fallacy. However, that's entirely wrong. We access it all the time through our memories. This is our mental capacity for revisiting the things we've experienced throughout our lives most of which you might presume you've forgotten.

Let's utilise second sight now to go all the way back to when you were a child. Just imagine you'd created a diary of everything that happened to you. It would contain all manner of new experiences hopes aspirations fears insecurities and problems. I'll bet many of the tribulations that troubled you so much back then seemed overwhelming and even unassailable?

Well imagine suddenly finding that diary after many years. Go on open it up and read it once again. Conjure up seeing it through the eyes of the adult you've become.

Imagine re-accessing all of those incidences and occurrences, events filed away in the deepest storeroom of your mind so long ago. I now ask how much empathy would you feel for that fledgling naïve version of you? While we're at it wouldn't it also be fascinating to revisit those seemingly overwhelming and unsurmountable problems which seemed so terrible at the time? They might have related to school or been issues with friends or family. They'd likely also contain silly things like not feeling good enough or having insecurities about your body appearance or future prospects. Yet

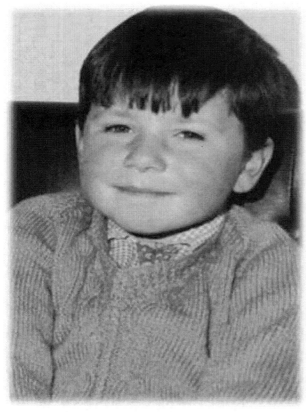

despite it all here you are regardless: Congratulations you made it.

I'll wager you'd now be able to laugh good humouredly at some of those things that seemed so unsurmountable. After all, through second sight many of them would seem silly. For this reason alone, wouldn't it be nice to step forward and put your arms around your younger self and hold them tight to then reassure,

"Listen it's going to be okay. Everything'll be alright in the end. None of it really matters too much anyway."

It's true. We all go through so much yet one way or another we somehow manage to endure it all. As I write this one particular page from my own internal diary springs to mind thus I guess I'm meant to share it with you. After Mandy lost our second child she went on to suffer a debilitating illness over the succeeding two years. A series of tests offered little hope and with a small child to look after whilst still grieving our recent loss I now dreaded losing her too. Bereaved I felt hollow bewildered and scared in equal measure. Wrongly assuming nobody cared I became indignant towards everyone else because they couldn't feel what we felt. I was prone to noticing evil everywhere except in my own heart and tended to punish the virtues of others just because of the anger soiling my dark thoughts. The damned world just kept spinning in mocking us and if the truth be told we had stopped living. Life had instead become one big struggle to just make it through one rotten day to reach the next. No surprise we grew apart for a time whilst occupying the same deep pit of despair as one was unable to look after the other.

Even though he didn't know what to say I found solace through sitting with Mandy's Dad for comfort. Back then boys were trained to suppress their feelings against the risk of being measured weak, so as stifled men we were equally wracked powerless by the other's inability to outwardly express what we were inwardly going through. Notwithstanding we shared the same loss and fear so I could discern his discreet care. Anomalous he was the only one who had noticed the storm in my eyes the emptiness in my words and the heaviness weighing down my heart. Because of this I found his company extraordinarily healing in some strange way.

Anyway, change remains a cardinal universal law regardless of the petty affairs of mice and men, so given time Mandy thankfully made a full recovery. Even so one tragedy was soon replaced by another as we then lost her Father in quick succession. Together we had no other choice than to plough on as we swapped places: She adopted my thorny throne of bitterness whilst I instead took her wounded pew. Irrespective as to whether or not we like it every diet requires roughage and life is often like that too - there can be no good without bad and no light without shade.

At this point I want you to now distinguish that your internal diary does actually exist. It's your subconsciousness and you can readily access it anytime you so choose. Chronicled within the storeroom of your mind you'll find everything that's ever happened throughout your lifetime. Even now your current experiences hopes aspirations fears insecurities and problems are all being documented there. So, now you know.

You might be experiencing seemingly overwhelming problems. They'll likely be the hitches of an adult. Perhaps they relate to the pressures and responsibilities that concern raising and providing for a family? Or maybe relationship issues blockages with work or your health? However, here's the thing - how silly will they seem when you look back upon them many years from now? Indeed, to your future self they will likely seem as inconsequential as the seemingly unsurmountable problems your younger version chronicled in your inner diary way back then when you were young.

This same concept has proven very useful for me throughout my own ordeals and surely you and I can't be too dissimilar. Therefore, it stands to reason second sight enables us to revisit the past in ensuring the future doesn't become some forgone conclusion. We shouldn't dwell on them but to forgo the lessons of the past is to imitate a fallen leaf which denies it was once part of a tree.

I have already openly fessed up to my stifled emotions a couple of times so feel I am entitled to assert with some authority that the act of eventually letting them go is indescribably healing. There should be no shame whatsoever in crying even for boys. On the contrary. Salt-water is purifying and the unseen, but obvious truth is that tears are a magical potion.

★

(A fictional Short-Story of Hope)

BETWEEN THE FOURTH AND SIXTH centuries

BCE an honest farmer named Aarav and his wife Prisha lived on the fringes of a small village within the Indian province of Karnataka. They had tried for such a long time to conceive a child before Prisha had finally fallen pregnant. In time she had given birth to a beautiful baby girl and the couple were completely overjoyed. However, within a month tragedy had struck.

Awakening through the night they experienced every parent's worst nightmare insomuch as Prisha stirred to discover their daughter had inexplicably perished. In a frenzied state of disbelief, Aarav immediately sent for the village doctor who upon arrival stipulated the child had passed from a neonatal cot-death. No other explanation was forthcoming.

Completely devastated afterwards Prisha completely withdrew into herself and otherwise became unpredictable aggressive and mostly surly. Worst still ever since the disaster she had not uttered a single word. Although sympathetic people tend to fear what they don't understand. So, after doing their best to rally around the couple and assist they found they were soon left well alone by the other villagers.

A patient and supportive man, Aarav somehow had to manage his own deep grief whilst wondering what more he could possibly do to help his wife recover – but sadly things continued like this for quite some time. Eventually seasons change. Indeed, one seamlessly blends to the other just as each sunset bleeds shades of red to a dying sky. Summer arrived and it proved unseasonably hot as the region found itself slowly gripped by a worsening drought. Indeed, no mortal mouth escaped the terrible curse of thirst as the dwindling water supply leisurely shrank away.

During this time a young travelling monk decided upon stopping off to rest in recuperation from what had been the incessant pilgrimage of travelling far and wide. Arriving unannounced at the couple's farmstead one morning he intimated to Aarav that he could not speak by virtue of a vow of silence he had recently adopted. In spite of his personal struggles and suffering, Aarav remained kind and charitable, so offered the monk a simple room to utilise for as long as he wished to repose. This was no mean feat considering doing so meant he unquestionably apportioned the Buddhist a share of their own dwindling supply of water.

Throughout this period Prisha soon found herself drawn to the monk. It was immediately obvious he was compassionate and caring, moreover he seemed to radiate a virtuous calmness and composure. Intrigued after a few days she came to hover by the threshold of his modest room silently watching him abide a basic daily routine whereupon he would light a small candle before meditating.

Of course, being acutely attuned to others the monk was well aware of her peculiarities. Logically he discerned her presence as she watched each day so on completion of his meditations would gesture her to sit and join him a while. On the first few occasions she took fright before turning on her heels to get away. That is until one day she finally approached to tentatively sit down opposite him.

Gripped by a terrible thirst they sat as one in silence for quite some time before he smiled then mutely reached for his well-worn satchel. Removing a small clay pot, it contained nothing more than a knot of earth. Regardless he smiled then placed it between them then clasped his hands together in prayer. After a while he offered a parched Prisha a drink from a small cup of the precious supply of water. Nervously accepting she took a sip then handed it back to him. At this he did likewise before doing something that caught her by surprise - he handed it back to her and gestured she should pour a small amount into the clay pot which she sheepishly did. Following this he smiled to retain the pot before placing it into the sunlight pouring through the window. Upon completion he effortlessly dropped back into meditation.

Quite fascinated by all of this for the next few days Prisha would attend at the same time in repeating the anomalous ritual – sitting silently with the monk as he meditated. As before they shared a sip of the dwindling supply of water before he encouraged her to pour a small quantity into the little clay pot. To her surprise as the days passed a small shoot was gradually sighted pushing its way to the surface and in doing so she strangely found she was beginning to feel just a little better within herself.

As expected throughout this Aarav noticed the time Prisha was spending with the monk. More importantly he was discerning a certain shift in her behaviour. One day he was visited by his sister. They chatted as they sat out back in the shade in a futile bid to escape the ferocious sun.

"How is Prisha?" his sister eventually inquired.

Aarav nodded his head contemplatively.

"Well, I don't know how and can't say why but something is definitely shifting. I'm not certain, however Prisha seems to be healing someway," he stated

Things continued in this vein for a while. Despite remaining silent Prisha started to soften and eventually came back to him as one night the couple unaccountably re-kindled their physical relationship for the first time since the tragedy.

Otherwise, each day she would proceed to sit with the monk as he meditated until she eventually joined in. Now their customary routine he would take a sip of the dwindling supply of water then watch her do likewise. This would always culminate with him encouraging her to pour a small quantity into the little clay pot. Therein each day a small plant gradually grew little by little and she inducted a genuine affection for it. She resultantly experienced a personal transformation as for the first time in what seemed an age she reacquainted the sort of inner stillness and peacefulness that can only be practiced from within.

In the interim the sun continually beat down and the drought intensified. By now the village well and the oven baked wizened riverbed had run completely dry. Nonetheless as was their routine they still sat silently meditating until at last there was no water. The silent monk showed Prisha the empty cup turning it upside down to emphasise its void. Disregarding her own thirst, she instead focused on the small delicate plant and became overcome by sadness. Too much to bear, she had started to cry for the first time since losing her beloved daughter.

The kind monk watched with compassion as the tears streamed

her face. At this he surprised her once more by gently lifting the little plant in the clay pot to her face to softly capture the tears. He finally placed into the sunlight streaming through the window and he nodded to her and smiled. Clasping his hands in prayer he returned to meditation, and she curiously found despite her crippling thirst she felt good once again.

By now the village folk were withering and much of the prized livestock lay idle in the fields shifting ever closer to fatality. Catastrophe loitered near yet despite it all the monk and Prisha sat together once more in silence to meditate together. After a time, Prisha opened her eyes to witness one of the most beautiful things she'd ever encountered as the small plant situated between them had blossomed into a beautiful lotus flower. Witnessing this phenomenon, the monk then clasped his hands together in joy. He then took her quite by surprise as he broke his vow of silence.

"Tears are useful!" he whispered in a serene voice.

She could no longer hold back so sobbed hysterically. All the while picking up the pot to hold the small lotus flower to her face in ensuring it captured the tears.

A short time later Aarav had begun to abandon all hope that the drought would ever end. He sat by the kitchen table whereupon a short time later the door lightly opened, and Prisha walked in carrying a delicate lotus flower in a little clay pot. She sat at the table by his side and to his astonishment spoke for the first time since their bereavement.

"Aarav please forgive my quietude and surly behaviour. I know my loss was your loss too. Thank you for being so patient and supportive I love you with all of my heart."

Overcome with emotion they proceeded to hug and later

consummated their intimate physical relationship once again.

Several days passed and as the drought escalated the oxen lay dying in the desiccated spartan fields. The couple huddled together on clay tiles by the relative shade on the kitchen floor in desperation. All of a sudden the monk serenely entered with hands clasped in prayer. He bowed deeply to the couple then in a sweet gentle voice heralded,

"Friends I have decided my vow of silence is complete and it is time to move on. I offer you my heartfelt gratitude for your hospitality."

Aarav stood up then impulsively hugged him tight with genuine affection.

"Brother I can never thank you enough for what you have done. Before you go tell me how you managed to help Prisha when all of my best efforts failed?"

The young monk appeared overtaken by humility.

"Aarav, when hurt people tend to invest too much energy into the denial of their emotions," he returned. "On the contrary your efforts were successful. You allowed Prisha sufficient time and space to process her sorrow whilst managing your own."

Now pointing to the small lotus plant now resting in its pot upon the table he furthered.

"Each tear is a gift because everything it touches becomes sacred ... and given time even plants respond to kindness!"

At that he turned to leave and when he opened the door a miracle transpired as the heavens opened and torrential rain began to fall upon the appreciative scorched brown land.

Just as rain is what happens when the sky reaches down to touch the soil tears are what happens when the heart reaches up to touch the soul. Both signify a truly sacred communion in which each downpour arrives just in the nick of time for things to recover just enough to resemble normality once more.

Even better an elated Prisha would soon reveal she was pregnant again and in the fullness of time would go on to give birth to twins, two beautiful healthy baby boys. The monk had slowly led Prisha to a state of acceptance through teaching her to release her pent-up grief through sustaining another living organism. In this he taught her to share her tears - the most highly prized commodity in a terrible drought of sadness.

Chapter Twelve

'Of Ants and Angels'

EARTH IS NEITHER HEAVEN nor hell.

Rather it sits somewhere in-between thus can be regarded both. In reality nothing is ever perfect in Gaia, God's bountiful garden of Eden. As for us I guess we occupy a seat somewhere in the natural order amongst ant's and angels for we too can be both.

A stark contrast to the fertile mature woodlands and rolling hills of my childhood home at the head of the Gareloch there was also a beachhead. For many of the village children our ritual was to frequently visit that place.

Being ever curious having relocated from the landlocked Stafford by the age of six I considered Garelochead's shore an endlessly fascinating place. Naturally, the word 'beach' may conjure images of golden sand palm trees and caerulean sea however, ours had none of that. More of a dirty old shoreline it mostly featured rocks flotsam seaweed and was usually accompanied by seemingly endless flurries of rain. Likewise an old sewage pipe perpetually mourned through weeping human waste into the murky brackish water. Nevertheless we frequented it irrespective all else just for something else to do.

I recall the summer of 1979 as being particularly hot humid and sticky. On one occasion accompanied by my friends we'd gone down to the shoreline to play. With the tide out you can probably imagine our surprise to discover a beached, Blue-Nosed Whale lodged there already in the initial throes of decay. I vividly remember being overwhelmed by its size and the heady stench. The unmistakable mix of brine seaweed and rotting flesh would accordingly emit the gargantuan mammals corpse and suspend over the village like a viscous shroud for weeks to come. Interestingly something else noteworthy transpired that would hold me transfixed as a seemingly endless quantity of aliens had arrived. At the time I was aged ten and simultaneously captivated and repulsed by the advent of interminable Hermit Crabs arriving to feast upon the rotting behemoth.

I vividly recall the different shapes and sizes; the appendages, colours and unique shells. Absorbed I craved to know more so sought out further information from the village library which was incidentally one of my very favourite haunts. Unlike conventional crustaceans I discovered Hermit Crabs seemingly didn't develop a shell at all. Instead featuring soft vulnerable abdomens they salvaged the carapace of others to make a home and find protection from predators. Then in time as they flourished the incorporated case would inexorably befit tighter and tighter meaning the crab underwent mounting pressure - a sure sign they must make a change by foraging a more appropriate upgrade.

Now this all got me thinking. I ruminated in bed at night over having to live in a scavenged secondhand shell all alone in the vastness of the ocean and the concept really struck home. Ironically it would later become incredibly pertinent as an adult. You see many years later I had lost myself whilst trying to find everyone else. The incessant pressure of the troubles and bad luck which always beset us had eventually gotten too much and I guess I had fallen apart. In all honesty looking back I think I had an emotional breakdown which fueled my injunction to push everyone else away. Damned fool my accursed pigheadedness and pride had also gotten in the way and begun to work against my own best interests. Don't get me wrong the difficulties which were troubling us were not necessarily our fault however, the way in which we were mismanaging them at the time probably was.

In any case I found solace in motion, and what I mean by that is I would spend an inordinate amount of time just aimlessly driving around alone in my car. In some way I had resolved to become exiled, but at the time this seemed the best decision on my part. Actually, fate had lit the bonfire of my soul as I subsequently combusted into an emotive wilderness. Indeed, for a time I would continue to blister and char by this same ardent flame. Then again the universe mostly works in mysterious ways and adversity often introduces us unto ourselves. Think about it by this I mean how can you know how strong you truly are unless you have no other option than to be as strong as you can be?

It's impossible to describe my vulnerability at that point. The loneliness was overwhelming and almost overnight I felt I had become invisible even to supposed friends family and associates. Insult to injury rightly or wrongly I felt a great many of mine had proceeded to mete judgement upon my character without any proper inclination regarding the actual situation. So when we were down on our luck and believed nobody understood nor cared what hurt most was those who then turned a blind eye to distance themselves.

'Don't judge us. Every saint has a past, and every sinner has a future!' I'd furiously thought all alone in my car.

Yup it seemed everyone had an opinion. However beware because never have more sinister words ever been spoken than when uttered by those who dispassionately peer in from the outside,

"No matter what you think I know what's best for you."

Don't get me wrong I'm not bitter at all. Thank goodness for small mercies as it's nigh on impossible for me to bear grudges no matter how hard I try. This is good because bitterness is self-destructive. It's a bit like drinking poison and expecting the other person to die. Instead consider this dialogue an ambivalent recital of how things were at that time. Witnessing others suffering from some downfall tends to either evoke schadenfreude pity or foreboding. It serves the bystander an uncomfortable reminder that the same could feasibly forgo them too should fate so decide. Hence, people tend to avert themselves from those embroiled in such circumstances because it's pretty damn uncomfortable.

In any case I posit each setback is sent to test you. Hence in that sense one way or another I simply decided we had to take it all on the chin. After all you can only begin to find yourself once you have become lost. It strikes me as I write these words that what I was really looking for as I drove around was myself.

Anyway this got me thinking about homeless people because it became all-to-easy for me to comprehend how one could end up in the gutter to then find the torrent of fate washing them towards the storm drain. In this context I came to realise how fortunate I was by comparison. Sure I had virtually cast myself out and was something of an emotional wreck - but in real terms I still had it all to play for. I had a crucial lifeline as against all odds we were still managing to keep the candle of our relationship alight, maintaining a nice home, my job and fund a reliable second-hand car. Definitely to me my car had come to symbolize the essential radical autonomy and privacy that I craved at that time.

At work I was highly specialised crewing an Armed Response Vehicle (ARV) and serving as the section Operational Firearms Commander (OFC). Given my circumstances I was functioning properly in a professional capacity. Then again Force Policy stipulated any officer going through personal difficulties was to automatically have their firearms authority rescinded.

My boss at the time was a Chief Inspector who knew I was having a tumultuous time. Even so he was much like everyone else insofar as he was blissfully unaware as to the inner workings of my private life. I had been faking it well enough to get by but in any case out of the blue he had proceeded to summon me into his office for an interview 'without coffee'.

"I'm sorry about this. I've been instructed from on high to remove your authorisation to carry out firearms duties," he had declared.

"Boss please don't. Come on cut me a break. You know this will kill my firearms career," I'd pled. "Is there nothing else you can do?"

"Look you know only too well if I put my neck on the line for you

I'm placing my own career in jeopardy should anything happen," he'd replied shaking his head.

At this I looked him square in the eye then reached out by offering him my solemn oath.

"Listen do this one thing for me, and I promise I won't let you down. Give me a chance to get over things ... please."

He was the former force Chief Firearms Instructor and held a reputation for not tolerating fools gladly. We had only worked together for several weeks as he was bedding in even so it's reasonable to say we had already developed a decent rapport. He appeared discernably taken aback by my informal request and proceeded to hold my gaze for what seemed an age at which point I became acutely aware he was penetrating my psyche.

"Right let's have some straight talking," he uttered lowering his voice with conviction to glance the door was shut properly. Satisfied he then returned to maintain eye contact.

"Make no mistake I've already read your file. I've got to admit I liked what I saw. I've also asked around about you and all I hear is you're universally known as being likeable honest and reliable. All in all I see an excellent operator sitting before me. You're committed conscientious and capable, and I respect that."

He then sat back and sighed. Pursing his lips he then drummed his fingers on his desk for a few seconds as he looked up toward the ceiling deep in thought.

"I want the truth," he demanded now suddenly looking intently at me again. "My gut feeling tells me there's more to this than meets the eye but spare me the details. It's your business. Even so don't bullshit me. What I really want to know is are you going to be alright or not?"

"Boss, honestly I guarantee it's all under control," I'd pledged with sincerity. (*Note: This was my belief amounting to certainty at the time but for full disclosure I couldn't have known for certain*).

"Alright," he impulsively announced following a split-second hesitancy. "Against my better judgement I am going to bat for you after all. But hear me loud and clear if you f**k up we're both going down - I'll make damn sure of it do you understand?" he'd emitted.

I agreed then in the coming days he took it upstairs to swing it my way. I presumed him the last person to query procedure, yet I somehow retained my position. To this day I don't exactly know how he did it. Of course there would be a price to pay. There always is and I'll discuss that a little later.

I momentarily flirted with betraying his trust, but only once. Double crewed in an ARV in the public domain between us we possessed enough weaponry ammunition and ancillary equipment to start a small-scale war. This was admittedly not exactly ideal given I was sometimes losing the internal battle I was waging against myself at the time. Feeling particularly down I desperately needed to take a leak so in-between operational deployments we'd parked at a remote woodland spot whereupon I alighted the vehicle to go into the undergrowth to relieve myself.

Momentarily overcome with sadness I teased myself to do something to make it stop. Sporting a holster containing a high-powered handgun loaded with twelve-rounds of 9mm hollow-point ammunition I became aware that my hand hung near the familiar cold form of the pistol grip as a seductive thought suddenly presented itself,

'What would happen if you drew it then held it to your head and gently squeezed the trigger? Your misery would end in an instant.'

Easy and painless the prospect almost seemed appealing. Then again I ruminated over the devastation it would cause Mandy and my daughter, my colleague, and the promise I'd made to my boss. Taking a few deep breaths to chase the ridiculous notion off I hastily unzipped my fly then being ever so careful to avoid splashing my boots took a leak instead. What a relief. I had instantaneously snapped out of it. Calmly strolling back to the vehicle I found my now obviously bored colleague waiting patiently.

"Is that better now?" he asked stretching and turning the ignition back on in preparing to drive off as I hopped back in.

"Yeah much," I'd responded.

Off duty I continued to spend a lot of time in my scavenged mobile home. Looking back I wonder how I got through that patch. In some way I reckon we must have had invisible support from somewhere. In isolation I recall the stars dispassionately looking down on me at night from their heavenly demesne and felt intensely isolated in the vastness of the universe. After all I often enjoyed parking up to sit and stare at the vast map of heaven from some layby or other. This essentially gave me hope as it was a constant reminder life was a giant adventure with so much left for me to see and do. I attempted to count them one evening whilst wondering about the vastness of it all. Strangely enough at that point I somehow had an epiphany and knew I would make it if I clung on just a little longer. So I steeled myself until I eventually saw the guiding light.

Oh the absurdity. When that beached Whale generated tens of thousands of Hermit Crabs to our beach in 1979 I never dreamt I was destined to become one myself in some sense. As for my mobile

mobile home I kept that car until it was practically falling apart. Long-standing sociological studies indicate males typically preoccupy themselves with things whilst females gravitate more towards people. This testimony indicates there might just be something in that because when I had to sell that car it literally broke my heart. Then again the pressure mounting on me at the time had indicated I'd outgrown it and had to move on.

On reflection I've come to realise that good experience amounts to good experience and bad experience is just experience. C'est la vie and all that.

★

EXPERIENCE MIGHT BE CRUEL but she's a damn

good teacher. My troubles taught me resilience which in turn served me well. I'd expand on this by attesting Mother Nature is an astonishing educationalist if you pay attention to her nuances. What I mean is nowadays people seem so preoccupied trying to cram as much as possible into their day often chasing meaningless causes with their heads stuck to their phones deaf dumb and blind to the miracle of life unfolding around them. I don't take a single thing for granted anymore. Furthermore I never save anything for a special occasion. All things considered I'm grateful to still be here thus every day is a special occasion.

I'll share something else with you. I was an unusually perceptive child and first noticed ants in my back garden at a young age. Henceforth I proceeded to watch them go about their business in fascination. At the village library I learnt biologists consider ants amongst natures highest order of organism: reasonable given they've been thriving on this planet for almost one-hundred-million years which is incidentally approximately twenty times longer than our own tenure. Antarctica aside they have colonised every single landmass of Earth. Their sociological organisation and ability to modify themselves no matter the habitat - and its life-sustaining resources, or lack thereof - marks them out as ingenious. Truly one of the natural world's most highly adaptable and resilient survival specialists. Why am I banging on about all of this? Simply put there's an awful lot to be gleaned from them.

You see to me it became apparent they were unlike people insofar as they just never quit. This became evident as I concurrently watched many of the people in Garelochhead scurrying about to then sacrifice their dreams and grand schemes for small desires. Even then I noticed people tended to imitate water insofar as they always opted for the easiest route before settling for their own level. Each one of them possessed some talent or other but when things got too tough they tended to just give up by going to prop up the bar instead. For the few who did manage to buck this trend it seemed they did so through acquiring good habits attitudes and behaviours like discipline determination and perseverance. So at the tender age of eight I had already compared people just enough to ants in arriving at an epiphany: If you never quit then failure was impossible.

So as a child the ideology of an ant clearly exemplified: '*I will never give up.*' Now I did warn you earlier I was an unusual child! Anyway go and try it yourself. Block their path this way and they will find another as they go around and under obstacles. Block that alternative and they simply find another. Over around or even removing or going through obstacles. Wash them away and they simply re-establish elsewhere. Moving beyond all opposition they are ceaseless and never give up. Certainly they always seemed able to bear incredible loads far beyond their own weight. The unspoken patterns of Mother Nature are always simple and easy to chart, and ants know this to never ever rest on their laurels. During plenitude they plan for famine: *'Gather collect hurry because winter is coming,'* is their summer mantra. Then in famine they plan for plenitude: *'Keep going endure prevail, it can't last much longer we're going to make it,'* is their winter mantra. Their innate ability for problem solving building and adapting is married to an extraordinary will as they have an instinctive awareness that the seasons of life constantly change and no matter what they just never give in.

Sure the truth is always a heavy burden to bear. Even so at least it remains consistent. Life is unquestionably scattered with sporadic happiness and joy but is ultimately governed by the fact it must come to an end: Therefore it always remains a tragic affair. It also combines considerable injustice heartbreak and malice. However I've also learnt what really matters most is how we respond by what we do about it. I learnt it's essential to not only accept our burdens but somehow learn to welcome them. We shouldn't shy away from suffering because to deny it is to amplify it. I know it's never pleasant however, it is necessary to lean into resistance and hardship for it ultimately shapes us into becoming more than we are.

There are all manner of ways to mitigate tough times with one prime example being through seeking help from others and finding strength in numbers. Actually, maintaining numerical superiority was always the first principal of Police Firearms tactics. The legendary American Football coach Vince Lombardi once asserted: *"Everyone has a will to win but very few have the will to prepare to win."* Well with a ratio of at least three to one police firearms officers will wherever possible manipulate each confrontation to their advantage before deploying into the arena. After all they aren't remotely interested in fair fights when it comes to protecting the innocent. Simply put the Police must win. Similarly, ants co-habit expansive colonies whereupon they are co-dependent on each other which imbues the exact same fundamental.

Therefore, even as a youngster I figured it was best to forge relationships with capable people and those able to actively compete with me. I mean had it not been for James MacDonald I would have not learnt the meaning of life, and had it not been for the faster boys competing for the school's athletic team the notion of becoming quicker wouldn't even have registered at all. Equally when seeking a lifelong partner, I contemplated the dovetail joint within woodworking with each element filling the others void in forming the strongest link of all. Almost impossible to pull apart I wanted someone who could provide the caulk I lacked and vice versa. Like the dovetail I reasoned such a relationship would be reciprocal by way of mutual exchange. I recollect after my Mum had met Mandy for the very first time she had become condescending once she'd gone home.

"Well, I think she's really nice - but much too tough for someone soft like you," she declared which I took as plainly patronising.

Completely missing the point for me that was a key part of the attraction. Even then I knew bad things would happen to us and if I aligned myself with a weak partner I would be sowing the seeds of our combined eventual downfall. In any case Mandy wasn't too tough in the least. Unlike Mum she just had her head screwed on and her wits about her which I think made her all the more attractive. What good is an alliance between two soft people when life bites them? A good marriage should be like a wrestling match at times - and it definitely does swing between coexisting as 'the best of friends' to becoming 'the worst of enemies' - yet this is normal. Life is no a fairy-tale and I don't care who you are nobody gets to live happily ever after. Instead of all sweetness and light it often requires sacrifice hard work and grit. In this context there's nothing whatsoever to be gained from an affiliation pairing you against someone you can easily best all the time. Each pyrrhic victory only undermines your principal source of support in times of trouble. An eagle surrounded with chickens eventually behaves like a chicken.

Here's the curious thing. Our difficulties were essentially good for us both. Don't misunderstand me it was taxing and became white hot at times however, let me tell you once we figured it out we were forged together as a formidable unit. As it happened we would eventually combine better together not worse as we had grown stronger as a couple. Much like weightlifting the resistance would build brawn.

I openly confess I can be almost angelic and what I mean by that is I'm intrinsically soft-hearted considerate and nice. My patience is legendary, and I'll almost snap myself in half to be helpful gentle and generous. Furthermore, I'm either blessed or cursed through always tending to see the good in others. Yet even I have a line in the sand because I retain the capacity to kick up a storm and wreak havoc if it is crossed. In fact, every properly integrated person should know patient restraint is not powerlessness and the best way of dealing with darkness is through becoming acquainted with your own darkness. Hence it's a terrible mistake for anybody to be completely harmless or surrounded by those who are. After all, if it comes to the crunch do you really want defeated people standing beside you on the ramparts? I figure at some point or other life will test the limits of your endurance. Seeing as the most powerful weapon of all is a soul on fire it was during our own hardships that we eventually awakened to the fact that our capacity extended above and beyond all circumstances. Ants teach us we don't fail when we fall we only fail if we don't get back up.

So, when you're on the rack those who depend upon you need someone fit for purpose not someone who will throw in the towel and surrender. Come hell or high water I eventually twigged I was capable of moving forward against all obstructions. To prevail hardship I decided to become an ant because I reasoned if they could persist in the face of overwhelming adversity then so could I. At that point I became an unstoppable force.

We are ultimately built by nature to survive. Something deep within us all encompasses the exact same capacity for occupying a place anywhere in the natural order between ant's and angel's and thank goodness for that.

Chapter Thirteen

'Weeds Never Rest'

GIVEN MY UNSATISFACTORY

relationship with formal schooling throughout my childhood many of my teachers presumed I was a bit on the dim side. Education felt like it went against the grain of my abstract logic and alongside my parent's low expectancies I had simply gone along with preserving a belief amounting to certainty that I must have been stupid too. I had resultantly accepted the expectations of others through unconsciously settling for what was in real terms an extremely low-resolution definition. Even so circumstance was about to ensure I would reach levels few of my teachers ever thought I could.

After joining the police I then discovered I was extremely good at weapon handling drills shooting and tactics then became an Authorised Firearms Officer. I joined the forces Special Weapons Group (the 'special weapons' in question being antiquated Sterling sub-machine guns and WW2 Browning pistols!) before graduating to being an Armoury and Armed Response Vehicle officer as the overall police firearms capability evolved. Due to my burgeoning association with Police Firearms Training by my late thirties I had become involved in teacher training with Teesside University whereupon Mensa officially measured my IQ as 148 then cited me a 'genius' - whilst extending me an invite to join up of course. Anyway it was at this point I discovered I could decide to be academic if I wanted after all. Who knew?

This was notable insofar as something dormant within me was finally roused. Like parched kindling paired to an eager spark my thirst for knowledge and learning soon burst into what could best be described a rapacious blaze. Indeed this soon raged into what would become an insatiable inferno.

Then again in another sense all of this bothered me too. You see I'm not boasting in the least as I found the Mensa stuff rather hilarious. As far as I was concerned anyone who seriously believed that an IQ test or Mensa membership indicated true intelligence had already flunked the real test.

Me a genius? What a ridiculous notion. I'm not even the cleverest person in my own house and am certainly not even as smart as my phone! Besides, the more I learnt the more I reckoned I knew nothing at all. So to me cleverness equated little more than a minor aspiration. As for wisdom? Well now, that did seem the interdependence of thinking and feeling therefore something really worth getting my teeth into.

Titles cannot elevate a man who is already great nor can the lack of the same diminish a man who already possesses greatness of character. Concerning Mensa I personally disapprove of clubs associations badges awards backslapping and trinkets. It's just not my bag. I prefer to do my own thing and take pleasure from doing it. Anything else is a bonus. For example as an author the secret to my contentment is realised through the act of writing books not selling them. For right or for wrong I simply don't care how many I offload because once I have my own copy I instantly have everything I need.

A lot of people miss the truth that it's those who control the marketplace that decide what books will become bestsellers or not just as it's those who control the music business who decide which music will top the charts. Like everything else it's all the type of rigged game that I enjoy refusing to play along with. On the flip side whilst congratulating each other on their superior intelligence some Mensa members miss the detail that everyone is clever in their own unique way. Consequentially no matter their educational standing each individual is perfectly capable of achieving a successful life (whatever 'success' might mean to them).

The ensuing story that I'm going to share was published in my second book: *This Dream, Reality*, (2017). Barring my previous disclosure it was reasonably well received and picked up on by a professor who worked within a prominent Glasgow University. This actually came about because her daughter - an accomplished professional cellist with a Philharmonic Orchestra - had come to see me for hypnotherapy to help with the anxiety that had been affecting her. I recall her as an exceedingly good-looking young woman engaged in a long-term relationship with an Olympic athlete. She almost comically continually used a rather old-fashioned bicycle to pedal to our sessions and seeing as it was summertime I'd always ensure there was a bottle of chilled water awaiting her arrival.

Vaguely quirky she was undoubtedly a talented and extremely well-read musician. Even so she wasn't immune to suffering from the disquiet of anxiousness. After all people are just people at the end of the day.

In a weird coincidence it turned out her Father was the very same architect who had drawn up plans for my house extension some years before. A charming and complimentary man he took a particular interest in the furniture I had hand built throughout my house from reclaimed oak floorboards. Anyhow as it happened she would reveal he was now in the latter stages of dementia which I recollect caused me to feel a bit blue at that time. Her Mother's expertise was business and having purchased my book from a local shop she had got in touch to request permission to use one of the short stories with the undergraduate students on her course. Naturally I was delighted to facilitate.

Having suffered the ignominy of being labelled a 'dummy' at school I was rather humbled she'd taken the time to read my story in the first place; even more so that she saw some way of putting it to practical use for the benefit of others. That's why I would now like to share it with you. I do hope you like it as much as she did.

★

(A Parable offering Life Advice)

THERE WAS A BUSINESS MAGNATE based in

London. He was held in high esteem due to what had been an outstanding and profitable career. Interestingly his financial success had been won whilst maintaining a favorable reputation for decency and fairness. Thus he was respected and admired not just for his professional achievements, but as a person by his associates, employees, and even his rivals.

Such was this prestige he was arguably the countries most revered businessman. Naturally, this type of success attracts those who wish to emulate such effective strategies.

Mounted upon the wall of his office was a small display case:

Within it was affixed seven brass penny coins. Whenever questioned as to why he displayed such a menial collection of worthless brass he would merely smile to avoid making any reply.

Childless he had mostly held his own counsel throughout. That said he did have a young nephew. Aspiring but well-natured he'd received many pleas from him asking to share the teachings of his accomplishments. On his part he had reasoned he might continue his aging Uncle's legacy. Well sure enough, after some time the businessman had measured him worthy thus relented. The time was right, so he presently invited him to a summit.

"I'm going to provide you the address of the guru who taught me everything, thus laid the foundations of my business empire," he revealed. "I cannot overemphasise the importance this man has played in my life," he continued. "I'm entirely indebted to him. His name is Mister Gardener and he's expecting you. I'd advise you listen very intently to what he has to say. Make no mistake if you do it will change your life."

Holding his Uncle in considerable regard the nephew was astounded to hear him talk so highly of another this way.

'Mister Gardener must be a man of almost God-like business acumen,' he inwardly reasoned. *'I will endeavor to become his follower.'*

Thanking his uncle profusely he immediately prepared himself. Determined to make a good initial impression he dressed in a most expensive designer suit, silk tie and handmade Italian leather shoes. Thereafter he made his way to the address his Uncle had provided in his open topped sports car.

Following a lengthy journey through winding country lanes he was surprised to eventually arrive at a modest cottage with a thatched roof situated in a rural setting on the edge of a remote country village.

Approaching the small house he happened upon a beautifully kept garden. Of a moderate size it featured a stunning array of colours and vibrancy. The hedge grass flowers and trees were impeccably tended, and shortly after he sighted an old man minding the ground with a hoe.

Of moderate height with a carefully trimmed beard he adorned a well-worn outfit of hat, cotton shirt, denim dungarees and leather boots. Presently noticing the young man he paused to look up from his work and smiled.

"Good afternoon. Can I help you?" he inquired cheerily.

"Oh, good afternoon. I'm a bit confused. I think I might be lost," he returned. "You see I'm looking for a businessman of great acumen named Mister Gardener?"

"Ah, and why might you seek him out?" questioned the elder.

"Well at my Uncles behest I am to become his follower!"
At that the elder gently laughed good humoredly.

"Well congratulations it seems you've found him. I'm Mister Gardener. Then again I know nothing of business. I only know about weeding."

Bemused the young man was momentarily lost for words and more than a bit crestfallen.

"... but I was to become your follower?" he eventually managed to stammer before adding, "My Uncle said that you taught him to lay the foundations of his business empire. I'm a bit confused!" he admitted.

At this the older man stood up then wiped the sweat from his brow.

"Well then herein begins the first lesson young man. Don't become a follower become a student instead. There's a huge difference between the two so it's best you don't confuse them!"

Surveying the younger fellow with kindness he was an exceptional judge of character. Self-satisfied after a moment he nodded to himself as he extended,

"Come on in I've just brewed a fresh pot of tea. Sit in my garden awhile and I'll talk to you about the importance of attitude."

Now seated together on the garden bench the young man found himself sipping a cup of the delicious, sweet tea and sharing in a biscuit as he listened intently to the sage.

"Attitude is everything. It separates the wheat from the chaff so to speak," he said. "An attitude is a habit of thought, and everything begins with a thought. For that reason you should always carefully guard the doorway to your mind.

"You see thoughts manifest through actions to become the material fabric of life," he went on. "Negative thoughts become negative actions so nurture, cultivate and regularly weed the garden of your mind. Be diligent, industrious, and always remain optimistic. Never complain because to moan is the outward expression of a fragile mind."

"I'm not sure I follow," replied the younger man after a prolonged period of introspection.

Mister Gardener took a sip from his cup then smiled kindly and continued.

"It's quite simple really. By way of analogy I'll explain the importance of weeding to you. After all, negativity is one of life's most pervasive weeds. Now here's the thing - weeds never rest but are no match for an industrious gardener.

"Of course weeding is neither glamorous nor pleasant but weeds remain easy to deal with. Of course it's far easier to ignore them – but mark my words ignore them at your peril. If you do they'll take over your garden whilst you're not looking!"

He looked brightly toward the sky scratched his silver beard then returned his attention to his present company.

"Mother Nature is patient and plays a long game. Without consistent maintenance she always reclaims any garden. Everyone has some form of natural talent or ability; however many forgo it through adopting bad habits like laziness or procrastination. Thus they sow the seeds of their own downfall. Perseverance on the other hand always conquers indolence."

They sat in silence for a while as the old man again sipped from his tea and nibbled some rusk. The young man thought on what had been said then to his surprise he sighted a beautiful butterfly flutter past then land right upon his shoulder.

As the gentle breeze rustled the leaves of the trees airborne seeds drifted past as he heard a pigeon calling in the distance. He next discerned a bee buzzing from one flower to the next then became aware that he had seamlessly become involved in an interaction that was incredibly meaningful.

Affording him the space to think after a while the old man broke back in.

"Everyone wants to be successful. But what is success? One person's is gauged in an entirely different way from another's. For me success is defined by maintaining a beautiful garden and keeping the weeds at bay.

"Everyone wants satisfaction, but where can satisfaction be found? Well for me it's born of the completion of little jobs! As for business? Well it's like gardening. If you become complacent or let your attention drift the weeds will overtake your garden and strangle the flowers!

"So to neglect the little things is to neglect the important things. Neglect leads to infection and infection to disease. Small instances of neglect might be easily addressed - but disease? Well, it can often prove terminal.

"The secret to properly cultivating anything relies upon one's purpose - that is having clear goals, being decisive, and acting with consistent care and commitment.

"Certainly some will say the things you are cultivating are not important or tell you to ease off and take a break. Who knows, they might be well-meaning – but then again, they might not.

"Remember some are always jealous or resentful of what you are working towards. A positive attitude and any attention to detail might cause them to feel inadequate because of their own inertia or procrastination.

"Hence you must also be prepared to ignore the nay-sayers and detractors."

At this point the young man furrowed his brow and interjected.

"Maybe that's true but what can you do when others try to derail you?"

Mister Gardener smiled then nodded as he replied.

"My young friend business is a competitive affair so you will always need to endure competition. The answer to your question is in your question," he declared. "Consider the word 'try'. It's a verb aligned with failure. Never try to do anything. Either do it or do not. As for those who denigrate you it's their load to bear so just leave it with them.

"You need to learn to disregard criticism whilst welcoming feedback. Those that criticise try to pull you down because they are already beneath you. Those who offer feedback are attempting to pull you up. One is a weed and the other a fertilizer."

"Ah, perhaps. But how do you know which is which?" went the young man breaking back in.

"Well now that requires wisdom my young friend," replied Mister Gardener as he burst into good natured laughter.

Almost overwhelmed the Nephew thought all of this seemed slightly surreal and quite the opposite from the type of encounter that he had anticipated. He mused upon what had been said for a while before finally clearing his throat.

"Mister Gardener, tell me ... how might I then become wise?"

The old man chuckled once more.

"Wise men are fools who were foolish long enough to become wise!" he stated. "Allow yourself mistakes. After all each mistake is a lesson, and each lesson should make you better."

They sat finishing their tea and after some reflection the nephew announced,

"My Uncle imparted you were the best. I think I now see he was right!"

"Oh dear. Herein lies the next lesson," went the sage, wagging his finger somewhat disapprovingly. "Becoming 'the best' only ensures perpetual angst. The label 'best' hangs around your neck like a millstone because it encourages an inflated ego. Given time a big ego weighs you down just as much as the unwanted weeds choke an untended garden."

"Oh then would you recommend as an alternative?" the younger man inquired somewhat surprised.

"Simple. Instead of aspiring to be the best, always do your best," Mister Gardener emphasised. "There's a significant difference between the two. I gave your Uncle this exact same advice many years ago."

Now enthusiastic the young man immediately caught the elders drift.

"That makes so much sense. My Uncle was right all along. It's quite clear now I have so much to learn from you," he acknowledged.

Gauging him with genuine affection Mister Gardener was quietly impressed by the immaculate younger man's humility and willingness to learn. Finally slapping his thighs he next stood up.

"Good, then this is just the beginning. Come back at the same time next week."

With that he put his hand into his pocket and produced seven brass penny coins. Handing them to the surprised younger man he explained,

"Each represents the components of a successful life: Goals, Attitude, Optimism; Nurture, Cultivation, Diligence, and Consistency. I recommend you mount these in a display case in your office to remind you to always stay on the right track."

Finally looking him up and down he then mischievously added, "Oh, and by the way next week dress more appropriately. We've got lots of weeding to do."

Chapter Fourteen

'Pulling Rabbits from Hats'

THE ROOM WAS DARK but comfortable, and the gentle hum of the air conditioning only served to lull them into a greater state of relaxation. In all there were twelve in front of me sat like a waddling of ducks in a row with eyes willingly closed and proceeding to downswing into a deep state of relaxation. Voluntarily acceding to this process some had initially chuckled before we'd begun – but that was absolutely fine. I was adept at affecting whatever response they extended and all that mattered to me was they had willingly assented to partake.

You see as far as I'm concerned hypnosis isn't a 'do to' phenomenon whereupon the hypnotist assumes control over the mind of the unsuspecting other. Not one bit of it. Don't get me wrong there are those who covertly manipulate others this way (advertising anyone?), but this is a limited and unethical practice. Rather I consider it a symbiotic process which centers upon interdependency ... or 'do with'.

Furthermore dissimilar another popular myth throughout trance you don't black out or not hear or feel anything then later wake up to confusedly probe "Hey, what happened?" No. That state is actually more akin to death! Rather you enter into a state of heightened awareness therefore are absorbedly aware of your surroundings and precisely what you are experiencing and what's being said etc.

"I can't help but wonder how my voice makes your ears feel as you continue to listen to me or what it might invoke inside," I softly coaxed. "Nonetheless as you continue to listen - and you let go deeper and deeper - in this relaxed state - wherever you may go my voice will go with you.

"And I don't know. Perhaps you might find all of this very useful … because a great many people enjoy the sensation of down-shifting into a comfortable trance. You might too."

Actually this was no ordinary setting, and these were no ordinary Police Officers. This was a Firearms Tactics course, and they were all Counter Terrorist Authorised Firearms Officers turned out for the express purpose of requalification. As course lead I was scheduled to deliver a nondescript PowerPoint presentation which would serve as the precursor to the forthcoming practical application - but was typically adding some flavour to mix it up in my own unique way.

More accustomed to the convention of didactic delivery my coworker had since shaken his head and rolled his eyes then softly left the room. He didn't approve but that was absolutely fine. Our methods were different which is reasonable given there are all manner of different ways of skinning a cat. In any case this wasn't about us this was about the learners. For me it always was.

I had witnessed the expediency of my all-inclusive approach firsthand many times now, and even those who scoffed would have to privately concede to its efficacy. Nonetheless I occasionally met derision from some despite (or because of) the fact a great many of the students enjoyed my lessons and I had consistently achieved good results.

Almost surreal as I sat in that room observing the group now in a collective light trance I couldn't help but think back to how it had all started.

I had been deployed to the Northeast of Scotland to deliver a tactical refresher course to a group of ARV officers. As a Police National Firearms Instructor I was one of three making up the instructional staff. Accompanied on this occasion by a familiar from my own department an ex-Metropolitan Police instructor named Alan completed the triumvirate.

Working with him for the first time I found him different in an absorbing way. It struck me he appeared the most relaxed person I had ever encountered. Proceeding to teach a lesson together I rode shotgun as he took the lead. His methods were unconventional yet observably fecund and along with the majority of the learners I was quite rivetted by it all. I needed to know more and given the instructional staff took refreshments in isolation from the core group the ideal opportunity would soon present itself.

"Hey, I really enjoyed your lesson well done," I offered settling down opposite him with a coffee. "Tell me I've not seen anything like that before ... what exactly was it you were doing?"

"Thanks I appreciate that. It's called NLP mate," he replied in his cockney drawl smiling between sips of tea and nibbling at a biscuit.

"What's that?" I explored interest further piqued. I'd never heard of it before.

"Neuro-Linguistical-Programming: it's a form of Cognitive Psychology if you like," he clarified cheerily. "It involves closely observing people's body-language, paying attention to their vocabulary, tailoring mine to suit ... invoking hypnotherapeutic trancework, you know that kind of thing!"

"What a load of old shit ..." the spare instructor listening nearby interjected having looked up from his newspaper in deciding to offer an appraisal.

Shooting harsh words as bullets his truculence came as no real surprise to either of us. He could be funny and good company but also tended to be a bit of an agitator if the wind blew the wrong way. In truth the department didn't have a fantastic reputation at this time and management were unwilling to arbitrate. They instead coerced fresh blood like me to join as an indirect attempt to dilute the problem as opposed to tackling it head on. This seemed counterintuitive to me as sometimes you need to prune a few rotten branches to save the tree, but there you go.

Alas I was embarrassed and also felt my temperature rising at his uncivility given he was openly insulting our guest. At that not sure what to expect I instantly switched attention back to Alan to see how he'd react to the slur. Nonchalantly disregarding the uncouth outburst he was completely serene as he smiled before calmly switching his focus back to me after a moment or two.

"Ahem, as I was saying John if you would like to know more about it I can always point you in the right direction?"

"Sure I'd really appreciate that," I replied as the other instructor shook his head and returned to his paper.

Later he remained in the office to work on administration whilst together Alan and I hit the ground to task the learners to coordinate a response to some fictional deployment or other. This was our way of testing their pragmatic means through experiential learning. Awaiting their arrival I decided to find out why he hadn't been maddened by the earlier outburst. After all despite being close to retirement he was a big fit guy and had felt a bit of heat in his time.

"Oh that?" he'd replied laughing good heartedly. "It's completely cool. He was just adhering to his model of the world as was I. You see I reckon a second of patience in a moment of anger always saves a lot of regret, don't you?"

I was immensely impressed by this bearing, and it was the beginning for me. He would later explain NLP was used to great effect by US Special Forces thereafter the Met had trialed its use in Police Firearms instruction. Utilised to improve officer's reactions and accuracy throughout live firing practices and in critical deployments of expanding conflict he revealed he had been part of a project entitled 'Operation Jedi'. In keeping with initial results the data was encouraging. Nonetheless funding was eventually cut before the project was finally wound down. Even so throughout he had qualified as Master Practitioner then persisted in its application.

Over the course of the week he tolerated my perpetual queries and taught me a few techniques – even going so far as to hypnotise me during one particular lunch break. In doing so he implanted an 'anchor' to manage some of the stresses taking place in my professional life which I found (and still do) particularly useful.

This had been something of an awakening. Finally here was an unconventional psychotherapeutic and holistic approach I could conjoin with conventional teaching to benefit others. Having felt out in the cold for what seemed forever I suddenly felt a kindred spirit was introducing me to a fascinating new trail of techniques. Suffice to say the kindling was lit and I was beginning to thaw out!

Already knowing it a lost cause but me being me, upon returning to the department I attempted to convince management to authorise sourcing NLP training for the instructional staff. Unsurprisingly my report fell upon deaf ears and the rest weren't in the least bit interested however, at least I'd tried.

Deciding to go it alone I carried out research before funding my own NLP training courses and qualifying as Master Practitioner. Furthermore I followed this up by attaining a diploma in advanced hypnotherapy and as they say the rest is history. I was up and running.

Effectively using NLP and Hypnosis alongside orthodox methods within adult learning I assisted thousands of students within my own organisation and other forces and agencies in this niche backdrop. Despite unaffectedly pulling many rabbits from hats and getting on well with everyone I sporadically met disdain from certain quarters. It didn't matter. By this time I had grown to welcome any opposition through inwardly reasoning,

'You are my teacher and I'm grateful for your noncooperation: it instils patience in me and provides a headwind to elevate higher.'

After witnessing the fruit of my labours for a while I subsequently decided to go for it and constructed a home office in my back garden with the help of my late friend Tony Stirk. Soon after I encouraged private clients in my spare time, and this was how my private practice began.

★

"BLIMEY, YOU LOT ARE A BIT aggressive aren't you?"

he declared following a live Simmunition firing exercise. "In fact if I'm being totally honest possibly the most uncompromising course I have ever taught!"

Coming from him this was all a bit rich. As a student participating in an eight-week police National Firearms Instructor Course (NFIC) he was no ordinary instructor. Actually he was the (in)famous Tony Long also known as the UK's most lethal Police Marksman. Dubbed 'The Mets serial killer' by his own bosses he had shot and killed more dangerous criminals than any other police officer. Illustrative at this time he was still mired in a legal process whereupon he faced charges of unlawfully assassinating a dangerous career criminal named Azelle Rodney, an incident that hit the front pages of every newspaper dominated the news and sparked civil unrest within the Black community.

The Met Predictably dropped him like a hot potato. I mean come on, to back him up would have been career suicide for any senior officer. It's just part of the game and therefore the way it is. Instead here he was now working freelance to make ends meet accompanied by an ex-SAS soldier who for the purpose of this text I'll call 'Thommo'.

I really enjoyed their lessons and learnt an awful lot which was no surprise given they had probably forgotten more about armed deployments than I knew. Highly knowledgeable and unlike his formidable reputation I found Tony extremely amiable relaxed and easy-going. Looking back God knows how he was managing the extreme pressure both he and his family must have been under at the time.

Thommo on the other hand was similar in some ways but in others completely different. Sure he was quiet and reserved approachable and humble yet there was something else about him. How can I explain it? Well, let's just say I find looking deep into the eyes of others a profoundly meaningful experience to the extent it can be quite overwhelming. I always reason in some way you are visiting their timeless soul, that is all that they ever were and all that they ever will be. Bear in mind by now I had been taught to harness my natural highly observant bent towards becoming a reader of people myself. The thing that struck me when scanning his was it

was like gazing into the void, as though I was somehow accessing a part of his soul that had been disbursed by a black hole. I've come across this on a number of occasions and intuitively reason it marks the owner out as being particularly dangerous if incited. Let me tell you it's hard not to feel like an imposter or a fraud when in the company of people like these. I could tell he had felt it too in that moment as he appeared spooked when detecting my oh-so-subtle intrusion: He didn't know exactly what I was doing but he felt it.

Nonetheless by the end of what had been a protracted selection process and succeeding programme of intense qualification I certified. This was the pinnacle of any AFO's career and as previously mentioned notably also entailed having to complete a prolonged process of adult teacher training with Teesside University.

My peers mostly hated this element and I have to admit to having severe misgivings beforehand too. I mean at this point I was still fostering the old improper notion I was stupid and incapable of any sort of academic practice. Damn, I hadn't been able to get out of school quick enough yet here I was now having to go back. But there's the thing once enrolled I was rather surprised to find I was actually enjoying it. Furthermore, I went on to attain 'firsts' for my dissertations alongside glowing reviews from my lecturers and assessors. Wow now here was a bolt from the blue. All at once I had discovered I COULD think critically and write effectively then take it further through finding comfort in expressing my ideas in front of a class. This all provoked an avid thirst for knowledge and a willingness to introduce radical new concepts to training. So much so it would soon become irrepressible.

A while later my NLP trainer graded my transcribed reflections "The best I've ever seen" and by now I had discovered I loved writing. This later conspired me towards becoming a published author in my own right and somehow now in my forties I was being reborn.

THE LEAD INSTRUCTOR FOR A REMEDIAL

Single System of Search firearms tactics course this was perhaps the most complex application in the curriculum. It required a team of

AFO's to deploy to a building force limited entry then proceed to find confront and neutralise ongoing violence perpetrated within by an 'active shooter'. A great many students struggled with this - no real surprise given half of the instructional staff didn't know what the hell they were doing either. Typically, during its inception it admittedly took me a while to get my head around it too yet once I had I would own it.

In fact, as one of only two national leads on Police Maritime Firearms Operations this would specifically lead to me working alongside the UK Maritime Warfare Centre, 45 Commando Royal Marines Boat Troop (including SBS), the Royal Navy, equivalent US Military Forces, and several regional UK Police Forces. You see, having personally authored the national tactics course relevant to boarding Maritime Vessels for the exact same purpose this had been highly lauded before being pilfered by a higher rank to aid his bid for promotion.

Interestingly enough I later heard he'd proudly paraded it around Police Scotland's headquarters at Tulliallan upon which my name had been deleted from the material to be replaced by his. To be honest I really didn't care as he was only cheating himself. Even so this is worth mentioning purely as an indication as to how these things often pan out in the plod: If you allow people to attain promotion through intellectual theft then you end up with intellectual thieves attaining promotion. My own personal view is individual ascension always usurps organisational advancement in this way. Then again who was I to say anything as I was just a very small cog in the machine. I simply left the crusades to the crusaders.

In any case back to the course in question. It had been specifically planned to accommodate officers who had been unsuccessful during summative assessments on preceding dates. For one in particular it was seen as last chance saloon. That is his livelihood was now on the line.

"Just to be clear I personally taught him on his previous attempt and he's useless. He hasn't got a chance," announced the Firearms Training Manager as he briefed me on the eve of the event. "You can train him until the cows come home but he still won't pass. If I were you I'd now get a head start by preparing the paperwork to flunk him."

Although seemingly callous discussions like this frequently took place behind closed doors at the department. Even so that didn't necessarily mean I was buying into it. After all, along with some other heretics I was able to work with 'difficult' learners in finding ways to overcome whatever difficulties were holding them back.

We had hit the ground at the inception of the course, and I had separated the individual in question from the group almost immediately. Fair to say I found him a little idiosyncratic.

"Come on over here and link up with me," I requested gesturing to him. Joining me I then continued, "Do me a favour and take your jacket off, won't you?"

This was a subliminal compliance check to which he conformed. As such I did likewise.

"Right," I announced. "Give it over and take mine," I offered as we swapped. "Good, now turn it inside out and put it on."

I then proceeded to do the same and by now we were wearing each other's jackets inside out. By this stage he looked completely bewildered and just as daft as I did! Moving close I placed my hand on his shoulder to whisper,

"Now how many armed cops in the world do you think are on a

tactics course right now wearing each other's jackets inside out?"

"Erm ... none?" he responded uncertainly completely mixed up.

"That's right. It's just you and me," I confirmed gently squeezing his shoulder. I momentarily noticed it trembling before continuing.

"Now what I really want to know is are *you open to suggestion*?"

"*Yes*," he automatically replied as his pupils dilated and skin tonus changed just ever so slightly.

This was all very promising as I'd just taken him to a mutually exclusive space – a shared model of the world - and followed my compliance checks - or 'yes set' - up with a conversational hypnotic embedded command ("you open to suggestion"). He had consented therefore I discerned I might be able to get him through this contaminated situation after all.

In a light conversational trance he would then more or less reveal he thought he couldn't pass the process because of being afraid of failing. This is very common and a great many people really zone themselves out like that when under the pressure of assessments and such like. First and foremost I realised a need to bin the fear.

"Okay listen to me. If you stick with it no matter what happens and give me one hundred percent I promise to get you through this," I'd offered out of earshot of the others. "Do we have a deal?" I asked extending my hand inviting a handshake (which incidentally was yet another compliance check).

"Yeah absolutely it's a deal!" he'd eagerly answered still mildly disoriented and instinctively responding by reaching out his hand to grip mine.

In the performing arts there is an imaginary space that separates the audience from the theatrical performance known as the 'fourth wall'. I likened this to firearms training insomuch as I had quickly noticed many of the instructors – often vying for the position of alpha - would encourage it before feeding from the separation by utilising trepidation in asserting their dominance within the hierarchy. Certainly this could be effective especially when enforcing safe practice throughout live firing ranges however, it could be equally ineffective with certain types of personalities throughout the same and during the formative stages of tactical evaluation.

Horses for courses notwithstanding I reckon the seat of any success on my part rested upon obliterating the fourth wall to make more profound and sincere connections: In short my own teaching concept was one of relevance not superiority or inferiority.

Binary it turned out his previous instructors kept trying the same couple of methods over and over again. True they had worked reasonably well for the majority, but he was different and just couldn't relate. They had subsequently become more and more frustrated, and he had been labelled 'useless' thus less likely to succeed. In short he'd been forsaken by their inflexibility. This reminded me of my own school days so to evaluate him he was initially embedded within the team so that I could then closely tune in to examine what he was doing. I noticed he was at a distinct disadvantage because he was kinesthetically ungainly, something he constantly compounded by attempting to rush everything.

"Woah there!" I coached. "Only fools rush in where angels fear to tread! The faster those are going," I furthered by pointing to his feet, "the faster this has to go," I concluded gently tapping his forehead beneath the oversize Kevlar ballistic helmet balanced askew on his bonce.

Anyway I guessed he was probably more inclined to visual means so reasoned the criterion was skewed to handicap him. Notably video footage was highly frowned upon during tactical firearms training given the restricted nature of the material. The hazards of it falling into the wrong hands needs no further explanation. Plus tactical methodology's are a perpetually evolutionary means. This means even cutting-edge footage soon become timebound and freeze dried.

Proceeding to try a couple of different things to no avail I suddenly remembered a quote I had once read of Nietzsche: "*A pupil repays a teacher badly if they always remain a pupil.*"

I now impulsively decided upon a maverick course of action. The best way to proceed was by demolishing the fourth wall and committing the ultimate sin. Pulling him aside I unzipped my hi-vis to offer him the coveted Firearms Instructors vest.

"Here put this on," I declared handing it over. Meanwhile the other trainers looked on both startled and mightily pissed. They'd suffered blood sweat and tears to earn theirs and here was an act of sacrilege - one being freely handed over to someone they didn't rate. On the other hand I simply didn't care. To me it was no more than part of some fancy-dress costume regime anyway.

"Right I'm taking your place in the team. From here on in I'm the student and you're the instructor, got it?" I announced to him as he stood astonished nearby.

"But I can't ..." he stuttered suddenly becoming wide-eyed.

"Whyever not? I questioned.

Looking nervously at the other learners and bothered looking instructors nearby he declared,

"I'm, I'm too embarrassed!"

"My friend you are now on a collapsing timeframe and the stakes are high so get over it, pronto ...." I ordered whilst taking then adjusting his weapons to fit me and shooing him away as he awkwardly sported my former attire.

I spent the rest of the morning running through a plethora of scenarios adopting a variety of formations by going time and again With the team. A complete role reversal following each scenario he had to debrief me and the others by offering detailed feedback on what we were doing as opposed to vice versa. Through taking this vicarious perspective he was able to further his theoretical understanding and by the time he slotted back into the team his own (along with the others) skills had increased no end.

None of this was rocket science by any means. Intuitive I couldn't have known for sure whether or not it would work. Nevertheless as it happens it did just enough and along with his peers he made it. Don't get me wrong he wasn't great but had improved enough to merit a pass. Predictably his response was relief which was wholly understandable. I would have been the exact same in his shoes. My primary motivation I reasoned if I had been him I would have hoped to meet someone like me willing to go that extra mile.

You know what? It's dead easy to be an instructor when things just fall into place. Why? Because you're not instructing. The alternative necessitates you have to step up and graft for your corn and I guess some teachers just can't be bothered.

In any case this all brings me back to the Training Manager as he almost seemed disappointed when I told him my man had made the grade. Actually, I couldn't help but get the distinct impression he was taking it as a personal slight. I have to admit on this occasion I had enjoyed proving him wrong which brought to mind a quote I'd once read of the Greek Philosopher Epictetus: *"Your boos mean nothing to me because I have seen what you cheer for."*

Then again this wasn't the first time he had grated me seeing as he had a tendency for damning me with faint praise. By now it was becoming tiresome. Where was the incentive in forever working against him in doing what we were employed to do in the first place? Venting to my closest ally throughout one of my most difficult times I recall him smiling knowingly before humbly advising,

"Healer heal thyself!"

I'm only human and as fallible as the next person. By now I was sensing this situation just wasn't going to work for me no matter what. I absolutely loved the role and my time with the students, but I was allowing the behind-the-scenes politics to crush me. A round peg in a square hole I arrived at the conclusion I was going to have to swallow some of my own medicine and do something else. I kept my powder dry then went home to discuss the implications over with the good Mrs. Hughes that night. She totally got it and agreed with me it was time to move on.

Time changes everything except something deep within us all which is always surprised by change and the following day I strolled into the Training Managers office to inform him I was ending my three-year tenure by returning to operations. Almost unheard of at the time it would be something of an understatement to say he was taken aback.

———————

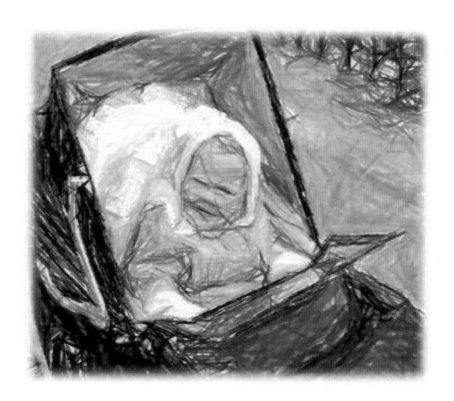

Chapter Fifteen

'Who's Harry?'

MY FATHER GREW UP in rural North Wales during World War Two. Despite being an enigma wrapped up in a puzzle he had a wicked sense of humour and particularly enjoyed a wind-up or two. Nonetheless being extremely awkward in a crowd he wasn't especially sociable or much of a raconteur. Even so he would occasionally indulge me by narrating stories about his childhood, none more so than when he was elderly and disabled and I would take him out for a Sunday afternoon drive each week. On one such occasion I'd professed,

"My goodness those were lean times. You must have often been hungry as a boy?"

"Nah not a bit of it," he'd responded.

It turns out they had no running water or electricity and would catch birds rabbits squirrels and fish every day then take them home to his Mother who would turn them into tasty dinners. You see they also grew their own vegetables potatoes and such like. Additionally, having no indoor toilet they would regularly have to fetch ice-cold water from a well situated almost a quarter of a mile away in two buckets. Despite the inconvenience he testified it was the most delicious water he had ever tasted.

To be precise I'll never forget one anecdote whereupon he

narrated his Father arriving home early from work one day with a tiny piglet under his arm. Interest piqued naturally I'd asked him where he had gotten it.

"Oh, we never asked," he replied thoughtfully as though such an inquiry had never even occurred to him.

The tale continued with cheerful recollections of how they named their new family pet 'Popper', and the fun adventures he and his siblings had with him. Fondly recounting serving him scraps each day he revealed how they loved Popper and explained he'd eventually matured into a great big fat porker. I'd never heard any of this before, so was fascinated. Given by this

time my Father had reverted to type and become distant again no further information seemed forthcoming. I wanted to know more so eventually probed him a bit further.

"So then pray tell what happened to Popper the pig?" I'd inquired.

"Oh him?" he re-joined furrowing his brow and watching the scenery pass us by as though he'd almost forgotten we'd only recently discussed the matter. "We slaughtered and ate him!" was his blaise reply lacking any suggestion whatsoever of irony or regret. Accompanied by a momentary twinkle in his eyes he went on to sentimentally add,

"Ah yes I recall we had beautiful pork sausages bacon and chops hanging from the rafters of our kitchen for weeks afterward," he went now almost salivating and licking his lips.

Open-mouthed I was still processing this unexpected turn of events for a few moments before deep in thought he had next continued,

"D'you know what was best of all though?"

"What?" I stammered glancing sideways at him now almost apprehensive as to what would follow.

"The day after we butchered Popper my Father arrived home early from work with another piglet under his arm," he chuckled. "To this day I still don't know where he bloody got them," he added nostalgically stroking his chin, and leaning forward to look out the windscreen up toward the sky as though it might offer some answer.

Lost for words I just shook my head then returned full attention to the winding road unfolding before us. It was at times like that I found him unintentionally hilarious.

Sure enough, he could be an incorrigible rogue at times and on occasion loved nothing better than being outrageous. Even so he wasn't a patch on my Uncle David who was a year or two younger than him. In fact, not even close.

Different from my Father insomuch as he was extroverted and something of a conversationalist, just like my Grandfather Dai was tall and thin but as hard as nails. He also held a penchant for revelling in his outrageous deeds whilst holding court to recount them in his own inimitable way. Let me assure you I have no reason whatsoever to cast any doubt on any of his misadventures. He visited Scotland a couple of years ago as an elderly man in his eighties during which he proceeded to narrate loads of stories. When together my reticent Father was always happy to play second fiddle to him. One such tale centred upon growing up alongside the River Dovey.

He explained as a young man a chemical spillage once polluted the waterway which resulted in a plethora of dead Salmon floating around inert upside-down in the stream.

"I thought to myself 'Now then what a great opportunity!'" he revivified, his deep brown eyes twinkling wickedly at the recollection.

"What do you mean?" I replied naively inquisitive as to what would come next.

"Well, I fetched a load of bags to fill them with dead fish of course," he clarified. "I then packed the car up to speed over the border into England before they rotted."

"Really? Why did you do that?" I continued still not catching his drift.

"To sell them cheap around the local hotels of course. It was a lovely little earner!" he chuckled seeming really pleased with himself.

"Right. Hold on a minute," I probed, becoming increasingly alarmed at the implication. "Are you telling me you sold contaminated Salmon for human consumption in restaurants? But surely that would have poisoned people!"

At this he looked at me intently blatantly stupefied I hadn't naturally gotten the gist of the story.

"Oh, for f**k sake John ... they were English who cares!" he stated with chagrin as though he was conversing with some sort of simpleton.

Another example featured his workplace where he was employed as a foreman within a factory. There for over thirty years he revealed his bosses prized possession was a priceless bottle of Sottish malt whisky that had been secured within a wall-mounted safe in his office for as long as he could remember.

"I often wondered what that whisky would taste like right up until the day I retired," he mused furrowing his eyebrows and smacking his lips.

"Well then did he offer to crack it open on your last day to mark the occasion?" I innocently inquired.

"You must be bloody joking he was a tight-fisted git!" he blurted dismissively in his Welsh brogue. "Anyway, luckily I'd watched him open the safe a few times and had memorised the code," he smiled with a wily grin.

"On my final day once he left I opened it up and drank the entire bloody bottle!"

"You've got to be joking?" I laughed. "What happened next?"

"Well, I drove to the pub then downed ten pints of Guinness for good measure".

Bearing in mind I was still a serving Police Officer at the time I was a bit incredulous.

"Wait a minute – are you telling me you drove after drinking a bottle of whisky and then sunk another ten pints of Guinness?"

"Yeah so what?" he replied truculently before becoming tangential. "Anyway, on the way home afterwards the bloody car ended up on its roof didn't it!"

He paused to take a sip of tea then satisfied settled back into the armchair to watch the TV and fiddle around with the remote control awhile. The outrageous story seemed to have reached a natural conclusion and nothing else was forthcoming. Unsurprisingly I wanted to know more nonetheless out of politeness gave him a minute or two before making further inquiries.

"So, Uncle David, let me get this straight. You drank a bottle of whisky drove to the pub, then had another ten pints of Guinness. I assume afterwards you drove again then crashed?"

"Well yeah that's about the size of it!" he openly declared as my highly watchful Dad listened intently nearby whilst chuckling away to himself.

"So then were you okay or what?"

"After the crash you mean?" he asked as though he'd almost forgotten what we were discussing.

"Yes after the crash!" I clarified rolling my eyes seemingly stating the obvious.

Repositioning himself forward in the chair he purposely placed the remote control down then scratched at his chin thoughtfully for a moment or two.

"Hm, I suppose I was alright. I only had a few scratches really," he declared. "However poor little Timmy came off second best."

"Timmy? What you mean your dog was there too?"

"Yup he went everywhere with me. He'd been sat in the front passenger seat and flew straight through the bloody windscreen!" he clarified without a trace of irony and now looking a tad regretful.

I was completely taken aback and before I could utter another word he had cut back in.

"Yeah such a real shame. Poor old Tim. When I came too, the first thing I saw was him missing and the blue flashing lights. I thought 'Oh shit!' and it was at that point I noticed the Bobby stood over me shaking his head".

"Ah right. So, you were arrested for drink driving then?" I proclaimed expectantly.

"Nah. Luckily enough he was the local copper and we'd shared a few pints of Guinness together in the pub earlier on to celebrate my retirement. As it happens he was almost as pissed as I was!"

Yes indeed. These shenanigans perfectly summed up my Uncle David to a tee.

★

THROUGHOUT THE 60'S AND 70'S we were

poorer than most families. Even so my Mother was an exceptional housekeeper cook and baker. We were spoilt insomuch as she always ensured we never went hungry and the interior of our threadbare home and handknitted / repaired 'cast off' clothes were always immaculately clean. Even so the words 'I love you' hugs kisses open support and encouragement were virtually unheard of. In this respect regardless whatever we were going through in our lives we were more or less just left to get on with it and manage things the best we could by ourselves.

At mealtimes huge portions of simple food - which always included my pet hate potatoes - were placed in front of us and it was a cardinal sin to not finish each and every bite. In fact you literally weren't allowed to leave the table unless you had. This was my Mother's way of showing us affection. Unlike my Father's background terrible hardship and hunger had featured throughout her upbringing on the farm near Southend in Kintyre where she was raised. I'm sure this later underpinned my unhealthy all or nothing attitude to food as an adult because to this day I can easily fast for many weeks before blowing out to gorge until I'm physically sick.

Born in Stafford during 1968 I was a big baby and had appeared sporting a thick head of long black hair. Apparently this caused a bit of a stir in the hospital whereupon the nurses unofficially christened me 'Beatle' after the mop headed fab four from Liverpool who were all the rage at the time.

My early memories feature some surprisingly vibrant recollections. These include playing outside to chew the dried spearmint chewing gum I'd picked from the pavement together alongside consuming the apples I'd find on the ground beneath our neighbours tree.

Having proven allergic to the mandatory Rubella vaccination distributed at the time I consequently caught German measles. Becoming seriously ill it was virtually touch at one point with an extremely concerned doctor deciding I should be hospitalised. Throughout this I still recall hallucinating an endless kaleidoscope of vivid colours and experiencing acute tinnitus for days on end. Thankfully I went on to make a full recovery. Even so afterward when sharing a small room with my sister I would undergo hallucinatory images of people on the ceiling then hear voices when tucked up in bed before falling asleep. I now realise this must have been a post-viral manifestation of childhood psychosis, a lingering symptom of having been so critically ill.

I possessed an extraordinary imagination and had seemingly grasped speech from a very early age (something my second born daughter Bethan also typified). For example when just over a year old my Mother had taken me to the shops in the old secondhand coach-built Silver Cross pram she'd used for me and my siblings. Sitting up proudly sporting the woolen hat that she had knitted, Mum proceeded into the greengrocers for provisions to leave me out on the pavement for a few minutes with my big sister standing watch. The story goes I'd soon caught the attention of a curious young woman walking close by and she'd stopped.

"My goodness what a beautiful big baby boy!" she cooed whilst admiring me.

"Me is Harry," I happily uttered typically enjoying the attention.

"Oh my, he can speak too ... how adorable!" she'd gasped wide eyed and lost in delight.

"Me is Harry Hoos!" I further responded much to her glee.

Now exiting the shop with a bag of groceries my Mum had returned to join us.

"Oh hello there I'm just admiring your beautiful big baby boy!" the lady extended friendlily still leaning close to me smiling and making clucking sounds.

"Thank you, yes he is lovely," my Mother responded pleased

turning her full consideration towards me.

"Yes and named 'Harry Hughes' too ... what a perfect name for him," the woman continued still giving me her full attention.

"Harry? Who's Harry?" asked my Mother stupefied. "Where did you get that from? His name is John!" she laughed good naturedly.

"Oh I'm so sorry? ... but he told me his name was Harry!" came the baffled reply from the now blushing lady.

As they briefly looked at each other legend has it I giggled then held out my arms towards my Mother.

"Me NOT John," I had proclaimed. "Me is HARRY Hoos!"

My Mother had no idea where I'd conjured that identity from as I had never mentioned it before. Obviously looking back I'm also at a complete loss.

Oddly enough my parents revealed from around age two I had begun to express serious misgivings about my appearance. I'm fairly certain this is unusual for an infant. Throughout my youth they endlessly explained there was nothing wrong with me to no avail. I was having - and still have - none of it. In short I suffer from Body Dysmorphic Disorder which is when a person has terrible objections about their appearance. I absolutely despise seeing my reflection or any photographs featuring me. Good at hiding it I have continuously felt intensely ugly and my body grossly disproportionate throughout my entire life. In private these flareups have been so intense they have almost crippled me. It wouldn't be for the first time I've ended up curled in a ball on the floor in desperation.

So what's going on? Well I've since discovered children who come from a troubled background typically toil with low self-esteem and have a poor self-image.

Initially tall and well-built for my age I was always termed 'Big

John' and 'John Huges' (a simple wordplay on my surname) by my school peers. Actually these were meant as terms of endearment. In fact to be termed 'big man' on the West Coast of Scotland is something of a badge of honour. Notwithstanding every time I heard these monikers it would stoke those deep insecurities I held about my appearance therefore I would became emotionally distraught. Embarrassed when standing alongside other kids growing up I would actually try to shrink down to their size. A bit daft given they would mostly catch up with me by our late teens anyway.

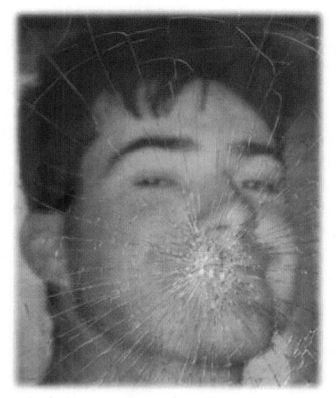

Throughout my life I have been persistently reassured as to my attractiveness. I have admittedly received a lot of attention from the opposite sex. Yet simple logic doesn't come into it. I've long since reconciled myself to the fact that nothing anybody can ever say or do will convince me otherwise. It's for this reason I always bat any compliments away. Not to be confused with arrogance or pride in truth it's the exact opposite. Regardless the context I can't assent to accolades because I deem myself undeserving and always will. When forcing myself to look in the mirror I've always privately judged *'That's not me.'* The only explanation I can offer is because I don't think my exterior aesthetics match the way I feel on the inside. It's almost as though I consider my outward resemblance to be somebody other than me.

Look, I know psychologists would have an absolute field day with this however, I consider every psychologist I've ever met to be more screwed up than I am so good luck with that! Actually during a conversation I recently held with one (who shall remain nameless) I had queried,

"Would you ever consider giving someone a clean bill of mental health?"

"No that's not possible," she instantly responded. "Such a thing doesn't exist!"

So there you have it. According to her we are all brilliantly mentally ill to some degree or other.

On one occasion when aged nineteen I was preparing for a night out. Having drunk a bottle of Eldorado tonic wine to get warmed up I'd spent time fixing my thick black hair in my bedroom mirror. Suddenly transfixed by my image I was momentarily disgusted by the ugliness of my likeness. I instinctively wailed then punched out to thrust my left hand through the glass. It shattered leaving my hand soaked in gore which also produced the scars I'll forever wear on my knuckles.

It sounds crazy however Body Dysmorphic Disorder is a highly intrusive and distressing illness. One of those curious people puzzles it has certainly caused me enough misery to impair most of my social activities and normal day to day events. It is yet another form of anxiety - which incidentally is what happens when we fanaticise suffering. How do I manage it? In short I am absolutely fine unless forced to encounter my own reflection. For this reason I do my level best to avoid stumbling across it at all costs. If and when this is unavoidable I just accept that when I do sight it it's going to be unacceptable, and my heart will sink.

Sheesh, I know this is a bit of a conversation killer nonetheless it's my cross to bear. Even so I do hope that through disclosing this it might help anyone reading this who can relate. After all if it affects me it's bound to affect others too.

In the Rush song 'Limelight' the legendary lyricist and drummer Neil Peart declared: *"One must put up barriers to keep oneself intact."* Indeed, he was bang on the money. His best advice stipulates we should never fully reveal ourselves to others especially regarding our weaknesses. Even so having now put this out there I feel a little bit better - thus sometimes the risk of figuratively exposing oneself for the express purpose of recovery is a risk worth taking.

Chapter Sixteen

'Be the Light You Want to See in Others'

YOUR BODY HAS A self-generated energy field and if you take a good look you'll discover it's even visible with the naked eye. All it requires is the conscious effort to expand your visual sense by fixing on an object then allowing your gaze to defocus. Go ahead then voila! I personally theorise this implies we are spiritual beings having a human experience: Each of us being a transcendent energy temporarily occupying some biological form.

I am willing to gamble you've always been able to discern auras too but at some point learned to ignore this phenomenon. We actually tend to do this quite a lot. Take your hands for example. Open them up to spend a few seconds looking closely at the unique lines on your palms. Go on. In doing so you might be surprised to know these were actually the first things you ever saw as a fetus in your Mother's womb. Naturally you already know this but have consciously been pretending you've forgotten for your entire life.

I've always seen subtle energy fields around people and inanimate objects. It's much like a translucent glow. Sometimes even a faint colour is perceivable. On occasion when people move their hands and such like I'll notice coloured tracers in their wake. For me it's interesting to note some people glow - or radiate more heat than light - than others. Of course conventions relating to societal norms judge discussing any of this stuff to be new age claptrap weird paranormal or plain outside nature's laws. Even so for me it's not supernatural at all it's just supernormal.

Before my firearms instructional career having learnt to read the Tarot proficiently I used to bring cards to work on night shifts. Whenever we had quiet spells throughout the wee hours I'd do readings for my colleagues as a bit of fun. In demand overall it generated an avid interest. At this point you might inquire *"Surely your supervisors should have stopped this?"* Actually they were too busy queuing up for a reading. Then again I once made the mistake of going a step further to mention the 'aura thing'. Afterwards I was advised to reign it all in because I was catching flak behind my back.

From that point I left the cards at home and stopped discussing the subject. It was a shame as there had been a lot of genuine interest from many of my colleagues. Even so I understand it wasn't exactly congruent within the typical work environment you'd come across in a police station therefore that was the end of that.

All of this aside – regardless what anyone says to the contrary – consciousness faith and spiritual beliefs consist key formative components of how subjective reality is realised and then expressed. To dismissively foreclose them is just plain arrogant lacks open mindedness and is overall very pessimistic. The overarching truth is that everything in the universe is almost exclusively comprised of incomprehensibly mysterious Dark Space and Dark Matter (95% all told). By the way everything includes us.

Now don't let them bluff you. Scientists don't have the first idea as to what any of this is. For this reason in objective terms almost nothing is beyond nature's laws.

A peculiar offshoot species of primordial primates we actually

237

know almost nothing about anything. Regardless we still insist an unfortunate trend for erecting arbitrary boundaries around the preconceptions we have established based upon our lack of understanding. We then proceed to inhibit ourselves by living within their means whilst ignoring what we can't comprehend. Doh!

Why is this? Well we are scared because more than anything we actually like certainty. It provides comfort. So as an alternative to the legitimate but unpalatable truth we instead choose to look inwards by distracting and deluding ourselves. After all it is a folly to be wise when ignorance is bliss.

Now remember I'm just a no-hope school dropout who someway went on to develop an interest in psychology quantum mechanics physics and religion. In any case hang tough as I'm going to play around within the boundaries of empirical science just for a moment or two. There is a point to this so stick with it.

We are all electromagnetic beings thus it stands to reason everything we do is enabled by electrical signals. Actually the entirety of the material world is constructed from subatomic atoms (each one consisting 99.9999999% Dark Space/Dark Matter).

The tiny percentage of substantive material that we do know consists an atom is made of neutrons electrons and protons. Neutrons have a neutral electronic charge, Electrons have a negative charge, and Protons have a positive charge. When these charges become unbalanced an atom becomes positively or negatively charged which allows electrons to flow from one atom to another. In short being built from this stuff we subsequently generate an awful lot of electricity.

When we ingest food it is broken down on a molecular elemental level in a process termed cellular respiration. These molecules and elements are then converted into the electronic impulses required by our body (which recall is built from 99.9999999% empty space) to function properly.

Cutting edge Medical Science utilises Electroencephalograms to record the electrical activity of the brain Electrocardiographs to measure the electrical activity of the heart and Electromyography to measure the electrical activity of the muscles. Guess what? More recently the exact same devices have been used to gauge the electrical human energy field or the aura ... and all of a sudden we are back where we started.

Certainly this energy field exists but it can now be accurately traced. The aura has been found to have a staggering potential for presenting a very wide range of frequencies which is gauged as Cycles Per Second (CPS), or vibration. Furthermore different mental activity has a significant impact upon a person's CPS or vibrational frequency. For example to concentrate on materialistic kinesthetic bodily function typically results an average vibrational range in the lower region of 250 CPS. Yet trance meditative and spiritual states including prayer can invoke higher vibrations ranging up to 900 CPS. Some of the most extreme readings of this type have astounded researchers by reaching 200,000 CPS! Interestingly the strongest recorded parts of the energy field center almost exclusively upon parts of the body associated with what the ancients called the chakras.

This all begs the interesting question: How did ancient spiritual traditions advocate chakras literally thousands of years before they could be scientifically proven? Anyway here's the crux. Have you ever wondered why you just seem to click with certain people – be energised or inspired by them? There's a strong possibility it's because they are vibrating on the same (positive +) frequency as you. Alternatively perhaps you've wondered why others seem to drain you turn you off or always drag you down? An argument can be made because they're vibrating on a (negative -) rate below you. Those skilled in establishing a strong rapport with others could be embodying an innate ability to alter their vibrations to match those they are interacting with on a moment-to-moment basis. You see in all of our communications connections and exchanges the law of personal attraction and magnetism consists so much more than the simplistic chemical reactions (there was chemistry between those two) which occur by virtue of our reactionary central nervous systems. Instead it's largely electronics and vibrations.

What is or is not possible? Scientific empirical evidence is based upon observable reality - or seeing is believing - yet despite sight dominating our five perceptual senses to the region of sixty percent it is perhaps the most fallible sensation of all: The eyes look but the brain see's ... and for example magicians fool it all the time.

The fact is universal existence is governed by intangible circular or cyclical movement. Atoms planets galaxies tides seasons – in fact everything that consists of our bodies – all rotate in cycles on an axis. Constant revolutions underpin the very nature of conception and birth itself. This is the flux of the cosmos. A common perceptual distortion is that we perceive ourselves as stationary. However, not only is the planet spinning at approximately 1000mph, but our entire galaxy is rapidly spinning in constant rotations through space like a corkscrew. It should come as no surprise then that our underlying subconscious processes mirror this, as I shall illustrate.

I once had a client who happened to be a manager for a large company. A mature lady she had been looking after her elderly

Mother for a long time. Providing all manner of intimate personal care right up until the end of her life was a formidable albeit commendable endeavour. It had taken a considerable toll upon her own wellbeing which I know only too well as this is a very common denominator for familial caregivers.

Mum had eventually passed away which left her struggling with grief. Worse still this was compounded by a range of difficulties at work. To be precise these mostly centered upon a particular regional administrator who simply had it in for her.

Anyhow we shared a few sessions which she found particularly constructive. Initially focusing on talking therapy we progressed to explore NLP techniques and finally carried out some hypnotherapy.

"Think about the emotions that are bothering you," I asked during one particular session. "As you do so where do you feel the sensations in your body?"

"Erm, well they start in my stomach and go up to my chest area and back again I suppose," she replied screwing her face with effort as she consciously thought it through for the first time.

"Alright. Now think carefully about this ... which way do the feelings spin and what colour are they?"

She thought about this for quite some time.

"Oh ... clockwise I think, and I guess they are black. Wow, I never noticed that feelings spin before now, but they really do!"

"That's right!" I agreed, genuinely pleased she was discovering this phenomenon. "Next I want you to stop them turning before making them rotate counterclockwise instead. I also want you to change their colour to pink from now on." (*Note: This wasn't arbitrary - I had already ascertained pink was her favourite colour*).

Afterwards she revealed this new technique was working particularly well by significantly quelling her distress. I recommend you also give it a go yourself sometime as it's quick and easy to do.

On another session I placed her into a deep trance whereupon I encouraged her to talk about her Mum. After a while I was astonished to discern my small consultation room was overcome with the strong unmistakable smell of perfume. Taken aback meanwhile my client who was still in a deep trance had begun to spontaneously converse with me.

"Mum's here with us right now. She is perfect and in a state of grace," she dreamily whispered eyes still closed tight but rapidly fluttering. "She's talking to me. Oh, it's so nice to be reunited and together again."

"That's good what does she say?" I queried by now totally fascinated by the phenomenon unfolding in front of me.

"She says I need to become a guiding light in the darkness for others and that my true purpose is to help those in need. She tells me I should take early retirement ..." she softly tailed off.

I should clarify at this point it's fairly typical for clients to access their inner resources during hypnosis with their subconscious outwardly proposing practical solutions to the alter ego of their conscious self in relation to whatever difficulties they might be going through. Even so this was unprecedented. What had begun as therapy had inadvertently merged into being an otherworldly experience.

The smell had lingered for a while after she retained a state of full waking consciousness.

"My God," she softly exclaimed placing her hands to her face in shock. "... that's my mother's favourite perfume!"

"I can smell it too," I had quietly admitted by now equally dumbfounded.

If you are anticipating my logical explanation regarding this phenomenon then I'm sorry as I'm at a complete loss. I could opine it might be some shared hallucination but to do so would be insincere. Simply put just like the scent it lingers on as a deeply meaningful shared phenomenon. We stayed in contact after her treatment, and she later revealed she had taken early retirement to assist at a hospice for those at the end of life with incurable cancer.

Mahatma Gandhi once declared: *"Spiritual relationships are far more precious than physical relationships."* It's true. Even so deep meaningful spiritual experiences instantly lose their significance once spoken aloud – just not so much when they appear in print. It is for this reason I included this encounter by sharing it with you.

★

MY BOSS WANTED TO SEE ME, and I'd gotten straight away this wasn't going to be good news. Stationed at the Marine Unit at the time I tread over to his office. Arriving outside as I knocked the door I consecutively thought,

'For Christ's sake, what now?'

"Aye John ... come in and grab a pew," he cried out from the other side.

"Boss, everything alright?" I asked walking in and glancing briefly at him before taking a seat in front of the large Mahogany desk now separating us.

"Not too bad, and you?"

"So far so good," I replied, "then again I get the feeling that could be about to change."

"Don't be so pessimistic," he scolded. "It just so happens I've got a great opportunity for you," he unconvincingly announced smiling. I now knew my instincts were right and this was going to be bad news after all.

"It seems there's a space begging on a forthcoming Firearms Tactical Advisor course delivered by South Yorkshire Police. I won't beat around the bush I want you on it!"

Shit. I'd heard all about this. The UK National lead for conflict management himself was delivering it, and word on the grapevine was it was rock hard with a high attrition rate. Resultantly everyone was avoiding it like the plague.

"What about the Firearms Training wing?" I came back thinking desperately on my feet in trying to offer a viable alternative. "Surely it's their place?"

"Pfft, that bunch of bluffers and posers?" he spat looking away and curling his top lip in condemnation. "Surprise surprise, they're all running scared and have graciously declined," he added frostily.

"Yeah well perhaps for good reason," I interjected. "So why me?"

"You're an Operational Firearms Commander with years of ARV experience. You're made for it," he declared. "Plus, it would be a feather in the Unit's cap having a Tac-Ad on board if you catch my drift," he said whilst winking at me.

Proceeding to dunk a biscuit into his tea several times he then took a bite. Remaining quiet he kept his eyes on me throughout in allowing his mild exploitation to similarly soak in and soften me up. Finally placing the mug down to recline in his high-backed leather chair he squinted cold blue eyes at me.

"A word to the wise there's big things coming down the line for armed maritime operations," he mysteriously concluded before winking once again.

My mind was racing faster than ever as I attempted to think of a way out of this bind.

"Yeah, but still, I could do without the complication right now."

At this he exhaled, then wordlessly shifted forward to pick up the phone. I sat there mystified as someone at the other end eventually answered.

"Yeah I've got him here," my boss uttered into the receiver. "Uh huh, yeah well just so you know he's not keen, but I'll stick him on."

Silently handing the receiver over I confusedly took it.

"Hello?"

"Hi John, long time no see!" It was the unmistakable voice of my previous Chief Inspector from my ARV days. He had since returned to the post of Chief Firearms Instructor in Essex. "What's this I hear you aren't up for the Tac-Ad challenge? That's not like you."

"Boss, the timings not great if I'm being honest," I bumbled. "... is there nobody else?"

"Nobody like you," he came back immediately. "You're one of my best officers and the division needs a good Tac-Ad ..."

"... yes but," I stammered, clumsily interrupting him.

"... but nothing." He had returned the favour by effortlessly slicing back in as sharp as a razor. "I'll cut to the chase you owe me remember?"

And there it was. The dreaded words 'you owe me'. Thus, the die had been cast and there was no way out. Later on, I was still in a spin as the arrangements were made for my two-week sojourn to bloody Rotherham.

As it happens the course lived up to its reputation. Actually, it was probably the toughest two-weeks of my career. Loaded with twelve Firearms Instructors from all over the UK I felt out of my league, and we were tested to the limit around the clock with a variety of formative tests hypothetical role playing 'paper feeds' and similar challenging methods. The fact I had gotten off on the wrong foot whilst typically daydreaming in class hadn't helped.

"Gentlemen this here is what they call a 'Smartboard'," went the course lead in his thick Yorkshire accent pointing with great pride toward the pristine looking device newly mounted on the wall.

"It cost us a bloody small fortune so under no circumstances whatsoever are you to use Blue Tack sticky tape or marker pens on it during your presentations. Got it?"

I was preoccupied whilst preparing my presentation the following day as I apprehensively stood in front of my peers and proceeded to stick some posters I was using as visual stimulus onto the same board with – guess what - Blue Tack. In doing so I dopily stood with my back to the group when all of a sudden a collective gasp went up which gave me quite a jolt. I froze for a split second before turning confusedly to face them.

"What's wrong?"

The instructional staff were gawping at me open mouthed. One of them managed to point at the Smartboard with a shaking finger before blurting,

"FOR F**K SAKE! NO BLUE TACK! Are you taking the piss out of us or something?"

Uphill from there I was regularly hammered at each and every opportunity. Thankfully I really clicked with a guy who I'll name David from the Serious Organised Crime Agency (SOCA). Alongside being a really lovely bloke, he also just so happened to be very high functioning which was evidenced by him powering through each challenge with aplomb. I was really impressed therefore attempted to latch onto copying his style.

Meanwhile two other participants from Leicester Police had singled me out - and what I mean by that is from that point on we had what could be coined a taut relationship. In fact, they took each and every opportunity to try and take the piss out of me. Don't get me wrong, I was up for the banter but in short knew they were bullies. Notwithstanding in my mind's eye I emulated a reed blowing with the wind throughout it all as I rode out their perpetual nonsense. Actually, this only served to embolden their incremental attempts in winding me up.

Both were burly intimidatingly tall rugby players with cauliflower ears. One wore a thick moustache and interestingly carried a picture in his wallet of himself in plain clothes standing beside the late Queen Elizabeth II as a diplomatic protection officer. Proudly producing it at every opening, he even used it in the hotel bar in a vain bid to impress the pretty young barmaid. Observing this I remained perplexed. In truth my abstract thought processes had by now kicked in and I genuinely couldn't comprehend what this posturing was all about.

"So then if you don't mind me asking, why exactly do you carry that picture around in your wallet then?" I authentically asked him over dinner one night. Good grief what a mistake this proved to be. All at once I became acutely aware that the rest of the group had stopped eating and were now quietly watching us intently like a column of classical statues. You could hear a pin drop as he glared wrathfully at me for a few seconds and looked as though he was just about ready to hit the roof.

"Because she's the most IMPORTANT F*****G WOMAN in the country of course. Are you F****G RETARDED or something?" he angrily growled with fury in his untamed eyes.

Okay I confess my query was a tad off-the-wall, but now realised too late what the rest already knew: He had taken my legitimate although naïve query as some sort of challenge to his legitimacy. I  thought about how best to react to this for a moment then instinctively produced my own wallet. Proceeding to open it I showed him a picture of Mandy and my girls as I calmly replied,

"Nope I'm not retarded, but I think you're mistaken because these are the most important women in the country."

At this the group erupted into hysterical laughter. Meanwhile he didn't see the funny side at all, instead furiously standing up to knock his chair over in the process of storming from the room.

In any case this was just a distraction. I was so stressed by the damn course and the random out of hours formative phone calls for tactical advice that I had barely slept a wink throughout. I openly admit I was struggling big time.

On the penultimate day I was paired up in a small room with a

Superintendent and a Chief Inspector for my final formative paper feed. They would act as Strategic and Tactical Commanders and I as their Tac-Ad. The scenario centred upon a bunch of armed terrorists driving around Sheffield City centre which lasted the best part of an hour. Floundering, the pressure had finally gotten to me. Resultantly the hypothetical Armed Police response had veered completely off-piste and gone horribly wrong. Afterwards I was given a tag-team earbashing which lasted for almost forty-five minutes. This culminated when the Superintendent looked me square in the eye and vehemently banged his fist on the table to conclude,

"Lad you'll NEVER be a Firearms Tactical Adviser as long as my arse points downwards. Take my advice and don't even bother turning up for summative assessment tomorrow."

Torn apart I had been mauled. I was devastated however, after a long night of soul searching I did turn up. Paired with the national lead himself for my summative assessment as I strode towards the designated room with him I ruminated,

'Typical. Just my luck to get him. In any case it is what it is. Do what David would do and just go for it!'

Something strange then happened. It all abruptly clicked into place just in the nick of time as the penny finally dropped. I somehow proceeded to smash the examination in considerable style. Afterwards when receiving informal feedback from my assessor he was extremely gracious.

"Where the hell did that performance come from? I'll be honest, I never saw it coming from you – but that was an outstanding implementation of what I'd expect from any firearms Tac-Ad. You really shone there, very well done indeed!"

"I'm not going to lie to you," I replied. "That's the toughest process I've ever been through."

He just smiled at me.

"Good I'm glad to hear it. It has to be," he proclaimed.

On cloud nine I modestly clutched my certificate as I made my way out and along the way bumped into a disconsolate looking David moping about in the corridor.

"Hey what's wrong?" I asked nonplussed.

"John I can't believe it," he uttered. "I've gone and bloody failed!" he continued shaking his head and looking at the carpet.

I was astounded as he had been 'the man'. Shortly after it next turned out only five of us had passed and I honestly couldn't believe I had been one of them. *(Note: Incidentally, I was delighted when learning a few weeks later that David had been recoursed and passed on his second attempt.)*

Anyhow, ironically as I drove from the carpark in my hire car to begin the long trek home the last classmates I encountered were the two Leicester guys. Looking crestfallen as they exited the building they spotted me and glowered my way. I already knew neither had made the grade so for a moment seriously floated the notion of cheerfully waving my certificate enthusiastically towards them as I slowly traversed past. Then again I discarded the idea in an instant as a cheap and nasty stunt. Instead, I simply raised my hand and nodded a genuine acknowledgement of 'goodbye and good luck' their way which in fairness they both returned.

What can I say. Sometimes you've just got to let your light shine bright by being the change you want to see in others.

Chapter Seventeen

'The Ladder'

MY WELSH GRANDFATHER David

Glyn - or Taid - was as tough as teak. I once heard a story about him centering upon a leak in his railway cottage roof. He couldn't place a ladder so being short-tempered instead became frustrated whilst proceeding to utilise a wheelbarrow to balance precariously in making his way up to do the repair. Once complete he shimmied back down and placed an extended foot onto the wheelbarrow only for it to abruptly skid away.

As he slipped downwards he caught his head on the slate roof and it sliced his ear near off. Naturally my Grandmother got in a right old state and screamed at my Uncle Dai who was a young child at the time to run for the doctor, who himself rushed to the scene.

"It's almost completely severed," he said inspecting it whilst wincing. "You need to get to a hospital then have it stitched back on straight away with some anesthetic!"

Seeing as there was no NHS at the time this would prove expensive, so the story goes Taid proceeded to drag the doctor into the kitchen and placed his head sideways onto the pine tabletop.

"No hospital and no anesthetic ... get it done here and now," he'd demanded.

The doc proceeded to stitch his ear back on and throughout

apparently flinched more than my Grandfather.

Incidentally my Nain - Welsh for Gran - was said to be the prettiest girl in Dovey Valley. Legend goes when my Grandfather first spied her he had to literally fight off his four brothers in a fist fight to win her hand. Nain and my Mother never saw eye to eye, but I have extremely good memories of her. I remember her as a very good-humoured generous woman who always spoiled me rotten.

Anyway like my Father Taid had a notoriously high threshold for physical pain. Even so he committed suicide when I was just a small boy, so I don't remember too much about him.

He'd apparently suffered from depression for a long time and had ironically begged the exact same doctor for help to no avail. Discussing mental health was completely taboo during this period in time consequentially people simply avoided doing it and that was that.

Recalling the physical potency my Grandfather had embodied

throughout the notorious ear incident the GP apparently repeatedly scoffed at him and insisted he get a grip of himself to snap out of it. Sadly my Grandad eventually decided he couldn't suffer any more therefore hung himself in his garden shed when I was three years  old. In fact one of my earliest memories is of my Father being informed of the tragedy in our living room: It was the only time I ever witnessed him cry and also one of the few times I ever witnessed my Mother willingly consent to hug him by offering some comfort.

Causality dictates every action must have an equal and opposite reaction therefore the aftereffects of recriminations sadness and shame would be felt for generations to come.

Depression is not only one of the most common and serious illnesses of all - but perhaps the most unresolved. Despite what some experts say they don't really understand its true origins or how to physically diagnose or treat it effectively. Importantly they do now know it runs in families which would seem to imply a genetic influence might be at play. Then again, they can't be sure.

I think this is only part of the story. A person not only inherits genes but also a familial setting. Underlying dysfunction often features throughout a great many families. Commonplace this also tends to result in general behavioural and/or mental disorders. Ongoing sociological studies reveal depression is much more likely to occur in domestic settings where abuse and conflict persist. Exemplars of this regularly occur between family members by way of emotional discord neglect and outright cruelty. This often leaves sufferers much more reactive to environmental stressors and more likely to develop depression. They are sadly also less likely to respond to existing medications or treatments.

I suspect this goes some way towards explaining why some people remain resilient in the face of severe stressors whilst others develop major depressive illnesses. This theory makes perfect sense to me given the highly charged emotional atmosphere which featured throughout my own upbringing. On reflection it's undeniable I had become conditioned to be exceedingly susceptible to the environmental stressors of the aforementioned.

I now reason this is why I zoned out so much: It was a form of avoidance. Possessing an exceptionally sensitive nature I simply had to in eschewing the overarching social political and economic anxieties which were constantly being passed on through the environment by my parents siblings and peers.

Deep breath. I've admittedly suffered intense periods of depression and even as a young child had thoughts of self-harm. At my lowest ebb in the depths of my despair I openly admit I'd become somewhat screwed up. Because of what my Taid did I someway deduced suicide must hereditary before arriving at a deeply held belief amounting to certainty that it had to be inescapable at some point or other.

I've already disclosed my inquisitive suicidal impulse as an operational ARV officer. Incidentally, don't try and tell me the same thought hasn't briefly entered almost every other armed cop's mind. After all the role itself compels each officer must afford a great deal of thought regarding the potential for utilising lethal force. Considering prescribed anti-depressant medication meant instant termination for any AFO's firearms career I know a great many secretly took them. Sure it's different nowadays because each officer assents to allowing the job full access to their private medical records however, in the early years there was no such requirement hence this data remained confidential.

Despite my disclosure even in my darkest moments I never decided upon self-destruction. Even so those hardships did test the limits of my endurance a few times. I guess you could say I had become capable of almost anything. During the tribulations of my private life no description here can adequately describe the emotional desperation or internal chaos in those instances. The suffering of life overrode the joy to the extent that joy no longer existed.

During this period I would also become haunted by PTSD and experienced flashbacks relating to a particularly gruesome fatal incident I dealt with as a first responder which received national media coverage. Throughout I recall fighting to save a man's life as a teenage girl lay dead nearby with limbs twisted into a grotesque distortion and neck snapped as her head swelled twice its normal size. Desperately awaiting assistance I worked on the man as his eyes remained wide open and his mouth somehow formed into a surreal smile. My desperate and exhausting attempts to save him via rescue breaths and chest compressions were continually met by that accursed grin as he stared at me with eyes glazed over like fisheye lenses. Afterwards that would smile torment my dreams and every time the tragedy was mentioned in the newspapers or news I was transformed to revivify it alongside the girl bent into contortion like some wayward doll. Even now can't help but wonder if he is still mocking me through grinning six feet under the ground.

Let's just say the warmth of my tender heart has been marred by the frostbite of cold reality and in those instances I have become momentarily broken. Many of those who I have loved so much are now dead which is exacerbated by the fact those I measure unworthy of living just carry right on doing it ... sometimes including me.

When mental health crashes down it's difficult to take an objective view of what actually remains and make the best of it. I'm not too proud to admit therapy helped me no end in sorting out my issues. Actively helping others afterwards helped me enormously too. Outwardly expressing my suicidal hereditary concept flipped it right on its head. So much so that it proved incredibly liberating for me. Anything extra suddenly became more which enabled me to shed a lot of the ascetic inhibitions that had dogged my younger self. In some way I was rejuvenated to be born again.

In reality most people spend their time living in a reactionary state of emotional unease ranging from mild worries to extreme suffering. Most sit at the lower end of the scale experiencing low self-esteem or insecurities based upon body image and such like. Consequentially most of us never quite feel good enough inside (that's right, it's not just you!) Built upon the framework of anxiety and stress depression is a response to an ascending inability to cope with the negativity which has led to persistent feelings of sadness and hopelessness. In extreme cases it leads to nervous breakdown and suicide. I've had to deal with both several times in my private and professional life so feel qualified to quantify that suicide is a permanent solution to a temporary problem.

How else do I surmount the dark moments that occasionally dog me? I openly talk about them and remain active. I also hold onto hope in the better times I know will come. Given change is a universal constant they always do thus it stands to reason all suffering must pass.

Furthermore unlike my Grandfather I don't use a wobbly old wheelbarrow to climb my way out of the blues. Instead I use a much more effective imaginary ladder to surmount the black clouds.

Having gone on to earn a reputation as a therapist in my own right it's important to understand you can't fix people. They already have all the resources they need to fix themselves you just guide them. Also, when dealing with depressed clients the first thing you need to ascertain is whether they are really depressed. You see the term often insinuates their life is just plain terrible and 'depression' is being utilised as a convenient way to carry the can for their true unmet needs. In either case I'll undeniably do almost anything within my means to grab their attention.

For example, I once had a young client from a very troubled background who had been self-harming. She had been diagnosed with Borderline Personality Disorder (BPD) and was Bi-Polar. On one occasion she turned up in my consultation room proudly displaying new cuts on her arm.

"I did it with a kitchen knife because my life has no meaning," she wailed. "I want happiness but what's the point? I've had enough so I'm going to kill myself!" she announced with certainty.

She had ramped the stakes up - but I took this as a challenge.

"Alright then why wait any longer?" I responded egging her on.

"In fact, let's do it right here and now. Come on sit down and I'll help you!"

This took her by surprise as her psychiatrist hadn't spoken like this. Changing my tone, I gestured her to sit then as she did, I tactfully leaned in real close.

"In any case I really don't think you want to kill yourself, do you?" I quietly whispered.

She replied she really did.

"Well then prove it," I challenged. "Go on, follow these instructions: Sit back and pinch your nose. Now keep your mouth closed. Stop breathing and in no time at all you'll be dead. It's that simple."

Stroppy she truculently attempted it and within less than a minute had given up by desperately gasping for air. No surprise really after all she had worked herself into a frenzy beforehand and I noticed she had been breathing hard.

I have often found silence to be a potent tool in highly charged situations. In fact, a meaningful silence is usually better than lots of meaningless words. Hence, we just sat quietly for a while before she eventually met my gaze.

"It seems I don't want to kill myself after all," she'd quietly confessed.

What a relief. Of course, I'd suspected this all along but couldn't be sure. Then again one should never underestimate the basic human instinct to survive. Sometimes we just need a subtle reminder of it.

With her consent I then placed her into a hypnotic trance and told her the story that will shortly follow. I'm pleased to say that in time she maintained a decent job met a nice guy and settled down.

I've no doubt whatsoever she still wrestles her dark nemesis from time to time. Even so I bet she will never forget my parting shot as we concluded our final session.

"Hey, you," I called out as she walked off. She abruptly stopped to quizzically look back over her shoulder at me as I concluded,

"Remember you don't become stronger by feeling good all the time. You become stronger by managing to feel bad better".

She just laughed then raised a hand to wave as she sauntered off seemingly without a care in the world.

It's true when she had come to see me, she had suffered from a powerful sense of negative emotions but underpinning this was the fact she had experienced a truly awful childhood. When treatment removes something, it ought to be replaced with something else. Therefore, I had influenced what she really needed - structure purpose direction and goals.

★

(Hypnosis story for depression)

IN ANCIENT TIBET somewhere between the fourth and sixth centuries BCE there lived a wise monk. He led a life of virtual solitude with several worshippers in a mountain retreat far beyond the great forest leading to an immense lake straddling the borders of the Himalayas. Despite this remote location his foresight was often sought out by seekers of wisdom and those wishing to follow a true path to enlightenment.

One such person had made the arduous trek and now exclusively found himself in the counsel of the wise man. He was middle-aged and despite being successful in business was experiencing an existential crisis. Having lost touch with meaning in his life he felt hollow and depressed and was worried he'd lost control.

Occupying a comfortable lotus position succeeding many hours of deep meditation the shaven headed guru eventually opened his benevolent eyes to gaze upon his counsel with tangible empathy and compassion. Returning to full consciousness he studied the querent inquisitively before his sweet voice resonated around the candle lit chamber in a rarified refrain.

"My friend, what do you seek?"

"Guru I'm so depressed," declared the man clasping his hands and dropping to his knees in desperation. "Everything seems so bleak," he wailed. "Please tell me what is the point of my life? I want happiness!'

Nodding his head the wise man cleared his throat:

"On a clear day you might notice and enjoy the beautiful vast expanse of crystal-clear blue sky and feel good however, there are days when we look up and all we see are clouds. True, you might simply observe and enjoy them as you interpret their transformational shapes and as such you might still feel good. However, there are other days when the sky is full of oppressive dark clouds and the beautiful expanse of crystal-clear blue sky is nowhere to be seen. On such days you will feel bad. Sadly, those are the days that never seem to end.

"Yet what would happen if you imagined you had a Ladder of such length it reached up through and beyond those clouds. Can you imagine standing at the foot of it looking up into the heavens ... seeing it puncture then disappear into them? I'll venture you would want to explore what lay beyond.

"Well if safe in the knowledge it was completely benign what would happen if you proceeded to climb that ladder? If you went up through those clouds what do you suppose you would find? Of course you would discover the beautiful vast expanse of a crystal-clear blue sky is still there and then you would feel good again!

"Regardless how things seem isn't it nice to know the crystal-clear blue sky never really goes anywhere? It's always there reigning imperious above the oppressive kingdom of the clouds. So, when you feel down you can choose to use your imagination and climb the Ladder to be there too.

"Just as a cloud is no more than an experience the sky is having; a wave represents an experience the ocean is having. As such you are an experience the universe is having. Inter-connected with the universe and everything else in it you are not a stranger misplaced in the infinite cosmos. You are it and it is you.

"Therefore, you must resist the inclination to feel like a stranger in the world. Those who do believe they were brought into this life against their will and fall into playing the worthless role of 'the wounded'. They then inevitably feel hostile.

"But it's now time for you to awaken. My friend life is made of time and yours is running out. You are not a *victim* of life; you are a *beneficiary*! You have freewill and so it's your responsibility to create a life full of the things you are passionate about instead of wasting it in a miserable way.

"A moment ago you posed the question, *'What is the point of my life?'* Well how on earth would I know? It's your life you tell me! What I can advise is you should spend as much time as possible doing the things you like and spend as much time as possible being with those you like. Failure to do so - irrespective supposed material success - will only ever cause you to feel hollowed out inside.

"From now on whenever you feel down I want you to stand at the foot of that Ladder then imagine climbing high enough to discover the magnificent crystal-clear expanse of blue sky imperious beyond the oppressive kingdom of the clouds.

"At first never look up to consider all ten-thousand steps required to scale it for you then attempt to overcome all ten thousand at once. Rather, take the first rung and then the next. One small step at a time summits any large obstacle and that is what life often seems."

Having imparted this the guru took a pause by closing his eyes in deep contemplation for a minute or two before nodding to himself and opening them again.

"Hm, your earlier statement went, '*I Want Happiness*'" he continued now chuckling. "Well by way of return I must outline that the word 'I' represents ego and the word 'Want' represents greed. Now, **I want** you to go ahead and remove ego and greed from your original statement before telling me what you are left with ..."

Pausing to look questionably upon the businessman with incalculable patience he allowed enough silence to compel a response.

After a period of rumination the businessman had palpably arrived at a realisation. Suddenly wide eyed he smiled then cleared his voice.

"**Happiness!**" he cheerily emphasised.

Audience concluded the guru wished him a safe passage before slipping back into meditative trance. The businessman enjoyed a simple meal and rested awhile before making the preparations to begin retracing his steps on the arduous journey home.

Given it was winter he encountered grueling weather along the way. Nevertheless he'd discovered a new sense of tranquility because he now distinguished the concealed expanse of a crystal-clear blue sky reigning imperious above the oppressive kingdom of clouds. Of course in his mind's eye he similarly knew he could always climb his internal ladder to be there too.

Secure in this awareness he thought of all the good things that now awaited him he looked skyward to cheerfully declare,

"Mister Sun, even though I cannot see you I still know that you are there!"

He then laughed because he now understood he could choose to feel good any time he wanted to.

Chapter Eighteen

'Holding Up'

WE SHOULD STRIVE TO know ourselves, to categorically understand why we are the way we are. Even so, I've found few people are readily inclined to do so in any meaningful way. Aldous Huxley rightly said: *"If we remain ignorant of ourselves it is because self-knowledge is painful, and we prefer the pleasure of illusion"*.

Actually, I was warned not to write this book and advised it was a foolish self-indulgent and potentially hazardous project. I initially struggled against this impression and was close to just binning it before establishing that contrary to foolishness it actually required courage to proceed. Hence stigma removed I knew I had to go with my gut instinct and proceed regardless of what others said.

To be honest what I unwittingly found took a hell of a lot more guts to confront than I had anticipated. Let's just say it seems they were right all along.

Carl Jung once asserted: *"In filth it shall be found"*. What did he mean? It implies the truth underpinning the semblance of self to be a terrible Monster loitering within the dark recesses of our psyche: He cautioned one should only reveal it if they are willing and able to confront it. Damn, I was fully committed when I realised he was spot-on as having picked at my scabs and scars I then ran headlong into my archenemy and there could be no turning back.

The clinical Psychologist Jordan B. Peterson warns: *"The gateway of self-analysis leads to the darkest place: a place that you fear, and which repulses you."*

Well, it was all of that. The profundity of what I discovered could only be truly realised once written out which was my way of making sense of what had surfaced. Then there it was - the ornery foundations of my life: My decisions motivations values beliefs thoughts fears and impossible aspirations manifest as an incredibly revelatory yet overwhelming personal awakening.

I would proceed to carry out a deep psychological analysis of this then go further by doing likewise regarding my parents own upbringings. I similarly unearthed repeating cycles of the same shared history playing out time and again.

It's astonishing how many people experience the same lonely fragmented and emotionally stifled childhood as I had. By now you'll know I read a lot as a youngster. I also listened to music and lyrics then spent an inordinate amount of time outside exploring nature. It was through these pursuits that I met my role models.

I was nearly ten years old when I concluded there was something wrong with my parents and that it would be up to me to bring myself up. This was a healthier choice than placing too much trust in them. As a consequence, I would inadvertently assume the role of 'responsible one' which irrationally led to them becoming increasingly more and more reliant upon me. As I grew up somehow the child was assuming responsibility for parenting the parents as time and again I had to ride to their rescue and hold them up.

Throughout I slowly came to a stark recognition of how unstable my Mother could be as I became closely acquainted with her controlling tendencies. On the occasions he was present she would attempt to goad my Dad into reacting. Despite mostly abstaining when he did take the bait they would really go at it as the arguments went on through the night and lasted for days. This sometimes culminated with her telling him she was taking me and leaving. I recall being pulled from my bed to walk the street hand in hand with her distraught in my pyjamas and barefoot whilst carrying basic belongings. Dad would then be forced to intercede and chase after us 'saving' me and ultimately providing her with what she truly craved ... attention and leverage. Heaven knows what the neighbours thought of us watching from behind their curtains.

From that point on I would listen whenever they fought through the night as I cowered under my bedclothes shaking like a leaf. I would wonder if Mum and I would be leaving again that night. This would eventually be accompanied by infrequent outbursts of domestic violence therefore you can imagine the anxiety of listening to this unfold as objects subsequently shattered in rage much like ill-fated plates at a Greek wedding.

I often used to wonder why Mum coerced us from the earliest age to acquiesce and just accept whatever others did to us. After all it left us as low hanging fruit in a rough housing estate. It now revealed her conditioning left us weak for the prime purpose of being even more reliant upon her. In short every crisis became a drama because she simply needed to feel needed.

Generational abuse plays out this way. She was renewing the exact exploitation her, and her siblings had suffered at a similar age by her own poverty stricken and increasingly desperate Mother. In the exact same way as my childhood Mum had I would come to view my Father as a heroic steadying influence. Then again he was mostly absentee because he wanted to avoid the difficulties of his marital and parental responsibilities. Therefore we were forsaken to be trapped in a vicious cycle.

Until my late teens I sometimes awoke to sight a shrouded figure standing at the foot of my bed in the night before the image faded away. I absurdly reasoned I was being haunted. Actually it wasn't until my own therapeutic training many years later I discovered this is a relatively common experience for those suffering from childhood abuse or trauma. To reiterate there are no haunted houses only haunted people.

Through writing this chapter it has been illuminating to carefully consider what was actually going on throughout this interplay of Jungian archetypes. Here is my simple analysis:

As the 'caregiver' my Mother could also become the 'tyrant'. We were the 'innocents' and my Father the errant 'hero' who would come to our rescue. Amongst my siblings I became the 'rebel' who would eventually have to cast his objections aside in rescuing the 'tyrant' and more importantly the fallen 'hero' during their difficulties in later life. Can you see the poignancy in all of this?

Now an adult my intercession on their part meant I had to put my own domestic and professional priorities on hold as I continually solved their difficulties. This wasn't so much requested as absolutely expected. You can then imagine the far-reaching repercussions this caused amongst my own now disgruntled dependents as they would frequently ask,

"But what about us?"

My troubled childhood still causes me guilt embarrassment and shame. It fueled my unhealthy all or nothing relationship with alcohol and food and appalling low self-esteem and depression. My entire adolescence was spent trying to firefight and fix my Mothers woes including her insecurities and health issues her never-ending dissatisfaction with her marriage; the poverty and additional worries that my growing siblings caused her. I had emotionally supported her throughout it all yet had received hardly anything in return. It's incredible how I didn't even notice this playing out because it became normal. I believed I was the unhinged one and what was wrong in the family. It wasn't until I started this process of reflection that I realised I have always felt unloved thus unworthy of receiving the same.

Laid bare here was the reason for my tendency of forsaking those that cared about me and detaching myself from those attracted to me. All along I thought there was something wrong with them because they favoured something as contemptable as me. It's almost perverse that I found it preferable to consider myself as deficient as opposed to admitting my parents flaws as being unstable incapable and unfair. I had become self-sacrificial in protecting the lie that was everyone else's superficial perception of them.

And then ... it is all too easy to play the role of victim and just blame others for all of our ills. Victimhood is far more dangerous than having been a victim and I am not a child anymore. Now a husband and Father, despite often finding these roles incredibly difficult to perform I have always taken them exceedingly seriously. When all's said and done nobody really knows how to execute the role of 'ideal' partner or parent. Some are certainly better at it than others, yet the source of reference is always to just copy what one has experienced oneself.

Armed with this knowledge I realised I had done likewise only with a twist. Mercifully mine was no sinful act of 'rinse and repeat'.

Instead, I had somehow redeemed myself with the help of my life partner through using my original familial template as a 'how not to' guide. It was in this way I managed to utilise the quirks of my abstract logic and unhappy childhood in breaking the generational chain.

It's also vital to acknowledge that no one is perfect. My parents were not bad people in the least. On the contrary in many ways just like their own they were thoroughly decent people. It's just that good people do bad things all the time. Through unwittingly fostering an unhealthy household they were actually doing the very best they could at the time in very tough circumstances.

I accept and forgive their deficiencies just as I hope my own children will forgive mine. They were just people whose flaws were compounded by virtue of the fact they themselves had been damaged. True my Mother far worse than my Father but only because nature and nurture conspired against her. Extraordinarily sensitive she was psychologically emotionally psychically and then physically crushed by her own formative experiences.

She would later undergo a hysterectomy in her early thirties however, through negligence the procedure went badly wrong. Suffering a catastrophic internal bleed, she died for several minutes before they somehow managed to resuscitate her against all odds. This then pitted her headfirst into all manner of menopausal and hormonal difficulties which also left her with permanent health problems. This would intensify her ongoing struggles and fragile state of mental health.

When all is said and done Mars and Venus are often not compatible on any practical level at all. Notwithstanding the absurdity of our innate biological imperative, this meant my parents

271

simply couldn't be apart. As a result, their shortcomings were exacerbated by the indignation of having to continually confront their own and each other's inadequacies from one day to the next. Regrettably, between them they were unable to muster sufficient velocity to breakout from the gravitational pull of each other's respective contamination.

I have always found that being of service to others has afforded my life a tremendous meaning and sense of higher purpose. Even so I now know I have really been attempting to help myself all along - that same lost frightened and insecure child who resides inside me. To be honest provoking the monster lurking within my personal history meant I was almost overcome by the truth it symbolised. A day of reckoning I had met my foe and it possessed a sharp set of teeth. Now roused it proceeded to masticate me. Even so in spite of the distress it has caused this process has finally enabled me to lay the ghosts of my haunted past to rest. As a direct consequence, the world no longer weighs upon my shoulders.

Despite being advised not to write this book I had no other choice. My past had owned me for too long therefore it was time for me to own it instead. After all it's easier to become a resilient adult than it is to turn back time and repair a broken child.

★

PRIOR TO ATTENDING INITIAL police recruit training at Medmenham in Buckinghamshire during April 1990, I had badly torn the ligaments in my left ankle during a New Year's eve Hogmanay party on the last day of 1989. Well-oiled and overly lairy, I had drunk an entire bottle of brandy by myself then proceeded to show off in attempting to vault a table. Yup you got it, it all went wrong. Taking me home in agony Mandy was furious as she flung me through my parents' back door and indignantly told my startled Dad,

"Here's your Son over to you!"

He then basically dragged me upstairs before flinging me onto my bed and declaring,

"Right Son there's your bunk, over to you!"

My latest self-destructive escapade had seriously exasperated Mandy no end and I momentarily thought she would ditch me. You see it placed my forthcoming induction into the Police Service along with our future plans into jeopardy. What an idiot. Thankfully she forgave me (white lilies always work!) however, the injury severely hampered my cardiovascular training insofar as I had no other option than to solely work on my upper body strength conditioning instead. Bulking up muscle I prayed the ankle would heal enough in time.

Upon attending the course physical training took place on a daily basis mid-afternoon in-between classes. This necessitated a vigorous warmup followed by a mile and a half run which had to be completed within eleven minutes. Then came circuit training. I hadn't ran since my injury and initially struggled by just completing it within five seconds of the allotted time. A bit humbling at least I made the standard. Moreover, I absolutely killed it during the circuits by easily exceeding the best efforts of all but one of the rest.

Then again one of my classmates an older transferee from Tayside Police named Alec really struggled and couldn't make the time at all. Nearing forty he was measured 'the old man' by the rest of us and seeing nobody could qualify unless they met the requirement he was playing with fire. Several weeks in our peeved PT instructor had summoned us and we stood to attention in file.

"There's still *someone* amongst you who hasn't made the grade," he announced making no bones as to who he was insinuating by looking directly at Alec.

"NOT GOOD ENOUGH!" he continued now glaring at the rest of us. "From now on Black Class runs each morning at seven a.m. until he does is that clear?" he barked.

"YES STAFF," we collectively barked despondently.

Shit. An early start and run before breakfast meant a double dose of training because the afternoon session was extant. For sure this was all part of the game. Even so it was their game therefore their rules.

"Guys I'm really sorry." It was Alec who broke the ice first shaking his shaved head and looking toward the ground after he had gone.

"Look don't worry about it. We'll run by your side and egg you on," a few of us reassured him.

He was a big guy with a sturdy upper body slim waist and legs and really looked the part. Then again some people just aren't born for running and he was one of those. Over the course of the next week or so we ran as a class by his side. Wincing in pain by the midway point he'd end up dragging his feet and wasn't making enough progress. No harm to him but by now we were becoming increasingly hacked off with this unwelcome morning routine therefore hatched a radical ploy.

The route consisted of an undulating road winding its way around the grounds of the college and three laps entailed the required distance. Significantly two-thirds of it was out of view from the PT staff who always remained at the finish line with their stopwatches. Our plot? We would revert to type and do our own thing with one exception: Accompanied by a rugby playing transferee from the Met nicknamed 'Gogsa' I would run by Alec's side then when out of view together we would literally take an armpit each and half-lift/drag Alec along.

By now my cardiovascular conditioning was vastly improved and the damaged ankle was holding up well. Even so I found it bloody hard work given Alec was a big lump. Anyway, as it happens it worked, and he made it. Afterwards Black Class would enjoy a morning lie in before breakfast for the remainder of the course.

Don't kid yourself. Our PT instructor knew exactly what we had done. After all his earlier pep talk was basically designed to put a surreptitious onus onto the rest of us to get our fingers out and help our classmate by hook or by crook. As far as I'm concerned it's never a bad thing to encourage togetherness in institutions like the Police. It's nice to know others have your back if you're in a spot of bother. Then again I did also come across some in the service who didn't act in accordance with that sentiment, especially towards the end as things slowly came apart by the seams.

I have an admission to make. I appreciated the quality of life the job afforded my family but hated most of my service. From day dot I always felt out of place and frustrated. I guess as a creative there was never really anything tangible to show at the end of the day which is why I threw myself headlong into hobbies such a furniture making DIY and music in my spare time. It offered a practical outlet and way of satiating my constant need to grasp new things whilst working with my hands to produce something.

Police recruitment campaigns will never tell you most of your service is spent in appalling conditions fighting the constant jetlag of working ungodly hours alongside having to deal with difficult people whilst getting little quality time off. Mandy ended up an exasperated youthful 'job widow' raising two young kids with no discernible social life and a constantly hacked-off husband. It seemed my laissez-faire attitude to school and lack of qualifications had now come back to bite me hard. Recognising I could do little else to change my situation I instead distinguished a need to change my attitude. I've got to admit what sustained me most throughout those tough times was one enduring thought: *'You now need to suffer so that Mandy and the girls don't have to.'*

MANY YEARS LATER AS A FIREARMS Instructor

I was acting as a Range Safety Supervisor conducting live firing rifle requalification shoots at the Barry Budden military range complex near Arbroath. Entailing varying shooting practices, a line of firers were allocated specific timeframes within a set procedure of 'exposures' to engage 'The Threat' (figure 11 cardboard targets) with accurate fire. The exposures naturally varied which necessitated contrasting disciplines to test the firers overall weapon handling and accurate application of fire within the fabricated pressure of a collapsing timeframe.

For what it's worth each Authorised Firearms Officer was required to requalify this way every three-months in line with national guidelines pertaining to the police issue and carriage of firearms. The rationale is they remain highly skilled practitioners as opposed to members of dangerous Organised Criminal Gangs and terrorists who generally speaking aren't in the least.

On this occasion one of the firers who I shall name 'Marky' posed a conundrum. Older with a recent history of ill-health and suspected mobility issues Occupational Health didn't want to deal with the issue therefore the predicament landed with us. Be assured we knew the job wanted him gone consequentially this individual was now a marked man. Virtually pre-empted to fail by management the firearms department were now expected to carry out the dirty work.

Instructors are meant to rotate and regularly adopt Range Conducting Officer (RCO) duty on range days. This keeps the collective 'current and competent'. Nevertheless, seeing as this involves assuming overall responsibility some tended to avoid it at all costs leaving the more conscientious to habitually shoulder the strain. Yet on the day in question, it just so happened one of the former had curiously positioned himself as RCO.

'Hm, that's strange!' I remember thinking to myself. *'What's going on here then?'*

Given he happened to belong to the same station as our problem child by rights he should have been the one managing him. Then again ...

With twelve firers in all Marky was craftily positioned out on the periphery in lane twelve to mitigate any negative impact he might have upon the rest.

"John I've placed you in charge of lanes ten to twelve alright?" our unfamiliar RCO dictated whilst looking at his clipboard somewhat over-casually. At this the rest of the staff looked away mildly - but only mildly - embarrassed. All they cared about was it wasn't them.

"Seriously?" I replied unimpressed only now sighting the angle. "I see. Everyone else makes the arrows but now I have to fire them?"

Assuaging themselves from the plot it was now clear it had all been contrived beforehand and I had been stitched-up.

"It's just the way it is," he countered. "Anyway, someone's got to look after Mr. Stupid over there," he stated nastily as he nodded towards him. "After all you're good with difficult students after all!"

"In that case I will look after him but only in isolation. I'm not taking care of anyone else. He's potentially too much of a handful," I avowed now deciding to dig my heels in.

"Aye okay, whatever," he came back rolling his eyes theatrically. "The rest of us will also manage lanes ten and eleven between us if you take care of him ... and I do mean take care of him if you catch my drift."

Meanwhile I cast a glance toward the guy in question standing awkwardly amongst his peers. Breaking away I strode right up to him then proceeded to pull him aside.

"Right, I want the truth. Is there any reason whatsoever why you shouldn't be taking part in today's activities?" It was off course an entirely rhetorical question.

"No not at all," he lied.

I expected no less. He didn't want to lose his job without a right good go at it. Even so his insistence was putting us all in a position and by rights I should have been angered. I had instead just resigned myself to circumstance.

'There's the way things should be, and the way things are - what are you going to do about it?' I inwardly ruminated.

I always maintain discretion is vital when adopting any position of authority therefore weighed this all up for a split second before sighing.

"Okay I'll give you a fair crack," I declared. "But if you pull any crazy shit on the firing point I'll put you straight off got it?"

"Yeah alright I understand," he replied in his unmistakable Aberdonian accent.

As I turned and walked away another couple of the firers - two ARV officers routinely partnered together operationally - smirked. It was undeniable that they were capable operators but otherwise they were also known as a couple of wise guys. The gobbier one proceeded to chortle my way.

"Ha, ha, ha, no luck big man. It seems you've got the care in the community case!"

"Shut up," I responded pushing past now in a blackening mood.

As we commenced one on one I watched Marky like a hawk. His alleged impairment remained medical in confidence, so I was none the wiser. That said I was pleasantly surprised as his handling drills were on point and he was following instructions. Moving freely his fall of shot was fine. Carefully spotting it splashing the sand at the backstop he was evidently there or thereabouts and cruising.

"Good shot you're doing well keep it up," I encouraged throughout by breaking the rules as coaching was forbidden during qualification shoots.

As we progressed the other instructors kept gawking over in anticipation. That said my man was bucking the trend. Not so much an avenging angel waiting to swoop with paws as sharp as a tigers claws I now found myself beginning to root for him. We then arrived at the final detail which was an 'advance to contact' with the firing party gradually making their way towards the threat. On each exposure they were required to kneel then engage the target with two rounds before awaiting the whistle blast to end the contact. At this they would apply their safety catch then cover the threat whilst standing back up. Seven exposures in all, it would culminate in the completion of the shoot.

Now on paper this might look straightforward enough but it's not really when you consider the firers were wearing fifty pounds of ballistic equipment and weaponry and basically navigating a myriad of rabbit holes in inclement weather. Crunch time and everything went fine until the fifth contact. Still maintaining his handling and shooting skills the whistle blast signified they stand back up however, Marky remained stock still.

"Get up ... move!" I hissed at him through gritted teeth. "Come on you're almost there!"

I clearly saw his legs trembling and they just weren't responding. Desperately groaning he was two exposures away from keeping his position a while longer but was done. I cast a quick glance toward the RCO loitering menacingly nearby and noted his satisfied grin. At this precise moment something snapped within me as instinct took over: I spontaneously reached down with my right hand to grab the back of his body armour with a clenched fist.

"Whatever you do keep that damned muzzle pointing down the range," I sizzled into his ear defenders before single-handedly heaving him up to his feet.

Watching open-mouthed for a few seconds the others were clearly shocked. Not knowing what else to do the RCO eventually broke his inertia by fumbling his whistle back to his lips then confusedly continuing with the shoot. For the last two exposures I did the exact same thing over again by lugging him to his feet in ensuring he passed.

Afterwards the RCO was evidently livid. To be precise you could cut the atmosphere with a knife on the long journey back - yet my stance remained clear. If you throw me under a bus to put me in charge of a difficult situation then don't complain when I deal with it my way. Along with the rest of the range staff he could admittedly have opened a can of worms by reporting me. Then again I knew he wouldn't. After all he had been attempting to avoid taking responsibility in the first place and the others didn't want to be seen as grasses. That said we don't live in a vacuum therefore rumour spread fast relating to my conduct. Consequentially the resultant furore polarised opinion and irrevocably damaged my reputation in certain quarters.

Over the succeeding days I was visiting a station armoury to do an ammunition stock check when I bumped into the two ARV officers previously mentioned. Don't get me wrong I overall liked them both - and had previously enjoyed some right good laughs with them - but on this occasion they were chuckling like a couple of naughty schoolboys as one shouted across the room at me.

"Oh, look everybody there's the 'gimp enabler!'" he cried out in front of a few stragglers. "Hey, John have you helped any gimps today?" he added.

I could feel my temperature rising at his slur however, held my tongue because it was neither the time nor place. Yet again my patience and willingness to go the extra mile for someone else had been interpreted as weakness. Would it never end? Nonetheless weeks later when I was acting as RCO delivering handgun requalification shoots lo and behold guess who turned up? Yup, they both swaggered as bold as brass towards the firing point. I quietly asked the other instructor accompanying me to take a walk for five minutes. Perfect it was now just the three of us.

"So then, what's that new nickname you've got for me boys ... 'gimp enabler' is it?" I enticed.

"Yeah well everybody knows what you did. He shouldn't be in the job anymore," officer two blew up defiantly.

"Really?" I clarified. "Tell me who put you in charge then?" I replied irritably suddenly becoming aware that my index finger was angrily pointing at him. Even though I was maintaining a civilised veneer I was actually struggling inside to contain the chaos threatening to overtake me.

"Oh, and by the way that's one of your COLLEAGUES you're talking about NOT some piece of dirt," I emphasised. "The guy has given years of loyal service and he's not done you or anyone else any harm HAS HE? Yet now all everyone wants to do is talk trash about him because he's had health problems!" I concluded spikily.

"Aye, alright, ALRIGHT CALM DOWN. We never really gave it that much thought," officer one intervened whilst attempting to square up to me. "At the end of the day IT WAS JUST A LAUGH ..."

"Yeah, IT WAS JUST A JOKE," his confrere now jumped back in customarily attempting to back him up.

It was now two on one, but I remained suitably unimpressed because their customarily humorous double act was suddenly turning sour and really starting to grate my gears.

"PEOPLE WHO DON'T THINK SHOULDN'T SPEAK!" I shouted back. "So, it was all just a joke was it?" I continued regaining enough self-control to proceed to outsmart them. "Well then here's a punchline for you ... I assume neither of you want me to cut you any slack if you ever find yourself down on your luck then?"

"Alright, ALRIGHT. Point made. WE GET IT," officer one now protested unconvincingly trying to simmer down.

"Oh, you do? Good. Next question," I went on deciding to hammer the same point home hard. "The gimp enabler wants to know if you'd both like to do this shoot and every other shoot and tactics course the easy way? ... or perhaps you'd prefer to do it the hard way instead?"

The implication was finally laid bare that I could easily make their lives hard by failing them. They evidently loved working together on ARV duties and I knew neither fancied a sudden career change. By denigrating me they had invited trouble.

"Okay John, okay," officer two finally submitted stepping back to also pull his neighbour away. He then placed open palms in front to placate me. "Enough already you've made your point!"

Three months after this had played out news broke that Marky had suddenly passed away during the night. Still in his forties this caused quite an aftershock for everyone that knew him. Not that it mattered but at least he'd avoided the extra ignominy of being humiliated in front of his peers at Barry Budden that day.

A framed picture of him was later mounted in his memory by his co-workers in his home station. Oddly enough some of the exact same supervisors who previously wanted him extricated began to speak of him with great reverence which left a particularly bad taste in my mouth. A bit of empathy in its place wouldn't have gone amiss when he was still alive and kicking. Schadenfreude is always an indication of weak character and remains just so much easier.

I'll put my hands up and admit according to force policy and procedure I was unreservedly out of line that day on the range. Indeed, you could easily argue my actions might have placed him in a position whereupon he might compromise his colleagues or even endanger the public. Then again this was mitigated by the unspoken truth that we all already knew he would never be operationally deployed again as an AFO regardless the outcome. That qualification shoot was his swansong instead and as such I had simply elected to make it less painful for him.

Make of it what you will. I know he was bluffing and pushing his luck that day on the range. Then again my soft pilgrim soul had noticed the bigger picture entailed he was down on his luck and needed a pick me up. What I did was wrong but in that instant I just didn't want to be right.

————————

Chapter Nineteen

'The Greatest Days in a Person's Life'

I LEARNT THE HARD WAY there's no place for honour amongst the dishonourable. Let's put this straight I'm no leader of men and never aspired to be. Even so circumstance conspired me to manage a team of National Police Firearms Instructors responsible for training the largest pool of counter-terrorist Armed Police Officers in the UK. This was my second stint in the department and unfortunately I'd taken the helm at the worst possible time.

A time worn proverb stipulates never go back. Even so in order to take proper care of my elderly parents I now required the ongoing security of a complimented day job and unfortunately this was it. When I was Training Sergeant my job was to lead the team in teaching armed cops how best to utilise the proportionate application of lethal force when faced by dangerous criminals and terrorists through weapon lessons live firing practices and the practical application of theoretical tactical training. I'll bet all of this sounds glamourous and in part I suppose it was. Then like most jobs it eventually just became plain old routine so often wasn't.

Anyway it so happened my tenure came just before the force descended into a total farce of nonsensical governmental budgetary restraints and increasingly absurd managerial diktats. Well I felt increasingly delimited by the stupidity unfolding around me. Under normal circumstances the environment was chiefly challenging because we were always understaffed and overworked but I just went about my business with a minimum of fuss and a degree of effectiveness. It was at this time I was forced to choose between my

core personal values and the unprofessional disarray of a department going into meltdown.

Our College of Policing firearms license had been suspended through organisational malfeasance, and it was clear to me I'd been selected to step up and steady the ship by the very same people who had broken it because of my standing. I'll be honest, domestic situation aside I really didn't want the post

at all ... I just needed it. Having distinguished the hierarchy compelled me because they anticipated I would accede to their increasingly daft decrees boy oh boy were they ever wrong. On the day I was appointed a friend who happened to be an Instructor from another placement took me for a beer to mark the occasion. It was over a pint and a burger that I took him quite by surprise.

"You do realise this is now the beginning of the end for me don't you?" I quietly proclaimed meeting his gaze over the table.

He stared curiously at me no doubt surprised by the underlying forethought which had fed such an unforeseen prediction.

Now I want you to know the UK's police service isn't a meritocracy in the least. After all you can feasibly attain the rank of Chief Constable by simply passing two exams - PC to Sergeant, then Segreant to Inspector - endlessly stealing other people's work and then navigating lots of interview boards by prostrating yourself to kiss the ring so to speak. It's often the sort of idiocracy and rigged game you either choose to play along with or not.

Not only has it always been encumbered with all sorts of old pal's acts it has more recently been infiltrated by numerous decadent ideologies. Consequentially a supposed non-political constitution is becoming ever more skewed and compromised by neo-liberal fiats led by a bunch of idealogue opportunists who will do or say anything to further their careers or status. I found that many of them invariably had no great talent imagination vision or discipline. For example this was never clearer than during the Manchester Arena terrorist bombing in 2017 to which we were deployed during Op Temperer in the immediate aftermath. I'll refrain from describing the placement as some sort of amateur hour as to do so would be a great disservice to amateurs. Anyway the less said about that the better.

I have always been a bit of a lone wolf and when I joined the police I had quickly figured out nepotism was rife so determined, *'Nah, not for me. I aint being led by the least of us. I'll be my own man then just do the right thing for the right reason.'*

On balance I'd noticed those who mostly sought to be in charge were frequently (but in fairness not always given I had some really good bosses) the worst candidates, i.e. many of them were the last people you would want to have in charge. In any case ground lain let's go back to the department.

Up until this point I'd sometimes worked up to eighty-hours per week and was constantly red-lining and burning out. Not enough management then made the decision I'd be duty-bound to work even more absurd hours along with the others by frequently relocating to Essex in doing so. Notwithstanding my familial obligations I had explained my caring commitment for my elderly disabled Father. Then again by this time organisational care and compassion were scant and they insisted I submit documents disclosing his complicated medical conditions. I clearly marked these 'medical in confidence' but once submitted I heard they were freely passed around by all and sundry at HQ. Worst still they then proceeded to lose them and eventually demanded a resubmission.

Incredibly disrespectful, this was deepened by the fact Dad was an ex-cop himself and when I challenged them they flippantly insisted it didn't matter anyway as the decision was firm and I must assent. By this point I'd given almost thirty-years of devoted service which had regularly required placing the job before my family. What a mistake. As far as I was concerned it was now all coming to a head because they had seriously pissed me off.

My own situation apart the noise of the group indicated a state of rebellion was brewing as they now also openly avowed they weren't going either. What to do? I thought long and hard about it before holding a meeting with the Deputy Chief Firearms Instructor.

"Listen I'm out. I've decided I'm not going," I stated.

"You're not out. Nobody's out especially you. You've got to go or else," came his curt reply.

"Or else what?" I evenly queried, maintaining an appropriate level of decorum.

"If you don't go we'll discipline you," he'd come back becoming seemingly surprised this usual mild-mannered subordinate would even question such a thing.

"Then you'll have to discipline me," I replied in a level tone.

"Take heed it's a lawful order. Failure to obey will lead to reputational damage and even cost you your job!" he blurted becoming increasingly agitated and even more red-faced than usual.

"Then I'm going to have to suffer reputational damage and lose my job," I stated in complete sincerity.

"For Christ's sake you're just going to have to do what you're told its nonnegotiable" he blustered before his sidekick the Training Manager decided it a suitable juncture to interject.

"Don't put your principles before your practical's," he declared. "You're one of the force's best instructors but you care too much. Stop caring!"

Wow. There it was, he'd just come straight out with it. I was genuinely taken aback.

"If something matters then it's worth caring about," I eventually replied. "Has it ever occurred to you that I'm good at what I do because I do care?" I then added.

He just stared blankly at me.

"Well it seems to me that you don't think what we're doing here matters too much then?" I went on. "Hey, feel free to correct me if I'm wrong ..." I enticed.

Silence. It had been a monumental tell from him so visibly discouraged he decided it best to just pipe back down.

In the ensuing period the shit really hit the fan as the department went into breakdown before the hierarchy tried everything within their means to pressurise me. This began with flattery and even the offer of promotion before it descended to insinuated threats and intimidation. In the end I remained true to myself and my family. For me the department had become a peculiar sort of circus insofar as it was exclusively inhabited by clowns. I mean as far as I could tell there were certainly no lions on show. Meanwhile I was assigned the trapeze with neither pole nor net as I precariously balanced above the drop. Good grief the notion of remaining part of this travesty was actually beginning to make my skin crawl. To my mind it was wholly unconscionable, and I had to get out.

It all came to a head when we held another meeting whereupon I was offered a final ultimatum. Come on, I'm easy-going but not stupid. I already knew my manager was hungry for advancement and had promised he'd deliver my partaking. In short through stubbornly refusing I knew full well I was blotting his copy book.

"Listen do whatever you like," I'd finally avowed. "You can discipline me tarnish my reputation or sack me. You can beat me torture me or even jail me - but if you do I'll just go on hunger strike. I AM NOT GOING and THAT'S THAT!"

I'd said this with total conviction and meant it. It was Friday afternoon, and he now lowered his voice to offer a final gypsy's warning as he glanced around to make sure we were out of earshot.

"Then in that case off the record it looks like we are going to end up in an employment tribunal," he uttered before leaning back and glaring at me with intent.

I felt this was a ridiculous thing to say. No matter what I never held any such intention and reasoned it said more about him than it did about me. Anyhow the following Monday a couple of goons were flown up from Essex for the express purpose of cracking the whip and overawing us. I sat in complete silence whilst their tiresome spiel laid it all on the line then once they'd finished I simply stood up and walked out of the room and my career was effectively over. They were incredulous as I hadn't uttered a single word throughout.

It was an incredibly stressful time and took a significant toll on my health nevertheless, I was determined to stick to my guns. The Force's Mission Statement lauded honesty and integrity its uppermost ethics yet I felt solitary in representing them to the highest rank.

Incidentally all of the other instructors predictably folded like a house of cards. I'd actually known all along that they would. As I lit the flare they instead opted to stay and burn as opposed to following it. Look at the end of the day this was entirely their prerogative, I mean they had their own livelihoods to consider. However, at that point my own personal choice was to epitomize a man of character as opposed to a man of means.

By now persona non grata on my last day I took a last look around the training suite before putting on my jacket and picking up my bag. Heading for the exit I bumped into my dismal looking boss in the corridor who just shook his head disapprovingly ay me.

"What a waste," he scolded. "I can't believe you're disappearing down a rabbit hole don't you realise you're really good at this?" he bemoaned.

"Don't you realise that I'm really good at everything I do?" I answered without missing a beat before turning to walk off for the last time.

Afterwards the Deputy and the Chief Firearms Instructor (*note: not my old Chief Inspector: his legs had been summarily 'chopped' long before this point*) moved heaven and earth to sabotage my return to operations and bring me back into the fold. My will versus theirs it was a mismatch. Albeit no rebel rouser when I say no I mean it and nothing could break my silent resolve.

At certain points in life circumstance dispenses us moral binds. As it happens I'd actually been in the right place at the right time all along. You see in some sense I'd been born to encounter that situation. Instead of compromising I made a stand and would do it all again. Throughout my life I had witnessed the beauty of good and the ugliness of evil many times. For this reason I decided from that point on no one would ever again implicate me in their ugliness and so I never consented to anything in firearms which would disfigure my soul.

In some way I'd also purposefully elected for adversity to prove myself a worthy adversary. After all I already knew my time was coming to an end so had decided to go out with a bang. A timeless moto of the performing arts stipulates one should always leave them wanting more and that's exactly what I did. I returned to ops to see my time out and my new boss tapped into my expertise by paring me alongside the exact same Instructor I had shared my earlier premonition with over a beer and burger. We couldn't have manipulated that even if we'd tried. As a proper team I was grateful for the endeavour of writing the key strategic documentation which countered the numerous challenges the division was facing.

I once read that the ultimate failure of leadership occurs once leaders stop caring. I disagree because it's worse when they never cared in the first place. I will always be grateful for my career but when my last day of service arrived it proved an overwhelming relief. Hand on heart without any doubt the single greatest day of my profession was the day it ended.

★

OKU MOTONARI WAS FACED with an agonising

dilemma. as a Buddhist he was able to still his mind yet each night he lost sleep and was in a state of inner turmoil. It was 1598 in feudal Japan and from a tender age he'd given many years loyal service to his noble master's service. Rising through the ranks of the Azuki clan he had proven an exceptionally honourable, and trusted servant. Throughout unwavering trials and sacrifice he'd eventually ascended to becoming his lord's most trusted personal aid: a master strategist, wise counsel, and military advisor.

His lord was Shimazu Azuki a strong and steadfast man with a reputation for always being fair and just. During his notable reign he'd ended what had been an era of conflict and unrest. Of course there was a price to be paid for such peace – it had been hard-won then maintained by the sword. Certainly Shimazu Azuki had been undaunted whilst using his military force to do what he considered necessary for the greater good of all.

As for Oku he'd excelled in the art of war. Nevertheless in line with the Bushido any violence meted out had been administered through legitimacy. Consequentially the Azuki clan was respected and admired by the common people especially given they now enjoyed an unprecedented period of armistice and tranquility.

Thus lord Azuki was synonymous with righteousness and balance, and under his stewardship the people had flourished. In privation the lord made no secret of his admiration and gratitude towards Oku. It was not uncommon for him to openly thank his righthand from the bottom of his heart for the exceptional service he'd given. Indeed so much so that he'd often breached protocol by admitting to his inner circle he considered the Samurai his best friend.

Flattered, Oku was also embarrassed as he shrugged off the admiration. He simply considered it his duty in line with his oath of allegiance to his lord, his family, and his obligation to serve and protect the people. Regardless he'd always privately felt deeply honoured by the platitudes.

Then things had slowly changed. His lord only fathered one child. The birth was a difficult breach and his wife had tragically perished in the process. Sadly the child, a boy named Saigo, proved an apple that had fallen far from the tree because his nature was entirely at odds with his fathers.

From a young age he displayed a total lack of empathy for others. Worse still Oku had caught him instigating acts of cruelty many times. As an adolescent the boy would trap and slowly torture insects. It was obvious he took pleasure from stripping them of their wings then their appendages to observe them suffer. This then gradually worsened as he matured. Despite the teachings and moral advice provided by his tutors Saigo had graduated to trapping and torturing frogs then other small animals.

Aged ten Oku discovered the boy had trapped a domestic cat. Dismayed he found he had bound its legs before cutting out its tongue and slowly extracting its claws with tongs. By the time he'd intervened the tormented animal had lost two paws. Worse still rather than being ashamed Saigo was unwavering as he stood defiant and unabashed – grinning as he elevated the bloodied trophies to the air like some grotesque trophy.

Lord Shimazu was under no illusion about his son's unfortunate nature. In privation he implored Oku.

"I know the boy is not as he should be. My legacy seems a cruel twist of fate. Please, in my name don't forsake him. Always try your best by doing what is necessary for him and the people."

"My lord it is my duty. I promise to always do this for you," Oku replied.

The years had passed, and the boy matured into a man. In time Lord Shimazu had become old, frail, and fevered. Finally on his deathbed he clasped his hands to plead with the now aged Samurai once again.

"Oku do what is right for Saigo and the people. Do whatever is necessary in memory of me."

Oku had held his hand and solemnly pledged then shortly afterwards his lord had died.

At that point Saigo assumed control of the clan to unceremoniously relegate Oku. Recalling the malevolence in his new lords' cold eyes he had been slapped hard across the face.

"Old man you are a fool and I consider you a has-been," he spat. "There will be no place for you in my new regime. Instead you'll live out your days as a lowly servant. Be assured I have no use for my weak Father's old-fashioned morals. Dare to cross my path again and I will strike you down with his own Katana."

He was then replaced by four young Samurai as the flag bearers of the new rule. The new lords' personal bodyguard and counsel, they mirrored his ways. Technically gifted, notwithstanding they were cruel and arrogant. And so as time passed Saigo proved an unjust and reckless lord who seemed intent upon imposing cruelty upon the land.

Meanwhile Oku lived a quiet life in his modest quarters on the periphery of the estate and filled his time by studying, meditating, carrying out menial tasks and rigorously training in private. His daily routine necessitated he would encounter the four young Bushi and on each occasion they would savour the opportunity to openly taunt him.

"Ha, look at the pathetic old man. We've heard ancient tales about his deeds as a fighter. Obviously lies ... and even if true I doubt he could even fight sleep now. Pathetic old fool. If you dared enter our dojo we'd annihilate you!"

They would spit at his feet then laugh hysterically in taking turns to kick his backside and legs or slap him repeatedly across his face and head. Throughout Oku would just look at the ground and take the maltreatment before scurrying past to continue about his business. In doing so the leader of the pack, a tall warrior with long jet-black hair would watch him go then sneer,

"Look at the cowardly piece of dirt go ... he's terrified of us!"

And so for three years it had continued this way.

"Old man why do you walk past them every day? You could easily take another path and avoid the daily humiliation," some of the other servants impeached Oku.

He made no reply by simply shaking his head and walking on. In truth the abuse never affected him. Easily stilling his mind he had transcended ego many years ago. Moreover from a distance he would often watch the young Samurai train in the dojo as they practiced their swordplay and unarmed combat. Working as a pack they would often hurt the lesser Samurai forced to spar with them.

The other servants noticed this and between them would sympathetically whisper.

"Look at the broken old man, he obviously relives his youth and reminisces past glories as he observes them!"

Despite this Oku remembered his oath. In line with his promise he still considered it his duty to serve the new lord in any way necessary. Even so things were now escalating given sinister events were taking place. For this reason Oku Motonari was faced with an ethical dilemma.

Bad enough the young lord had become embroiled in actively agitating the other clans in an attempt to reignite tribal feuds rumours insinuated he was involved in an unimaginable perversion and was becoming more unhinged.

Well connected, Oku heard verifiable accounts averring Saigo was abusing the population in horrific ways. Backed up by his personal bodyguard the lord seemingly abducted then mutilated young girls. It was rumoured he would cut out their tongues before amputating their arms from the elbow, and legs from the knee. Applying tourniquets to keep them alive he was using them for his own twisted pleasure before throwing them alive to the river to drown. Bodies had been discovered washed up by the local populous, and the outpouring of outrage portended an uprising was brewing.

Oku had sworn a promise to his lord Shimazu on his deathbed to protect his son. Yet in spite of this – following a period of agonising dilemma - he'd now decided Saigo had to die and that he had to be the one to kill him.

The following night beneath the light of a full moon copious snowflakes gently drifted to the ground as a graceless draft occasionally sighed around the palace grounds.

The four Samurai of the personal bodyguard were drinking sake in the reception hall outside the lord's personal chamber. Under strict instructions to ensure he was not disturbed they drank to be entertained by a young Geisha. Her sweet voice was accompanied by the cheery tune of her shamisen as they meanwhile discussed their master's latest plan to provoke a feud with a rival regional clan.

The conversation turned to how they had watched their latest tortured victims drown in distress the previous night and they'd become lost in mirth. Suddenly the outside door gently slid open and there in the snow armed with sheaved long and short bladed swords stood Oku Motonari ... and the laughter and music stopped.

Surprised at this most unexpected appearance the young warriors quietly watched bemused as the bare footed old man purposefully stepped into the hall then turned to smoothly slide the door closed behind him. The stupefied leader of the group looked at the others.

"Well, well, well!" he eventually sneered. "So it seems the old has-been comes to share some sake with real men - or perhaps it's a severe beating the pitiful fool requires?"

Oku remained unmoved and made no reply.

Now shouting the leader proclaimed, "Get lost while you still have your miserable life," and hurled his half-filled cup towards the older man.

Rattling at his feet an unperturbed Oku ignored this before silently removing his kimono. Slipping it to the ground his upper body was laid bare. Deceptive for a man of his age he had a magnificent physique. The only hint of fat was around his midriff and his torso and arms were decorated in scars. Additionally etched into the skin covering the entirety of his chest and back was a massive tattoo of a dragon and tiger embroiled in deadly combat.

Meeting the group directly he now serenely addressed them.

"The Master is insane, so I've come for him. Best you don't try to impede me, or you'll get hurt."

Stunned to silence the young Samurai momentarily looked at each other then their inertia cracked as they burst into hysterical laughter. Finally they menacingly stood up drawing swords to hand. Adjusting his stance accordingly the old warrior did likewise as he countered them closing the gap to encircle him.

"You retard living on past glories ... you DARE to disturb us?" spat the leader of the pack. "The audacity! How dare you attempt to annoy the master. This is an OUTRAGE!" he added barely containing his rage. "You treacherous dog prepare to be cut down where you stand for your insolence!"

Then it happened faster than anyone thought possible. Without warning the old Samurai struck like lightening.

Consecutively feinting right he then altered course in a move that completely defied his age. In doing so he removed the lead warriors' right hand still holding his long blade whilst simultaneously plunging the shorter into another's chest. Such was the astounding skill and speed of the old man neither had been able to react.

A dramatic turn of events the leader was now rolling around on the blood-soaked floor crying for his Mother and the other lay dead. Momentarily pausing the wide-eyed remnants exchanged a glance then screamed in fury to bear down on him in rage. Moving with grace and poise Oku easily blocked several furious blows before counterattacking. In a move neither warrior had witnessed before Oku flicked one blade upwards concurrently slashing the other diagonally in the opposite direction to push the nearest man's blade aside and slice his stomach open. Calm, confident and relaxed, Oku momentarily noted his opponent desperately dropping his blade in trying to prevent his intestines spilling to the floor before he next utilised his legs to sweep the final astonished man to the ground. Bringing his entire weight to bear upon his face with his elbow he dislodged several teeth and broke his jaw and nose. Knocking him completely unconscious he had immobilised him but ultimately spared his life.

The entire engagement had lasted less than thirty seconds, and with the bodyguard now neutralised a blood-soaked Oku stood up then gestured for the hysterical Geisha to disappear.

Leaving the dead and injured behind he elegantly strode through the mayhem to slide the door which led to the masters' quarters open and impeccably stepped inside. Closing it behind he turned to peer through the gloom toward the waiting Saigo before walking towards him then bowing deeply.

Dressed entirely in black silk the young man was seated upon a highly decorative antique chair armed with what had been his Father's antique Katana. He coldly regarded the older man prostate before him as he wiped the sweat from his face and ran his spare hand through the unraveled long hair framing his pale narrow face.

"Old man before we begin," he stammered. "If you don't mind, I want to know how you defeated my personal guard so easily?"

"My lord repetition is the mother of all success," stated Oku.

"What do you mean by that? They were younger, technically gifted, and outnumbered you four-to-one!"

Oku raised his head.

"Master if they had numbered eight then they might have stood an outside chance. Your personal guard were proficient in the art of talking and cruelty - less so in the art of war. They regularly engaged minions in the dojo which fed their illusion of invincibility. In doing so they lost sight of the fact that sycophants and amputees can't hit back.

"Oh ..." went Saigo despondently.

"I overcame them by following a simple procedure," Oku continued. "I continually observed them train to identify the repeating patterns of their movements which allowed me an intimate knowledge of each man and how they fought as a collective.

"Furthermore I frequently walked past in allowing them to assault me which confirmed the things I'd noticed about their physicality. They confirmed it all in the way they moved, kicked, and beat me."

"I see but surely that alone couldn't guarantee success once you confronted them?" went the cruel lord.

"Quite correct," Oku agreed. "But afterwards I would proceed to fight them a great many times in my minds-eye. I knew them intimately by this time so mentally rehearsed engaging and defeating them in combat.

"They were predictable during our engagement a few moments ago insomuch as they allowed their emotions to overwhelm them. Only a fool allows anger to overtake him because it clouds his judgment. I on the other hand remained alert, calm, and composed."

"Ah," stammered lord Saigo nervously.

"True they were technically gifted, younger, and outnumbered me four-to-one," the old warrior continued. "But they were fools. Weak thoughts lead to weak purpose and weak purpose to weak action. Complacent, they were doomed before a blow was struck but just didn't know it."

Saigo assessed the old man for what seemed an age before finally standing up. He resignedly loosened his grip on his Father's sword which echoed the chamber through clattering to the ground.

"You know my Father was right all along. You truly are a magnificent man," he bitterly stated. "No, I won't fight you. There would be no point so just go ahead and end my miserable life ... who knows perhaps you'll afford me eternal peace."

Advancing purposefully upon his young lord with a poised blade Oku stated,

"Master I shall keep my pledge and do what is necessary for the greater good of all."

Moments later he had discharged himself of his dilemma. In a final act of honour he peacefully knelt beside the decapitated body of his young lord and bowed his head for several seconds. Eventually breaking the hush he outwardly affirmed,

"The two greatest days in a person's life are the day they are born and the day they discover why, and this is what I was born to do."

Duty fulfilled and loyal unto the bitter end Oku Motonari nodded to himself then proudly used the discarded Katana of his old master Shimazu Azuki to commit the ritual suicide of seppuku by disemboweling himself.

Chapter Twenty

'An Uncommon Man with a Common Name'

MY MOTHER'S FATHER was John, and I was named after him. Apparently my Mother and Nain had a major falling out over this which by all accounts wasn't particularly unusual in of itself.

At the time Nain insisted the name John was much too common, instead insisting I should be called Glyn which was my Taid's middle name. My Mum on the other hand had different ideas. She had promised her Father that should she ever have a son he would be named after him. Digging in her heels by the end some compromise was struck whereas I would become John Glyn. Personally I'm not too bothered about any of this. As far as I'm concerned you can call me anything and I have been called much worse.

My Scottish Grandfather was born in 1910 to a farm which housed a very large and desperately poor family on the Kintyre peninsula on the West Coast of Scotland. Every day was a battle for them to scratch together enough food to fill their mouths and shrunken stomachs. Their only source of sustenance my Great Grandmother would make large pots of vegetable soup which lasted the entire family for weeks on end. So I guess their perpetual tussle with famine was one they frequently lost.

The unspoken truth is they were country peasants. As such my fledgling Grandfather was well acquainted with hunger and hardship. Anyhow despite never owning much he remained a person of the highest worth.

Painfully shy self-conscious and reflective he was as honest as the day was long. Certainly he was unbendable in the way he was reliable conscientious and trustworthy in all of his dealings.

An incredibly poor child he had to walk two miles to school and back bare footed; his little collection of books tied together by a tatty piece of string. Yet at the tiny rural primary school by the sea it was identified he possessed a considerable intellect, and he won a regional literary award. Consequentially upon reaching his early teens they wanted him to go to into further education. I might say for the poorest class of society in those days this was almost unheard of. Courted by a raft of decent universities he simply couldn't go. His family had no money and as the eldest child his parents needed him to labour on the farm to help fill his younger siblings' emaciated belly's.

He had to forgo this one-off opening but did so without complaint. Then again because of this I reason he must have known all about a different sort of malnutrition – the emptiness that is unrealised potential. Nonetheless he remained admirable and grew into what is surely the rarest of things in this mean world, an honest man of his word.

Unobtrusive yet incredibly authentic as a young man he met my Grandmother and together they would parent eight children which he supported through working tirelessly as a Shepherd. Combined they possessed very little even so they would openly share what they had without hesitation with those even worse off. Their door was always open and if someone happened by their meagre fare was unquestioningly divvied up to provide an extra portion.

Together they endured tremendous hardships and suffered countless setbacks and tragedies. People were so resilient then. Someway they just bore out the pain whilst picking themselves up and carrying on. Then again what else could they do? They simply had to. No matter what befell them he remained an absolute rock and was completely upright.

During the Second World War rural shepherds and farmers were forbidden to enlist. Throughout this he wanted to play his part but simply accepted it for what it was. He instead minded the flock admirably as his own grew.

There were no favourites amongst his children. That said because she noticed him and felt his burden he shared a special relationship with my Mum. It's fair to say they worshipped each other. Desperately poor nonetheless he invested the greatest of parental gifts in her ... time love and attention.

My Mother accompanied him everywhere and during her more cogent moments would recount tales of their especially close bond with me. Regaling how they would go fishing in his little rowing boat for mackerel and endlessly walk the hills with his dogs they certainly made the most of the complimentary fresh air and open space that surrounded them.

A man of few words I recall he once sat opposite a similarly shy boy as we quietly convened by his kitchen table in Campbeltown's Crosshill Avenue.

"Ah silence is golden," he eventually revealed between sips of

307

tea. "Lots of people chatter all the time but never listen. For this reason it's much better to save speaking for when you have something meaningful to say. Then when you do you'll be more likely to say it well."

"I had never considered that before," I answered clearing my throat. Generations apart I struggled to process this assessment after all I was only fifteen years old at the time.

"Well think about it now," he tactfully replied. "Most folk ask 'How are you?' when all they care about is when you are going to afford them the chance to talk all about themselves. So if you forget about yourself to take a genuine interest in them for a while you'll always earn lots of affection."

Together we then sat reflectively. I actually didn't quite know what to say so decided to follow his sage advice by simply holding my tongue.

"Here's a tip for you," he eventually concluded. "People mostly forget what you say but always remember how you made them feel."

Now if ever there was a truism that was one right there. These words resonated with me so much that I still hear them even now loud and clear. Indeed I would remember to put this to good use throughout all of my succeeding undertakings.

Another similar interchange we shared springs to mind as I write this, so it must be pertinent. Discussing his own difficult upbringing throughout he would emphasise the importance of finding a sense of higher purpose through looking after those less well-off wherever possible.

"John there is no shame whatsoever in being poor - but there certainly is shame in being ashamed of it. Anyway the poor become rich through sharing what little they have with each other," he philosophically declared. "Meanwhile those who covet money are impoverished through tightening their fist on wealth."

Make no mistake he was a very clever and insightful man and well aware the affluent would have scoffed at such a noble sentiment. Nonetheless that didn't matter to him in the least. His words perfectly epitomised the modest viewpoint of an honest and straightforward character. An uncommon man marked by a common name.

★

OUR MASCULINE BURDEN TO BARE, my

Mother always had a way of making me and my Dad feel we could never match up to her Father's benchmark no matter what. At least that remained my honest interpretation of the situation. Then being complete opposites by nature it stands to reason we would proceed to handle this indictment in our own unique and separate ways. Typically blasé and freewheeling my Dad seemed insensible and dismissive of any vitriol that came his way. Primarily batting it off with a brief shrug of his shoulders and a shake of his head he would usually simply amble off without a care in the world by either whistling gayly or humming some tune of or other which evidently drove Mum mad.

As for me? The familiarity of never being able to meet the grade in her eyes was a tremendous source of unhappiness. After all she continually implied she would always love him more no matter what. It cut me deep and I suppose it was for this reason I stopped looking for her approval from a relatively young age.

It was the exact same dissatisfaction which fed my deep conviction to resist her perpetual coercion. A fine partition divides love and hate the extreme ends of ardour. Given she barely afforded me affection encouragement and validation I would pettily deny her what she craved most ... the exact same. I'm ashamed to confess in this respect I dwelt as soft as a dove whilst skulking as sly as a serpent. It seems the punishment of conscience is to suffer from acknowledging one's own sin.

I openly admit she was incredibly gifted in so many ways. Excelling in the sport of bowling she won county and national championships and even represented Scotland. Eventually succeeding as a highly regarded umpire she would often return home triumphant in adding ever more trophies to her burgeoning collection.

"Och I suppose nobody will want these when I'm gone anyway" she would usually declare for my benefit. "They'll all end up in the bin won't they?" went her mantra as she watchfully tested my response.

I knew full well she was enticing me to protest to the contrary however, I would meanly ignore her because I deemed she had always meanly ignored me. The folly of youth as two wrongs never make a right. I now regret not being the bigger person. Besides she was right all along as I actually have no idea what became of them. Anyway I now distinguish this sort of thing isn't exactly unique in family dynamics therefore have stopped feeling quite as bad about it. Simply put it's just the way it was.

Poignantly I'm certain my Grandfather would never have endorsed the issues her deep devotion to him had triggered between us. Thus the high esteem in which I held him was never sullied. No surprise really considering he always remained modest in speech whilst exceeding himself in conduct.

Even so the heaviest burden for any child to bear is the unlived lives of their parents. Unless proper care is taken the older generations paucity is always handed down to the next by way of the poverty of their aspirations.

In tending his family my Grandfather had to work incredibly hard for inferior men. He did so whilst having to witness his own children mirror his footsteps as they tread the same two miles to and from the same rural primary school by the sea with shrunken stomachs and holes in the soles of their hand-me-down shoes.

Having starved as a child Mum made up for it by serving us huge portions at mealtimes and ensuring we were always immaculate. If nothing else we were well nourished on these her solitary expressions of love. Moreover she also instilled the importance of maintaining a strong moral compass. As my roguish Father exemplified 'rules are for the obedience of fools' she would endlessly countenance 'no, they are there for the guidance of wise men'. I am grateful seeing as many of the other kids in the village weren't as lucky.

My goodness my Grandfather must have ached when providing

his own the exact same sustenance. Sadder still seeing as they were accustomed to poverty they grew up to expect little else.

It's odd how history repeats itself. Like him my Mother excelled at school and later won the same regional literary prize. Being awarded a certificate and book meant the absolute world to her. She recounted the story to me many years later outlining her disappointment of having proudly taken her prizes home only to later discover they had inexplicably gone missing.

"As much as I tried they were never found," she mournfully confided as I quietly abided nearby.

God I loved her so much when we were able to connect this way. During those periods we would become extraordinarily close. Then again it was a case of here one day gone the next as her moods swung unpredictably from one extreme to the other. She was sadly incapable of maintaining any real level of consistency. Only now as I write this does it strike me I ultimately feel cheated. Damn her, we could have been best friends if only she had held it together more often. What exacerbates losing her most is the fact I hardly had her in the first place. The validity of my heartbreak is underscored by the truth that when still alive she abided nearby like an inaccessible island of paradise lost. Perhaps worst of all is my own persistent but entirely inappropriate nagging thought,

'I really should have done more.'

In any case for her sake I'll now share the following accounts of her dear Dad. He was so clever but unlike me never had the opportunity to commit it to print so it's the least I can now do in trying to make things up to her.

Approaching middle age he re-trained as a mechanic. Modest to a fault he would never have admitted it but was the best in Kintyre. A hugely talented man an incredible creative force burned inside him, and he found simple understated ways to incorporate this into his life, such as woodturning playing his accordion and the beloved hobby of golf which dominated his later years. Indeed he would express himself in all manner of practical pursuits.

Opportunity knocked twice more. On the first occasion he was offered a joint partnership in a bold new garage in Campbeltown. He wanted to grab this with both hands but weighing it against his extending parental responsibilities deemed it too risky. Here the tragedy of always being poor was reflected in his unwillingness to take a chance and he regretfully backed out. Instead he requested the position of chief mechanic which was agreed: In fairness he was more comfortable in the role of employee. Sod's law the garage went on to become a huge financial success making the owner a millionaire. Alternatively my Grandpa's only consolation was that of earning a reputation for integrity and talent which spread far and wide.

The second opportunity defies belief but like the rest of these memoirs is completely true.

During 1966 he was offered a pleasure trip on the now infamous motor-cruiser 'Quesada' as a favour for outstanding service. He was to dine in luxury as they sailed to Northern Ireland with a group of contacts and business associates. Uncharacteristically excited it dominated his conversation for weeks. Yet when the designated day arrived an urgent work commitment he'd previously promised to fulfil at a later date arose. A man of his word he put others first and changed from his best Sunday clothes back into his overalls to meet the guarantee. Finishing the job as quickly as possible he hurriedly changed back before rushing to the harbour where to his dismay he discovered they hadn't waited. Missing the departure by a matter of minutes he had to witness the stern of the vessel leisurely slip from the harbour just as his heart sank.

Attempting to hide his disappointment he sat that evening at home listening to the radio when terrible news suddenly filtered through. An unforeseen storm had arisen, and tragedy had befallen the Quesada. The Port engine had failed and as they'd desperately attempted to fix the fault they had made a run for the safety of dry land. Tragically the vessel subsequently lost all power and now at the mercy of the heartless sea she had become flooded. Less than ten minutes later she was overwhelmed before being condemned to the unforgiving hidden depths alongside her luckless passengers.

A lifeboat had been launched and anxiously making his way to the quayside to await the rescuers return my Grandpa knew had he been onboard he might have been able to fix the engine and avert disaster.

In spite of an incredibly brave attempt to salvage survivors a great many of his contacts and associates perished that night as the Irish Sea condemned them to its remorseless murky mausoleum. Thereafter he never got over it and would live out the rest of his life suffering from an entirely unfitting sense of guilt.

In a mindboggling coincidence the vessel was skippered that night by a fellow named John McMillan - the exact same name as my Grandfather. Intervening it seems fate had determined my Grandpa's willingness to keep his word would spare him whilst condemning his namesake and the rest to Davey Jones locker for not waiting a few more minutes for him.

Anyway we are tied to this world by such slender threads. In the end having barely suffered a single day of sickness throughout his entire life my Grandad took a massive stroke then passed away at a relatively young age of seventy-six. I was just eighteen years old when he drifted like a moth towards the bright light of heaven. I awkwardly put my arms around my trembling Mum as I tried to console her by his freshly dug grave. Meanwhile my Dad stood impassive nearby and completely ignored her. I often wonder if this was his revenge? I can't be sure, but if so it was served ice cold. However don't judge him too harshly. I'm sure similar acts play out every day in families just as complex as ours across the land.

Once the coffin was lowered her youngest sister became hysterical and attempted to jump into the deep hole in the ground with it. Throughout this theatre my diminutive Mother just sobbed with dignity in my arms before I heard her quietly whisper two words.

"Goodbye Daddy."

I recollect discerning her bristling beneath my sincere but unwelcome touch. Yet another dagger through my fraught young heart I was almost overwhelmed by all of this and thought,

'Dear God, you might as well just bury her as well now. She has surely died with him.'

And so it proved as she would never be the same again. Afterwards going through his meagre private possessions lo and behold she discovered the perfectly preserved certificate and little book she'd received as a literary prize all those years before. It so happened he'd been so proud he'd simply had to have them. To his eternal credit this proved his only dishonest deed throughout a life well lived.

You know me well enough by now to know I've thought about this a lot. Well I finally arrived at the conclusion the cheaper your pleasures are the richer you'll be. What I mean by this is I don't think great people are defined by what they have at all: Instead I think they are defined by what they give. The only possession my Grandfather truly coveted was his childhood daughters academic prize. Hence in relative terms he'd owned almost nothing but been incredibly wealthy. The great Greek philosopher Plato once stated: *"There are three classes of men: lovers of wisdom, lovers of honour, and lovers of gain."*

My Papa's legacy was that of a good shepherd in that he was unquestionably wise and honourable, and two out of three is entirely fitting.

I must also add that it just so happens my Mother was spot on all along. I never could meet his benchmark no matter how much I tried because I could never be him. All I could ever do was strive to be the best version of myself. Anyway the last time I ever saw her she completely took me by surprise as she reached out to hold me tight. I'll never forget that loving embrace.

"I don't know what I would have ever done without you thank you for always being there," she whispered in my ear as we caressed each other.

Shocked it is almost as though she had a premonition we were parting for the final time. Nonetheless as we separated on the very best of terms in that instant I finally understood that I had been enough for her all along … it's just that she hadn't known how to show it. How ironic that in the end the one person who had always caused my turmoil would prove the exact same who caused my peace.

Coda

THE MOST POIGNANT PART of

aging is I have realised the potential fun life holds. I must acknowledge I have less time to appreciate it and less strength to take on the escapades my spirit has awoken to: I'm ageing too soon and becoming wise too late. The greatest miracle is we are here and able to live at all as the odds against this occurring are astonishing. Yet here we all are, so it seems we can either live as if nothing is a miracle or as if everything is a miracle. I choose the latter thus there will always be part of me sitting by McAulay's Burn as the wind whispers through the leaves. Who knows if you happen upon that spot some time you might even feel my presence or sense my still beating heart float right on past.

I reason everything we do and everyone we meet is placed in our path for some purpose or other hence there can be no accidents nor coincidences only consequences. Equally we should be willing to regard the lessons presented before us because these are probably what we have been put here for.

Pensive as I write this dying embers flicker the hearth as my wistful gaze is drawn toward the sky lit with a magnificent sunset on fire. I contemplatively meditate on what I have acquired from life thus far so for what it's worth I'll now share it with you:

Trust your instincts and take risks. Don't let fear govern you. If something scares you it's a sign you should go ahead and do it anyway. This is sometimes how we attain the things that matter most. Live and love; laugh and cry. Allow yourself to feel how you feel whilst figuring out how to manage it. Life necessitates we celebrate and mourn in equal measure which is just as it should be. That which is remains so much better than that which might have been: Foresight is the best insight to hindsight

A good life is not without suffering it is full of meaningful suffering. After all what would being be without a challenge? So never hope for who or what you want, instead hope for who or what you need. It's okay to aim low as long as you shoot high after all the stickleback in the jar is worth more than some trout in the stream.

Be patience where there is none and impatience where there is too much. Don't hide behind yourself as that's just too easy. Take control when required and relinquish it when not. The world is not out to get you it doesn't care about any of us or what we do. Life is a blank page, and you are the headline act so go ahead and write your own story before someone else does.

In the not-too-distant future we'll all be gone hence it will be as if we were never here at all. Hardly anyone really cares about what you think say or do therefore you might as well just cut loose and chase your dreams. Most important of all whatever means the world to you right now might mean the world but ultimately means nothing at all.

I'd like to finish by telling my children how much I love them and really hope they will tell their own and theirs not to forget about me.

ACKNOWLEDGEMENTS:

Nothing worthwhile is achieved in isolation. To this end I would like to extend my gratitude to my family and true friends for their patience and just being there. I love you all.

I would especially like to thank Michelle MacDonald for allowing me to tell a little piece of her own story. Her encouragement and friendship is greatly appreciated, and I wouldn't have done it without her endorsement.

A hand-picked few offered me feedback as I shared a few bits and bobs with them throughout writing this: I am sincerely obliged for the precious life energy that they traded. I chose to share it with them for a good reason.

Finally, Mandy McTernan you always let me soar as you watch from the wings. I want you to know the truth that I really would be a nobody without you.

Printed in Great Britain
by Amazon

17141775R00183